Cruel Attachments

Cruel Attachments

The Ritual Rehab of Child Molesters in Germany

JOHN BORNEMAN

The University of Chicago Press
Chicago and London

John Borneman is professor of anthropology at Princeton University. He is the author of many books, most recently *Political Crime and the Memory of Loss* and *Syrian Episodes: Sons, Fathers, and an Anthropologist in Aleppo.*

The University of Chicago Press, Chicago 60637
The University of Chicago Press, Ltd., London
© 2015 by The University of Chicago
All rights reserved. Published 2015.
Printed in the United States of America

24 23 22 21 20 19 18 17 16 15   1 2 3 4 5

ISBN-13: 978-0-226-23388-8 (cloth)
ISBN-13: 978-0-226-23391-8 (paper)
ISBN-13: 978-0-226-23407-6 (e-book)
DOI: 10.7208/Chicago/9780226234076.001.0001

Library of Congress Cataloging-in-Publication Data

Borneman, John, 1952– author.
   Cruel attachments : the ritual rehab of child molesters in Germany / John Borneman.
      pages ; cm
   Includes bibliographical references and index.
   ISBN 978-0-226-23388-8 (cloth : alk. paper) — ISBN 978-0-226-23391-8 (pbk. : alk. paper) — ISBN 978-0-226-23407-6 (e-book) 1. Child molesters—Rehabilitation—Germany—Berlin. 2. Incest offenders—Rehabilitation—Germany—Berlin. 3. Psychosexual disorders—Treatment—Germany—Berlin. 4. Psychosexual disorders—Treatment—Germany—Berlin—Case studies. 5. Child sexual abuse—Psychological aspects. 6. Incest—Psychological aspects. I. Title.
   HV6570.4.G3B67 2015
   616.85'8360651—dc23

                                                       2014026043

♾ This paper meets the requirements of ANSI/NISO Z39.48–1992 (Permanence of Paper).

CONTENTS

ACKNOWLEDGMENTS

Grateful acknowledgment is made for permission granted to reprint the material in chapter 2, a slightly revised essay initially published in 2012 as "Incest, the Child, and the Despotic Father," *Current Anthropology* 53 (2) (2012): 181–203. I thank audiences at the Berliner Institut für Psychotherapie und Psychoanalyse, and in anthropology departments at the University of Edinburgh, University of Manchester, University of London, Martin-Luther-University Halle, University of Konstanz, and Princeton University, who commented on early work. This research was supported by National Science Foundation grant # 0921817, and approved by the Senatsverwaltung für Justiz in Berlin, Germany. I would also like to thank the therapists and their clients at Kind im Zentrum, who trusted me to observe their group therapy sessions. Personally I thank Jürgen Lemke, the late Achim Perner, Sigrid Richter-Unger, Irene Berkel, Barbara Kowalenko, Peter Bischoff, and Christoph Wulf for much help and vibrant intellectual exchanges, and Andreas Marquardt for sharing the story of his life with me. Michaela Stiepel was immensely important for help with psychoanalytic concepts and literature and for a close and critical reading of the first draft of the entire manuscript. Parvis Ghassem-Fachandi shared with me his insights on the sacred, disgust, and ritual, and I am grateful to him for being a wonderful and supportive friend and partner throughout the research and writing. Finally, I thank Nancy Scheper-Hughes for taking the time to discuss with me a draft of the prolegomenon, and the two anonymous readers for the Press for some very helpful feedback.

Prolegomenon

On August 22, 2008, in a museum in the former public bathhouse of Berlin's Neukölln district, I attended a reading from a book about a man who had been sexually abused by his mother from the age of six and one-half to fourteen. It was a rainy evening, requiring umbrellas, though both the writer of the book and its subject, who sat at a small table to the writer's right, typically prefer never to cover their heads. The subject of the book, Andreas Marquardt, became, by his own estimate, one of Berlin's wealthiest and most ruthless pimps. For crimes committed in this capacity, he served eight years and four months in various prisons, during which time he betrothed one of his former prostitutes, Marion Erdmann, and underwent rehabilitation, involving a fundamental psychic change with the help of therapy. After release from prison, he built a foundation, *Helfen Macht Stark* (Helping Makes You Strong), dedicated to protecting children from sex abuse. The writer, Jürgen Lemke, also Marquardt's therapist, read selections from the book. Although Lemke had written the book, the publishing house, for marketing reasons, insisted on giving authorship to Marquardt, with Lemke listed clumsily on the cover as assistant. They both answered questions from the audience, some thirty adults, mostly women, including a few who identified themselves as abused, a few who counseled abused women, a couple retired prostitutes, and several social workers. Most of those present were strangers to the two authors, and most had not read the book, though they had heard about it.

Marquardt considers this kind of event *Wiedergutmachung*, a term that translates literally as "making something good again," roughly meaning reparation for past behavior. He also considers the writing of the book and its public reading a continuation of therapy, and Lemke concurs with this assessment. Another way to view the event is as a novel attempt to bring the issue of child sex abuse into the public sphere (*die Öffentlichkeit*). Both concepts, *Wiedergutmachung* and *Öffentlichkeit*, took on special meanings in Germany after the experience of Third Reich. German intellectuals have argued that the failure of the public sphere, which had been democratic and vibrant in the Weimar period, was one of the primary reasons the Nazis had come to power, and that after the defeat of fascism reparations to those who had been harmed was one way to restore the integrity of the public. With the 1962 publication of *Strukturwandel der Öffentlichkeit* (translated into English and published in 1989 as *The Structural Transformation of the Public Sphere*), perhaps the most consequential work of Germany's major postwar philosopher and sociologist, Jürgen Habermas, scholars began to debate with renewed vigor its origin and meaning. In this first of his many books, Habemas explored the origins of *Öffentlichkeit* among the emergent bourgeoisie in the transformation of feudal into democratic society. In his interpretation, the public sphere emerges as a bourgeois space where opinions are formed and discussed, a location for intervention between the structures of private life and the authority of the state.

What kind of intervention was I, an American anthropologist, observing in this public reading of the personal reflections from someone's therapy? What kind of treatment is this, where the private details of the patient's life are discussed in public and justified as having positive therapeutic effects on his well-being? What are we to make of the alleged psychic change of this man? Does presenting the story of Marquardt's abuse in public constitute a form of atonement for his pimping, facilitating his goal of *Wiedergutmachung*: making amends for his past, modifying his hate of women, transforming his self, and protecting children from a fate such as his?

Displaced Voices

There have been more than forty public readings of *Härte: Mein Weg aus dem Teufelskreis der Gewalt* since it was first published in 2007. A book of fifteen chapters and 260 pages, *Härte* translates into English readily as "tough," but it also connotes "strictness," "harshness," "hardness," "pitilessness." Audiences in a library, a church, a university, a house of culture, schools, theaters, at meetings of therapists and social workers, in two golf clubs and nine prisons, as well as on radio and television, have heard selections read from the book. It tells the story of Andreas Marquardt, who, as the book's subtitle explains, has found "[his] way out of the vicious cycle of violence." The literal meaning of *Teufelskreis*—the devil's circle—points clearly to the redemptive narrative the audience is to contemplate: Marquardt no longer does the devil's work of pimping; through therapy he has found a way to depart from his violent past. Indeed, without therapy as part of his rehabilitation, this personal transformation would have been impossible.

The readings publicize this redemption. Lemke brings into the readings his own experience, though not consciously or directly, acting as a conduit for the voice of Marquardt in the text. He reads, *"Ich bin sechs, da zerquetscht er mir die rechte Hand,"* describing the scene before Marquardt's sixth birthday, when his father sadistically squeezes his right hand until the bones crack; or the scene as a one-year-old, when his father places him naked on the balcony of the apartment in the freezing cold, causing a lung infection and months of hospitalization; or the scene when his mother teaches him how to please women sexually and praises him for his excellent service; or the scene when he terrorizes into submission one of whom he now ironically calls "my whores."

Lemke reads what Marquardt had said about himself in therapy, generating an autonomous third voice, independent of the two men, that enables the public to register the brutality of Marquardt's experience without identifying with him as a person. They listen to a story about the fundamentally divided character of a man who has been both a victim of traumatic physical, sexual, and emotional abuse by his parents and a vengeful executor of cruelty toward women, what Marquardt calls *"mein Haß-Program Frauen."* My Hate-Program: Women. Lemke, who is older, taller, gentler, more cerebral, and more empathic than Marquardt, temporarily inhabits his words while reading, including his brutality, his resentments, his lusts. The audience would be less likely to listen if Marquardt voiced his own words. By hearing the words from elsewhere, they are able to separate Marquardt's words from both the therapist and the person sitting by him, effectively shielding the listeners from a direct relationship with the man who was abused as a child and then later abused women.

"Marquardt is not a *'Sympathieträger,'*" Lemke explains to me, meaning he does not prompt widespread sympathy. Yet, if not sympathy, then at least empathy, the capacity to feel sorrow for another's suffering, must be aroused to reach a public who will listen without first judging. Lemke establishes a connection to Marquardt and to the audience by reading the first-person account of *Härte* in a grave, slightly hurried delivery, swallowing words and fusing sentences, with little changes in intonation. That voice lacks the succulent tones, the warmth and reassuring timbre, the humor, of his normal speaking voice, which he reverts to in answering questions. What the audience hears in the reading is the feeling of a third-person account, words initially spoken by Marquardt but narrated and read by Lemke, a therapist and an author. When Marquardt answers questions after the reading, they hear short succinct sentences in a rushed voice that is eagerly straightforward, anxiously understanding, never vague or evasive. The multiple displacements of voice in these events enable the public to establish a conscious distance to Marquardt and his story, and at the same time they produce for this public an unconscious proximity to the therapist and his client that is usually not wished for.

This unconscious proximity is necessary for empathic listening and learning from the other's experience. Empathic listening is not gullible listening. It is not belief in what you hear. It does not require abandonment of your critical faculties. But it does demand suspension of immediate judgment. Empathic listening is necessary not only for the audience in these public events to be able to relate to what is said but also for the initial work of therapy to have any purchase. For the anthropologist, empathic listening is necessary to be able to gain access to and construct an account like this.

I met Jürgen Lemke in 1986, on my second day of dissertation fieldwork on the divided city in the former East Berlin. He quickly became one of my very best friends. This friendship gave rise to the trust that makes possible my unusual writing about his relationship with a client, and about their attempt to transform the self of the client. At that time, in 1986, Lemke was a lecturer in economics and foreign trade—"a topic about which I know nothing," he says, modestly—and only several years after the Wall came down, and following a nervous breakdown, after millions of East Germans had lost their jobs or were forced to reeducate themselves and seek new forms of employment, did he begin retraining as a therapist.

Although Lemke had told me about his book project with a client at the time he was contemplating writing it, I never met Marquardt until the reading in Neukölln, which I attended as I was starting new research on child sex offenders in Germany. In that first encounter I was immediately struck that a large part of Marquardt's public appeal rests not with his story of child abuse, and certainly not with the abuse by his mother (which invokes the desire of and for the mother, a taboo that continually shocks and surprises members of the audience, including therapists present). Rather, his apparent appeal seems to be in his history of resolve and redemption: from one of West Berlin's leading pimps in the 1980s and 1990s to a man dedicated to helping children. Without knowing him, I had in the late 1980s frequented the district in which he made his prostitutes work, around Stuttgarter Platz in West Berlin. If I had taken any interest in the hookers who routinely propositioned me while walking home from a café or bar or restaurant, I might have met the violent criminal, pretherapy self of Andreas Marquardt back then.

But I did not. So it is that some twenty years later through Lemke I met Marquardt, who subsequently welcomed me at his readings and publicity events—even taking me along to a reading at a maximum-security prison in another part of the country. He also agreed to discuss his life and therapy with me in between training sessions with children at his sports studio and to let me tape our conversations. Many psychoanalysts claim that the first experience of unconscious proximity is the reverie between a child and its mother, the unspoken dreamlike elicitation and attunement between them, which conditions us for the development of a capacity for empathy. How did two men like Marquardt and Lemke, with nearly opposite relations with their mothers and very different empathic capacities, traverse their experiential divide to create the kind of proximity necessary for therapy?

Marquardt and His Mother

To avoid entering directly into the traumatic relations of Marquardt with his mother, I began with his memories of separation rather than attachment. I asked him to describe how he experienced the death of his mother. A year after his release from prison, after his forty-eighth birthday, Marquardt's mother died—alone. He refused to attend her funeral, although, as the only child, he was charged with organizing it. A few weeks before her death, Marion Erdmann, Marquardt's betrothed, had suggested they visit her once more, but Marquardt kept postponing the date until it was too late. On notification of death, he says he carried out the burial "hastily, without ceremony." He purchased an urn, had the corpse burned and the ashes buried in an anonymous grave. He knows the particular cemetery in which her remains rest underground, but he says that today he could not find the exact burial plot within it even if he wanted to.

Marquardt, as we know, had been seduced into sex, including sexual intercourse, by his mother, beginning at the age of six and one-half. This development he describes in great detail in *Härte*, but he offered to tell me many of the events again. The two versions, told from 2003 to 2005 and 2009 to 2011, are remarkably similar, which is to be expected given that repeated public presentations will tend to standardize narratives. Despite the easiness with which we can be fooled by other people's stories, I do not doubt the veracity of Marquardt's story. He has an acute interest in understanding what went on, for no greater reason than to rid himself of the

Figure 1. At thirty months

repetitive nightmares in which his mother appears, invariably with the same wish, or in which *das Ding*, a dark amorphous blob of nothingness, hunts and tries to kill him.

His mother was lively and caring during his childhood, and, as the picture at two and one-half suggests, he was an earnest child but capable of joy, at least some of the time (figure 1). Shortly after his first birthday, Marquardt's

Figure 2. With Opa

Opa—his mother's stepfather—kicked Marquardt's father out of their shared apartment, and his parents separated. Marquardt's father did pay alimony occasionally, however, and they saw each other "maximally ten times" he says, over the course of the next five years. The last time was just after his father crushed Marquardt's hand. Yet he was closer to his grandparents anyway, he says, especially to his Opa, whom he still "loves above all others." One sees in the photo of him at one year and nine months that his grandfather sits with him in the enclosed playpen, indicating an affectionate closeness with his grandchild that few German men of his generation sought (figure 2).

After his parent's divorce, Marquardt and his mother shared a bed in the very large apartment of his grandparents until he reached the age of fourteen, when, with his grandfather's support, he moved into an apartment two floor above theirs.

Marquardt shared with me two photo albums, one of his own and one he had inherited from his mother. He remembers "absolutely nothing, nothing at all" of his infant years, but he supposes, "It was a nice time. They paid a lot of attention to me." His memories begin with Christmas, at age four, when his Opa gave him a deep red pedal car, purchased from the German

Figure 3. As automobile driver

department chain Hertie. The photo of him as a precocious automobile driver evokes a very special German fantasy of freedom on Europe's only Autobahnen without speed limits (figure 3). And of being admired by others. "I was very proud," he says. "Everybody looked at me, all the kids looked." It is shot in front of the steps to the City Hall in Neukölln, where he grew up, and not far from his sports studio.

Two photos at the ages of fourteen and fifteen were taken less than a year after he had completely stopped his mother's advances. He had tried to end the sex unsuccessfully a year and a half earlier, by refusing to share his mother's large bed any longer and sleeping instead on the living room sofa. By then he found sex with her disgusting. She had developed a routine for them to the accompaniment of the hits from the musical *Hair*. From "Aquarius" to "Sodomy" to "Air" to "Ain't Got No"—all sung in German translation—she directed the foreplay. After "Hair" they took a short break, followed by "Black Boys" and "Three-Five-Zero-Zero," with an orgasmic climax sometime before "Let the Sun Shine In." Hearing those hits or smelling her perfume now made him particularly nauseous. He warned her, "If you don't stop, I will tell Opa and Oma."

"Who will believe you?" she asked him. "You should be careful what you say. Will they believe a mother or a wayward son who has nothing in his head but his sports?" And she praised him for his mature grasp of sexual techniques, which she had taught him, claiming he would have a huge experiential advantage over other young men when he started having sex with girls.

Even after he began sleeping in the living room, she still knocked on the door and begged him to return. When that didn't work, she threatened: I'll send you to an orphanage. I'll stop you from going to the sports studio to practice.

His grandfather had introduced Marquardt to boxing at the age of six, about the same time Marquardt's mother began to abuse him, but boxing wasn't tough enough for him. He switched to the martial arts, more rigorous, more severe, specializing in Tae-Ka-Do-Kan, full-contact karate. By nineteen he was the middleweight European champion, by twenty-five the Asian champion, by twenty-eight the World champion. But as an adolescent, he still feared his mother.

In the photo at age fourteen, Marquardt stands triumphantly by her, chin thrust out and up, right arm around her neck; she looks away from the camera, left arm wrapped loosely around his waist (figure 4). Several months later, she wanted another picture with him, but he refused. So she instead took a picture of him together with Oma (figure 5).

This second photo suggests a sullen and uncooperative youth (figure 6). His mother typed out a label to place above it in her photo album, which he inherited after her death. *Stur wie ein Panzer.* Stubborn as a Panzer. Surely a metaphor for resistance to more than having his photo taken.

During the years Marquardt was imprisoned he had little contact with his mother, and his friends and acquaintances abandoned him. Before he entered prison, they had indulged his every wish, a deference he then construed as a sign of respect. But in prison he realized they were merely impressed by his money and his ruthlessness. They feared his absolute resolve to achieve his ends. Only one person remained loyal throughout, and that was Marion Erdmann. He had initially recruited her as a teenager to work the street. For the first period of his imprisonment, in the detention center, he was not allowed any visits. So he arranged for Marion to appear at a specified time on the street corner where the bus stopped outside the prison. She remembers those visits as the most romantic of their relationship. They exchanged looks through the window of his cell. From outside the prison,

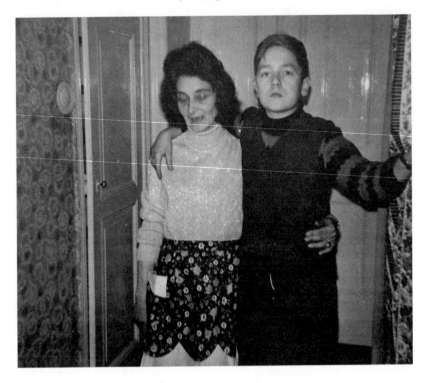

Figure 4. With Mutti at fourteen years

she took over his responsibilities and effectively ran the legitimate part of his business, his sports studio. She even moved in with his mother, who had just been released from the hospital and needed daily care.

I met Erdmann several times in the afternoon at their sports studio, where she worked with the customers and did the accounting. She tries to keep her distance from Marquardt's publicity work, but she agreed to talk to me about her relationship with him. Erdmann says she "fell in love with Andy the first moment" they met. Although he was extremely malicious, she tried to see the other side of him, how he must have been as a child, and compared him to "a small dog that bites" but need not become vicious. She tried to see him "in the round." I asked Erdmann whether she thought of herself as one of Marquardt's victims. "That is too strong of a concept," she replies. "He made too many decisions for me. Today I will say I would have preferred deciding for myself." She speaks in a measured, melodious, high-pitched voice, which, together with her alertness and large childlike eyes, does not betray her own history of work as a prostitute or

Figure 5. With Oma at fifteen years

experience of sex abuse as a child. Marquardt claims this latter history binds them together as *Leidensgenossen*, partners in suffering, "two sides of the same coin."

Erdmann thinks that she already knew about Marquardt's abuse by his mother before he told her, but that she had not openly acknowledged it. In retrospect, she says, some of the conversations with Marquardt's mother during the year of the mother's convalescence were about the abuse without describing or naming it as such. The mother was always quite curious about Erdmann's sex life with her son, remembers Erdmann, and she inquired about details. Erdmann thought the questions were odd, "That was too much, private, a no go for me, but she would make these comments: 'Andy liked to do this, and Andy liked to do that.' I realized later, she was telling me about her own likings as she experienced them with Andy."

A bit over two years into his sentence, Marquardt proposed to Erdmann

Figure 6. With Oma: *Stur wie ein Panzer*

in prison and arranged a prenuptial engagement. In her opinion, that engagement proposal was "really sweet," she says, and the ceremony he staged around it had "as much imagination as possible within the prison setting." The prison time, then, both Erdmann and Marquardt reiterated to me, was the most cherished time of their relationship since they, says Erdmann, "actually communicated," making the best of the few hours a week they were allowed to be together. They are still engaged, and Marquardt alternately calls Erdmann "my partner" or "my woman," as if they were married.

On the advice of the therapist, and with Erdmann's encouragement, Marquardt relented and called on his mother a last time about a month before her death. He wanted to confront her about the abuse. For the first time, and from his present perspective, he says, he acted "like a prosecuting attorney," verbalizing all the things he had never trusted himself to say to her. "No mother is allowed to do such things," he told her, and asked, "Have you understood?" For forty-five minutes she sat silently, avoiding his stare and any sign of a reaction to his reckoning. Finally, looking him in the eye, she stated, "I hope you can forgive me."

Lemke and His Mother

Jürgen Lemke's separation from his mother, in turn, was in an entirely different register of experience. Whereas Marquardt is trying to dissolve the memory of a mother whom he cannot forget, Lemke is still recovering such a memory. Lemke was told sometime early in his childhood that a Soviet soldier shot his mother as she and her two sons, together with her two sisters and her twenty-year-old niece, fled the approaching Red Army in March 1945. They were unaware that Soviet troops had created a great cauldron, encircling a large area that also contained their village, Bohsdorf-Vorwerk. In the confusion of that moment near the war's end, the women took flight with the two small boys, alternately encountering a quickly dissolving German *Wehrmacht* and army police, as well as units from the Waffen-SS-Panzer-Division "Frundsberg"—the armed wing of the Nazi Party, to which the eighteen-year-old Günter Grass, later Nobel Prize author, had been assigned—and the First Ukrainian Front of the Soviet army they thought they were escaping.

Lemke was nineteen months old at the time, barely walking. Several months before this shooting, he had accidentally pulled a pan of boiling water off the wood-burning stove in his home and scalded the entire left side of his body—the scars are permanent and still clearly visible today—meaning that he needed special care unavailable to him the entire time he was a refugee in flight. The picture he presents of himself at the time is of a relatively unpleasant, whiney, always hungry, fetid baby boy, a difficult child, under these circumstances, to love, and a child who learned how to suffer silently, to accept what he was given.

When I ask Lemke to clarify the circumstances of his mother's death, he keeps telling me to talk to his brother, who is seven years his senior. That is, only his brother knows Lemke's experience of childhood and can enable him to access it. Together with Lemke's partner, we had the year before visited the brother and his wife, who live in the same house where the two brothers grew up. I wrote out a list of events for clarifications about which Lemke had little memory, and we reached him first by phone. That conversation raises even more questions about the time of flight, so we drive to visit his brother again at his home in Bohsdorf-Vorwerk. The older brother then begins to talk of what he said he vowed never to speak about. He tells us that on their escape, one day, the three other women for a reason he cannot recall went ahead, and the boys found themselves suddenly alone with their mother, shot and dying. A bullet also hit Lemke's brother, though it only grazed the left side of his head. The mother said to him, "Keep going, I am

Figure 7. With mother before accident

nearing my end (*Geh weiter, mit mir geht's zu Ende!*)." Lemke's brother then resumed the flight, pushing him in a small wagon in the direction the other women had gone.

After several hours, the boys caught up with their aunts and cousin, and together fled further, hiding in ditches and in the woods, eventually heading in the direction of Dresden, which the British Royal Air Force and the American Army Air Forces had firebombed two months earlier, destroying 1,600 acres of the city center and incinerating between 22,700 and 25,000 residents.

I ask the older brother to retrace their route on a map. Closely inspecting the map, he recalls other details and images as if he were remembering them for the first time, jumping across places and times and then backtracking again. From Bohsdorf-Vorwerk they walked to Sellesen, and from there crossed the river to Bülow, eventually following the *Wehrmacht*, the German army. They ran into their first Russian soldiers in the next village, Gorden, and from there through the forest to Staupitz, where they first encountered scattered soldiers of the Waffen-SS, who, he says, "could have cared less about us." There they waited with other civilians, caught between Russian and German forces, and saw some heavy shooting. They turned back to

Figure 8. With mother and brother

Gorden and then continued in the direction of Hohenleipisch. After a very cold and wet night in the forest, he and his brother and mother had stayed behind while the other women went ahead.

I am still confused as to why they were twice separated from their aunts during the escape, the second time for two full days when the two brothers appear to have been abandoned. Lemke's brother says he learned nothing about what happened from his two aunts. They refused to talk about their experience, even later in the presence of his grandparents. Nonetheless, he is now intent on speaking what he knows, and says he can comment only on the first separation, of several hours, which was because, he says, "She wasn't finished yet (*nicht fertig geworden*)."

"Finished with what?" I ask. Lemke gestures that I should be silent, and his brother simply repeats, "She wasn't finished yet." What she still had to do, he says, he does not know, but adds that she "once turned around and rode the bicycle back home; she forgot to lock the house or something like that." He continues with the story and reiterates, once more, "In any case, we weren't finished."

"Finished with what?" I ask, again, noting the switch in agency from "she" to a collective "we."

Suddenly they heard shooting and Russian soldiers appeared from right and left, and they noticed they were the last ones there. The mother, he says, "suspected what is coming. I must say, now, very clearly, it was all out of the blue, that we really didn't understand, but the soldiers were abruptly standing around her, and we didn't know what they wanted, that we don't know. And then she didn't want [it] so (*wollte nicht so*), and they shot her."

On hearing this, Lemke exhales loudly, emitting an odd sound that punctures the air and reminds me of an abscess that has burst. I am brought into an emotional proximity to an event from which Lemke had been spared full impact for more than seventy years. I feel as though I am intruding on something very private, and I struggle to remain silent and to prevent my eyes from tearing. This struggle suggests that I am entering into Lemke's current emotional register, as in the original German term *Einfühlungsvermögen* into which the English word "empathy" is later translated. Yet I am bothered that, in touching some affective register of my own, I may be blurring the line between his devastating experience and my sadness. My sense of trespass leads me to keep the tears from flowing, blocking a further show of emotion.

Lemke's head plunges, and he says, quietly, "I always thought this." The soldiers had also wounded Lemke's brother, which he doesn't mention here, but says, tersely, "We stood there alone." Their mother's death, then, was not evidently the accident Lemke had always portrayed it as in his mind. The question that had shadowed Lemke, whether his mother resisted sexual advances to spare her boys this vision of violation, had been answered. Now Lemke has even more reason to believe that he and his brother were responsible for her death. In any event, she was not the only victim of the shooting, adds Lemke's brother; many German and Russian soldiers, horses, and civilian corpses littered the road.

The two boys caught up to their two aunts in Hohenleipisch, then went on to Groß-Buckow. As I listen, Lemke's brother peers over the large map patiently, searching for villages that have since been eliminated, sacrificed in the 1950s to dig up the then-valued brown coal on which they had been built. Sometimes he remembers the name anyway, along with scenes he has attached to those places that no longer exist. Before they reach Straußdorf, they, along with other civilians, are subject to Russian aerial bombardment.

They saw more retreating *Wehrmacht* soldiers along the way, who shot any Russian they encountered. "No prisoners-of-war were taken at that point," Lemke's brother says matter-of-factly. In one village, some civilians had hid in the church. Soviet soldiers took them out and shot them all. In another, he saw the dangling bodies of young soldiers—"I see their faces still, how they whimpered. They couldn't have been more than seventeen or eighteen, punished for desertion. They didn't even shoot them, just hung them up" as examples for other soldiers who might pass through. "I must be honest, though, hundreds of dead Russians on the street, but of the [dead] German soldiers, I didn't see a single one."

The family kept changing direction. After Plessa they passed through Elsterwerda, and finally, picked up by a military van, landed in Dresden. They quickly passed through the incinerated city and headed south to Ausig an der Elbe, today called *Usti nad labem* and integrated into the Czech Republic. Along the way, his aunts and cousin were most likely sexually violated, he acknowledges in response to his brother's question. But he only saw it happen to the one aunt, the one who later raised them. He says he will never forget the "Mongolian face" of the man who raped her. The blood on his own face from the bullet wound he suffered at their mother's death was not wiped off until they reached Dresden, when a Red Cross nurse attended to his wounds.

From Ausig an der Elbe they went back through Dresden to Chemnitz, which Americans reportedly occupied. But there had already been an agreement for the Russians to take over and the Americans to retreat 20 kilometers each day. In Chemnitz an unknown woman took off his shoes while he was sleeping, needing them for her own son, and from thereon he walked barefoot, eventually with a thorn lodged in one foot. After a few days he could no longer walk, but he found a pair of women's shoes, with high heels, which he then wore. On leaving Chemnitz he remembers seeing Russian and American troops stationed on the two sides of the Autobahn. And there he saw for the first time a black man. North, from Bärenborg to Wittenberg, Lunzenau, Geithain, and Leipzig. From Leipzig they caught a train to Hildesheim, on to Lehrte, where they were put in a hotel overnight. He recalls how he and his brother, thoroughly chilled, wet their pants every night. At the hotel, the women were particularly ashamed; they were guests, it was an actual bed. From Hannover, they went to Idensee and stayed in what became a German refugee camp. He thinks they were the very first to arrive.

Approximately a year and a half after the flight began they received a letter from Oma and Opa asking them to return. We have a big house and enough to eat, they wrote. The two boys and two aunts took a train back to Bohsdorf-Vorwerk, which since had become part of the Soviet occupied zone. Shortly after returning, Lemke's aunt contacted the mayor in the village near where the shooting of Lemke's mother had taken place. He pointed to an unmarked mass grave. She could identify the remains only because her sister had been wearing a raincoat with a fashionable Shepherd's plaid, black-and-white checkerboard pattern that in the interim had not fully disintegrated. The aunt bought a casket and organized the remains to be transported for reburial to a cemetery near their home. All of this is to say that Lemke's mother was dead before he could speak, before he had memories, before he became conscious of what a mother might be. For all intents and purposes, Lemke was denied the holding functions of a mother, someone whose intent is to make him feel secure, to accompany his entrance into speech and the world at large. Instead, he was accompanied, as we shall see, by an emotionally distant aunt and by the spirit of an absent father. In his late teens, he took his stepfather's name—the second husband of the aunt who raised him—obtaining the name of the father after he no longer needed it. All three figures—aunt, absent father, stepfather—were intrusions from the outside and never created the holding environment that Lemke himself tries to create in therapy sessions with his clients. Hence the strangeness for Jürgen Lemke of Andreas Marquardt's experience of having a mother who was too close.

Lemke and His Aunts

The theme of the absent father, *Vaterlosigkeit*, runs through most German families due, in large part, to deaths in the two world wars. We can add to that the theme of the absent son. The absence of the father usually alternates with his powerful, authoritarian presence, minimally in the imagination. The absence of the son is instead intensified by an accumulative aggression, an unconscious erasure of memory of the father along with the concepts *paternity* and *inheritance*. Sons inevitably have unconscious connections to their mothers, but they regard with ambivalence their relation to fathers, and often resist defining themselves in the terms fathers set forth. Both Lemke and Marquardt were unable as adults to reconcile with their fathers, and neither fathered any children. Such a son, caught between aggressive erasure and the need to reduce his estrangement with the father, is unable to reconcile with the authority of the father. Lacking any act of appeasement or atonement appropriate to redressing the wound created by this absence, he can neither locate himself as a son to a father figure nor assume the father function as an adult.

Despite having extended family albums, neither man has a single photo of himself with his father. The closest to such a picture is the photo, taken around 1958, of Lemke's father, dressed in a suit, walking gingerly alongside an elegant automobile, in front of the medieval Cologne Cathedral, one of Europe's most impressive Catholic churches that stood tall despite some seventy hits during World War II in a city otherwise flattened by aerial bombs (figure 9). Lemke had taken a train from East to West Germany to visit his father, and then accompanied him on this day trip to Cologne. But Lemke was left out of the photo.

Following the death of Lemke's mother, the care of the boys was entrusted to the two aunts, provisionally, until the father, who had fought on the West Front and initially sat in an American prisoner-of-war (POW) camp, could come and retrieve his sons. By 1947, both aunts knew the fate of their respective husbands. One would return from a Soviet POW camp in 1948; the other was declared dead, fallen in a battle near Leningrad. The aunt who had lost her husband was charged with raising the two boys. Not long after, she remarried, to a general in the East German police (the army had been dissolved and not yet reconstituted), who spent most of his time away from home defending the new border with West Germany. During the 1950s, the family—two aunts, the niece (who had since married a soldier she met during the flight), three husbands, and the two nephews—lived in an extended household together with the grandparents. Lemke grew close to his grandparents, especially to his Oma, whom he now thinks had the most incisive intelligence of all his relatives. She was able, for example, to solve complicated problems he encountered in mathematics in the school long before others.

In his early years, Lemke's relation to his father taught him, above all, that he had to deal with absence. He had already learned quiet sufferance in waiting for his skin burns to heal and then patience during the entire two years of flight at the end of the war. This patience was put to a test in waiting for his father who, after release from a Canadian POW camp, worked as a cook for the British army. The father had promised to return to retrieve his sons after he found them a *neue Mutti* (new mother).

Until 1961, with the erection of the wall around West Berlin and another wall to divide the two occupied Germanys, the situation of family separations and visits was ambiguous and open-ended. The boys saw their father

Figure 9. Father at Kölner Dom

sporadically. He would either send for his two sons to come and visit or take the train himself to see them on a weekend. On the visits they usually met one of a series of girlfriends, whom they were encouraged to think of as potential mothers. Lemke was told to call them *Tante* (aunt). He got to know two of them: Tante Ria and Tante Gretl. This photo from one such visit shows Lemke at age six asked to stand between two aunts, the Tante on his right who is his real aunt, the acting mother who actually raised him, and the Tante Gretl on his left who represents a prospective mother (figure 10). Father never returned with a *neue Mutti*. In fact, he stayed in the West and left the care for his boys to their maternal aunts and grandparents.

At fourteen Lemke moved into a state boarding school and visited his family only on weekends. With the building of the Wall, he faced a new dilemma: He could pursue studies at the university only if he had no contact with relatives in the West. The state feared that children from divided families like his would take advantage of a free education in the East and then join their relatives in the West, which many in fact had done. To secure his education, Lemke's aunt and her (new) husband, the army officer, adopted him so that he could change his name, ridding himself of his birth father's name. With "Lemke" as his new surname, he could disavow any contact, or wish for contact, with both the father in the West who had abandoned him and, should it be problematic, with his older brother.

Figure 10. With Tante Ria and Tante Gretl

Between 1961 and 1989, the years between the building of the Wall and its opening, many of Lemke's very best friends left East Germany for the West, and again Lemke learned patience and how to manage absence in his own life through a combination of unconscious erasure and an openness to developing new friendships. I am one of many people who has benefited from this openness.

Seven months before the Wall came down, Lemke was approved to travel in the West for the first time since the border had been closed. He reached out to his birth father, who, in the meantime, had remarried, fathered another son, divorced, and was now retired and living alone. "He was a stranger to me, an old senile man. We had nothing to say to each other. Nothing. We knew nothing about each other," explains Lemke. When this stranger died and was buried next to Lemke's mother five years later, Lemke was not told of the death or the funeral. He had in the intervening years lost contact with his brother, who took care of this father the last several years of his life.

Meanwhile, the aunt who had raised Lemke had since divorced from her second husband. Finding herself no longer capable of living alone, she moved to Berlin, into an apartment near Lemke, where, for the next seven years, he and his partner catered to her every need. His partner actually developed a closer relationship to her than Lemke had. She eventually moved into a care center for the elderly. Lemke saw her five days before her death; his partner was with her the day before.

I ask Lemke whether he experienced her death as the death of a mother. He hesitates. "I gave the eulogy at her funeral, it was very emotional. I had to stop and gather myself after a few sentences. We had a certain distance from each other. She noticed that I helped her in her old age as she had helped me as a child. The same relationship but reversed. She is buried here in Berlin, cremated, as she wanted. She was not sentimental."

Marquardt and His Grandfather

Marquardt does not know when or how his father died since his last contact was just before his sixth birthday. However, like Lemke, he kept in close touch with his grandparents, and it was their deaths that have left marks; it is for them he has truly mourned. Marquardt's grandmother died while he was in prison. He petitioned for release to attend the funeral, but, as he was classified a high security risk, prison officials insisted on handcuffs and shackles. And they were adamant that guards accompany him to the funeral. Marquardt refused to go, and on the day of the ceremony a pastor visited him in prison instead.

His grandfather's funeral has always been more troublesome for him, in part because, as he loved him the most, that loss was his most deeply felt, but also because he thinks that he could have prevented his death. At the time, Marquardt was working in the mortuary business. When he began to earn a lot of money as a pimp, his tax accountant told him that he needed to claim a legitimate income also and therefore to get a regular job that paid well. He found work picking up corpses and preparing them for burial. While his colleagues drank heavily to make their work bearable, Marquardt was, in his words, "cold in the head," which enabled him to do things that unsettled others. His colleagues, for example, were often unable to even touch the dead bodies of babies. This work made him sad, he says, but it was still something he could do.

Marquardt's grandfather had a heart attack while walking his trusted German shepherd in the woods. The loyal dog would not allow anyone to approach the dying man, so he died before emergency personnel arrived.

Marquardt volunteered to do all the preparation of the body for the funeral. He washed him, shaved him, dressed him, placed him in the casket, even lowered the casket underground. At the funeral, his bereaved grandmother spontaneously tried to jump in the grave. He says, "I had to bite my lip to avoid crying."

"When I talk about this, do you notice?" he asks me, "I am not doing well. I am shaking, I really don't feel well." I suggest we switch themes, but he is firm. "It's okay," he says, and goes on. "With the dreams, it's funny. I talked about this with Marion. You moved something in me. I don't know if that comes across. Lemke noticed it in discussions about Oma and Opa. I found it difficult to talk. You are a stranger, yes? I did not find it easy to talk, it is a weird situation. I began to shake, almost to cry. When I talk about that, like Opa's death, I am no longer myself but someone smaller, helpless. I am still there."

Nightmares

Within days of recalling these scenes of death, both Lemke and Marquardt complain to me of nightmares. Lemke says, they recurred only twice, and both times contained the image of the exhumation of his mother's plaid shepherd coat. Marquardt says, he now rarely sleeps without being awoken by nightmares, despite taking up to twenty different kinds of pills to help him sleep. Those pills are also to anesthetize him some from the pain of injuries sustained in karate competition. In other words, the physical pain inflicted by karate training, an activity resulting from a direct reaction to his mother's sex abuse, has now merged into the psychic pain from that abuse awoken through therapy and his attempt at reparation. His dreams contain recurring scenes of past events, for example, of his father crushing his hand or of sex with his mother; they are ongoing and he discusses them with Erdmann, but he does not know what to do.

In earlier conversations, I had asked both men about the content of their dreams, including daydreams. Marquardt initially maintained he has no dreams, but nightmares he readily admits to. Yet even these do not resemble the classic notion of a dream, where the scenes are distorted, everything mixed up. Marquardt insists his dreams, or nightmares, are real scenes of real events. Nothing takes place in them that did not take place exactly as it happened—except for one new dream that began several years ago, after he had had a heart attack and lost consciousness.

His heart attack provoked a feeling of death. In a matter of seconds, he says, his whole life passed by like on a film reel. His Oma and Opa were there. "Opa said, 'My son, fight.' My grandparents said, 'Go back, go back, it's not so nice here, you are needed.'" Since then, he has been having the dream of something dark and shapeless running after him. I tell him it is *das Ding*, the Thing, which I explain to him as the frightening radical unknowability that confronted him in his experience of deadness. He is unable to imagine the shapeless thing that pursues him. He then began to use the term on his own.

Shortly after these disclosures, I was having a discussion with Marquardt at his sports studio when Lemke happened to stop by. It surprised me to find him politely waiting downstairs for our discussion to end. It surprised me even more when Marquardt promptly grabbed Lemke, brought him upstairs, and asked him to comment on the discussion we had been having. It was an awkward situation for me, not because the three of us were together—we had shared space many times before—but because my presence had occasioned an event that forced me to comment on Marquardt's therapy. I turned my recorder back on:

MARQUARDT (IN A RUSH OF WORDS): We were just discussing my dreams, I woke up at night, sweating, crying out. I see my father, he crushes my hand, my mother and pictures of her, I cannot sleep. Das Ding comes, a black form with a huge pitchfork that will kill me, it also does kill me. This worries me. I don't know how to figure it out. I go out, in the public, I answer questions, before 100 people there in the audience. I am authentic: I am here, I am like this, I am strong enough to withstand what they say. Perhaps these dreams will stop, these dreams are threatening. Now they're more frequent, since a week ago.

LEMKE: The unconscious is at work here. You also have them a few days before a [new] reading, so after a reading they should go away.

MARQUARDT: They don't go away, but they are better. But they resurface, and disturb my sleep again. I am able to take this. That's how I see the readings, as a form of *Wiedergutmachung*, to tell people to be attentive. I want to torture myself, because I have hurt so many people, tortured them in my life. I see my victims in my dreams, whimpering before me.

LEMKE: Perhaps you should see a psychotherapist. That is not what we did. It is more intensive than our therapy was. Perhaps that is the key to going further. What we did is not classical psychoanalysis.

MARQUARDT: Therapy.

LEMKE: Yes. But psychoanalysis is a kind of therapy, too, more concentrated on your childhood. What do you think, John?

ME: You have no control over your dreams, and therefore they offer access to the unconscious. Herr Lemke tried to make you conscious of what you already knew but didn't understand. A psychoanalyst would work more with what you do not already know and cannot access.

MARQUARDT: I assumed I was guilty for Opa's death, and this guilt is still there, still present.

LEMKE: You know, we did work on that.

MARQUARDT: And that was good.

LEMKE: Grandfather was your great savior. He gave you orientation. And the readings are a continuation of therapy. I thought the readings would resolve some of these dreams.

MARQUARDT: They have not been resolved.

[They look to me to say something.]

ME: I am not a therapist, you understand. What I think? The readings are perhaps a form of becoming more conscious of yourself. But dreams are about the unconscious, and the readings are unlikely to access those thoughts. You want, I think, to be less emotionally stressed by these dreams.

LEMKE: Marquardt is capable of reconstructing many processes and of talking about them. But the unconscious, it doesn't follow [these reconstructions].

MARQUARDT: I have never before had such dreams with *das Ding*, which is persecuting me.

LEMKE: Child abuse. Such abuse in childhood is experienced as a deathly danger.

MARQUARDT: At the moment it's all very stressful. I am unsettled, especially while sleeping. I wake up at night. With Opa, it's morbid, he grasped me.

[Lemke talks about different possible therapists.]

MARQUARDT: It's ok now. I am a fighter.

LEMKE: I'll put you in contact with some psychoanalysts.

MARQUARDT: I was recently in the cemetery where Opa lies, and his grave doesn't exist anymore. It's been over thirty years. I know the tree [near where he rests].

LEMKE: I was in the cemetery of my Oma and Opa recently, and their graves also don't exist anymore. I think it's after twenty years and they're erased.

The Anthropologist's Craft

The primary craft of the anthropologist as fieldworker is to listen, but sometimes that is not enough. We can be easily distracted by being embarrassed, to the point of feeling distress, when we are told of an intimate event that asks us to contain the emotion of the other or when we are asked to disclose our opinions or elaborate what we in fact think is going on in the real time of our research. The request that I speak in this encounter, and that my speech should help, unnerved me. The three of us stand in unconscious proximity to one another, yet our relationships to each other are ambiguous, asymmetrical, unsettled. Marquardt asks Lemke, his former therapist, how to stop the nightmares preventing him from sleeping. Some of them seem to have become more intense, more frequent, since he began talking to me. Lemke interprets the persecutory figures in Marquardt's dreams as elements of his experience of abuse as a child, and he suggests further treatment by a psychoanalyst rather than other kinds of therapy. They ask me what I think. I elaborate what Lemke had said. They end this short dialogue in a moment of mutual suggestion and free association, commenting on the disappearance of the dead in Germany, how the graves of their grandparents have a planned life, like a dissolving time capsule, and then will be erased—an association likely prodded by questions I had posed earlier to each man separately.

This story is not about me, and I work to confine and delimit my place in it. But I am, at this point, an integral audience for the two men. And Marquardt and Lemke are integrating me into their stories by asking me to help. They are linking this idea of help with me, and this link makes me uncomfortable. It seems to distract me from my task of listening. They project onto me an expertise they feel they need. I do not welcome this projection, but also I cannot disclaim responsibility for it. Indeed, my ambiguous location—listener, friend, scribe, anthropologist, professor—encourages such projections. When I am alone with each man, my exchanges seem to call on multiple and relatively unbounded registers of my being. In the presence of the two men together, however, I feel more constrained to be an anthropologist. But what that means is determined only as our encounters unfold. Even as I try to avoid responding to their requests, they seem to sense what I am thinking. I look down but am aware that they continue looking at me. I am not there to tell them what to do. How am I authorized to advise the two men, who have spent years working together to reconstruct the wreck of a life, the decimated self of Andreas Marquardt? Yet their needs are palpable and pressing: how to proceed at this critical moment after formal therapy has ended but perplexingly dark messages from past experiences threaten to blow up a present stability? Marquardt has largely displaced his destructive energies into love and legitimate work, but the past, and the subject of his unconscious life, continues to erupt in frightening dreams and speak with such vehemence that his waking life is disturbed. He has problems sleeping because he has problems dreaming. His dreams are less about the thoughts of his waking life than nightmares of past events that he has now brought into speech but retain an unconscious affective charge against which he is helpless. My knowledge of the psyche is limited, I explain, as are my options here. I offer a summary and a few ideas about the unconscious.

Marquardt and Lemke are public figures in Germany. In a wide array of public settings and in visual and print media, they are asked to talk about their experiences of and knowledge of child sex abuse. They became public persons through the revelation of private details about the development of Marquardt's life and psyche in the book Lemke wrote about him, through the public readings they do together, through Lemke's professional work, and through the activities of Marquardt's foundation. My interest goes beyond this public activity to another realm, that of unarticulated private details. Without those details I cannot explore the nature of empathic communication between a therapist and his client. Without those details I cannot ask what kind of transference makes therapy efficacious and enables audience identification during readings.

Without becoming another point of identification, I am increasingly integrated into their dyadic relationship as an unsettling third member. I address Lemke with the informal "Du" and by his first name, but Marquardt with the polite "Sie," and they address each other with "Sie." To address Marquardt with the polite form grants him the respectful distance he warrants being the central subject around which our relationships unfold. To use the informal Du, as I do with the therapist, also implies respect but not the same distance. Lemke and I have been friends too long to ignore the proximity created through time. In writing I initially followed anthropological convention and anonymized their names by assigning the two men initials—"Herr M" for Mr. Marquardt and "T" for Lemke. I had promised them, and Erdmann, Marquardt's partner, not to use their names. But as they are public figures any number of details can be easily found through a Google search and even seen on YouTube, as a colleague warned me. This convention can no longer protect their privacy, and it might even make my writing appear deceptive, perversely opposite to my intent. But in attempting to be relentlessly honest, in using the real names of people in real time in revealing descriptions and interpretations of their lives and relationships, I risk, as an anthropologist, breaking an important axiom of the discipline: to disclose without harming.

Therefore, I asked the two men and Erdmann whether I may use their real names in my writing; all three agreed without hesitation. In fact, the conundrums of disclosure for them keep changing as the publicity surrounding their persons expands into new venues. Rosa von Praunheim, one of the most prolific and radical experimental filmmakers from the New German Cinema of the late 1960s, is, as I write, making a film based on Härte, with actors playing the personas in scenes of the past involving Andreas Marquardt, Marion Erdmann, and Jürgen Lemke. The real people, in turn, "play" themselves as adults in the present. Von Praunheim himself shares an uncanny unconscious proximity with the two men with respect to his relation to absent parents. His mother told him shortly after his fifty-eighth birthday that he was an adopted child. He was extremely close to his adoptive mother, having, as an openly gay man with many different lovers, shared with her an apartment until her death. That story is the subject of a film he made called *Two Mothers*, released in 2007, which documents his search for his biological mother, who died in 1946 in a psychiatric hospital in Berlin.

In any case, nominating—my use of real or fictive names as well as the renaming going on among the people I describe—has aspects of magical power and presents inescapable moral dilemmas. By using last names throughout this text, I lose the different nuances of distance and closeness in address available in the German language but not in English. Also, to sustain the unique immediacy of this kind of research, I use the present tense of the fieldwork situation when repeating dialogue, an older anthropological convention that has nowadays, without adequate reflection, largely given way to historical conventions of past tense in writing.

In fieldwork, anthropologists are usually positioned in a manner similar to the above scene, awkwardly, in between already existing relationships and outside the normal hierarchies, yet close and always in relation to them. Who knows what we are up to and for how long? Entering the spaces between the people we study can shift the questions they ask of each other. Precisely because we remain so ambiguously situated, we may either stop talk or open up a space for a new perspective. At best, alternative configurations of speaking and listening emerge to lend some depth or clarity to the present by exposing wishes that would ordinarily not have been communicated. Our entrance can provoke a moment of perceptual arrest for both the anthropologist and those studied, casting a new light on the multiple selves at play and drawing attention to the displacement of voice that characterizes and enriches the everyday. At worst, however, our presence can facilitate paranoid fantasies of being watched, even spied on, and forebodings of abandonment and betrayal, given that we nearly all depart at some point and return to the academy or other professional worlds. In response to this dilemma, many anthropologists today try to collaborate in their representations with the people they study. Integrating them into our research and writing may alleviate some moral anxieties, but this level of complicity inevitably leads to censorship of uncomfortable details and, in many cases, the sacrifice of insight, even truth, for harmony.

In addition to listening and at times offering something vaguely helpful like an understanding, I also serve as a container for the painful affects attached to the experiences Marquardt and Lemke recall in my presence. This is no minor role. Unlike Marquardt, I do not see myself as a "fighter." I do not see myself as "strong" or "tough." Their expectations of help threaten to overwhelm my own fragile sense of self, especially when I feel constrained to fill simultaneously the ethical imperatives of friendship and of my profession. Both men remind me of my own limited abilities, and of the ethical constraints of an ethnographic sensitivity, and how unlikely it is that I, in any way, can satisfy their requests. They make me feel guilty for not being there sufficiently for either of them. In this situation, and often, I decide that the best I can do is to remain compassionately silent.

Both men are trying to be brutally honest with me to arrive at the truth of their lived emotional experiences. I am trying to turn their truths into knowledge. I think that I am experimenting with a better way to communicate with them and about them than merely extracting information or data. Communicating with them in a way that facilitates their search for the truth about themselves. Communicating about them in a way that encourages more complex thinking about worlds that are not mine. Communication of this sort demands not only sensitivity to the inner worlds of those with whom we speak, but also the capacity to think through those worlds together, taking into account, however partially, our various past and present selves and senses of reality.

In several subsequent conversations with Marquardt, I sympathize with his inability to sleep by telling him more about what I think. I encourage him to see his dreams as a healthy attempt to work through experiences he is incapable of thinking through while awake. He seems unable to withstand thinking about these experiences, even in sleep—hence the nightmares. The only resolution possible, I say to him, is to find a way to make the dreams tolerable and to dream the experiences in them to the end. For that he might make use of a psychoanalyst, not to help get rid of his dreams but to help him think in dreams. He listens, friendly, but becomes distracted.

I share with Marquardt what I know while trying to contain the emotional alarm he is sharing with me. I insist I am only an anthropologist and disavow the expertise of a therapist, who may tell him something rather different, knowing that this distinction probably does not make that much sense to him. My commitment to engage with him is primarily about knowledge, I explain. The question of how I can come to know Marquardt is not in the pragmatic register in which he seems most to operate. My interest in knowing in order to theorize, moreover, entails a warrant to remain alert to what I do not know. Lemke understands this well. But with Marquardt, I am reluctant to offer any premature conclusions or advice that might lead him to act as though I could substitute for a qualified therapist. Another way to put this is to insist that my engagement is a form of open-ended discovery of the conditions of communication.

Yet Marquardt and Lemke wish to know or obtain something quite specific from me, including, in this case, help. On this level, anthropological knowledge intersects with but deviates from the knowledge of therapeutic efficacy. To think, to discover, to know, to understand, to help—these essential capabilities are called on in both the therapeutic session and the ethnographic encounter. What differs in the two settings, significantly, is the imagination of intimacy and connection. Especially among psychoanalysts, the therapeutic relation between analyst and analysand is thought of as temporary, a way of simulating and preparing for life outside the session. By contrast, the ethnographic relation of anthropologist to interlocutor is thought of as an ongoing engagement in life itself, where the anthropologist and, in varying degrees, her interlocutors risk reimagining themselves through what they might discover in an open-ended exchange. The limits to this exchange are by no means clear, and its ethical parameters can be determined only in real-life interactions during fieldwork. To do otherwise, to assume one can know unambiguously ahead of the encounter is to make the anthropologist into a machine of knowledge production and to reduce the anthropological subject to a use-object, a source to manipulate, even exploit, for our own, usually well-intended, purposes.

The dilemmas of intimacy—attachment, separation, closeness, distance— mark the professional relations of both anthropologists with their interlocutors and therapists with their clients, but the taboos between therapists and those they analyze are much more constricting if not considered absolute. While the initial taboos of the therapeutic profession continue to be enforced, other aspects of the relations between therapists and their clients have changed considerably since Freud's early twentieth-century experiments in what he dubbed "psycho-analysis." The room is still an enclosed and secure space; those analyzed still pay therapists for getting them to talk of things they would rather not reveal to themselves, much less to others; the content of the discussion is still considered confidential; and sexual intimacy between therapist and patient is still perhaps the most serious of violations. But often there is no longer a couch; often therapists no longer sit behind their subjects but across from them; and although classic psychoanalysis is prohibitively expensive, other forms of therapy informed by psychoanalysis have become available, including group therapy, which cost much less. And, as Marquardt and Lemke are demonstrating, it is possible to transgress the prohibition against taking the content of therapy outside the consulting room, in their case through the coauthoring of a book and its regular public readings.

Lemke calls Marquardt a "client," following conventions developed by German therapists, like him, who are not classically trained psychoanalysts but who draw eclectically on different analytic traditions. The term "client" emphasizes the active service dimension of the relationship, a type of relationship more maternal than paternal, and also more material and idealistic. In the development of the relation between Lemke and Marquardt, they have had to sort out these different dimensions, including maintaining private lives independent of each other's needs, as well as the sharing of royalties from the book and honorariums from reading engagements.

The two emphases, on the maternal and material, have become especially important in framing interactions with the administrative bureaucracies of contemporary welfare systems. In personal interactions, however, therapists tend to avoid abstract language and simply use proper names. Many types of therapy in Germany are still funded by the national health insurance system, which relies on both private contributions and state subventions. To qualify for reimbursement by the national health care system, however, analysts must increasingly speak in medical terms, of a doctor treating a "patient" to find a "cure." Some psychoanalysts are also medical doctors, as Freud was. Most important, and regardless of their training, therapists are charged to address wounds in the psyche, which, unlike many physical wounds, tend not to disappear. Even medical doctors are often skeptical of the appropriateness of equating psychic change to a cure similar to the healing of an ulcer or physical bruise.

One of the most innovative areas in contemporary psychoanalytic treatment, which is very relevant for anthropologists, has been the added attention given to empathic communication and the role of projections as well as the transfer of emotions between analyst and analysand. Freud initially found emotional transference and countertransference to be potential procedural obstacles in therapy to overcome. Awareness, in particular, of countertransference—the emotions the analyst invests in the patient—can appear to undermine the authority of the analyst as an omniscient observer and all-knowing interpreter. But countertransference also invites the patient to enter into the investments of the analyst, the thinking and emotions produced in the sessions. Analysts have thus increasingly found the interpersonal investments themselves to be the most direct way to access the patient's unconscious, and therefore an essential diagnostic tool for all successful treatment. As the analyst becomes aware of what specific emotions and roles are being projected into him, he seeks to understand his own projections and reactions to the patient, and, rather than withholding them from the patient, discusses them in the session. Therapeutic efficacy then depends more on symbolizing and understanding more deeply what is going on in the analytic session than on reconstructing the past, as in Freud's initial idea of treatment, by interpreting symptoms or locating the origin of particular problems. It would be wrong, however, to oppose the two activities of understanding the transference in sessions and interpreting symptoms. Any analyst must give some weight to both. The empathy that grows in such communication has the potential to cut through the mirror world of projections by demanding precision in sensing and responding to the emotional life and needs of the other without dissolving one's own integrity in the process.

Anthropological work also requires access to people and their worlds, and this access equally involves, similar to therapeutic work, emotional transference and countertransference. But while the anthropologist may befriend and help his interlocutors, even fall in love and marry one of them, he does not usually "treat" them. Thinking through the transference, as I am attempting to do here, has an altogether different purpose for the anthropologist: to bring one closer to the nature of lived experience. It enables learning how the histories and emotions of therapist, client, and anthropologist create affinities, identifications, or misunderstandings as we enter into different settings, with the ultimate goal of reframing our understandings and representations of experience. This reframing may indeed change the future. We and our interlocutors may become transformational objects for each other, in which case the therapeutic and anthropological relationship may come to resemble each other in important ways. On reflection, the various projects of Marquardt (reparation through self-knowledge and publicity), Lemke (treatment and publicity), and myself (knowledge and publicity) may no longer appear to be so radically different.

Similar issues have arisen throughout my ethnographic encounters in this project on the rehabilitation of child sex offenders. In this particular case, my investigation entails a series of encounters between Lemke and me, Marquardt and me, Lemke and Marquardt, the two men and various public audiences, and audiences (listeners and readers) and me. Each of these encounters revolves in some way around the treatment of child molesters. Children, sex, abuse, and rehabilitation—the four objects central to this study—provoke a wide array of emotional and intellectual responses, and bring forth phantasmagoria independent of what I actually say or write. Often these responses involve projections *onto* me of an intimacy with the issue—assuming, for instance, that I have been a victim of abuse, am sexually interested in children, or am obsessed with sex—all of which I very much doubt to be true. And they involve projecting *into* me certain negative feelings others have about the issues at hand, disquieting elements of experiences or phantasies that listeners or readers wish to get rid of. I am asked to contain those unsettling thoughts in a way similar to Marquardt and Lemke at their readings. The difference is that my unconscious proximity to readers is not displaced by another voice, as Lemke's voice displaces Marquardt's. Readers of this book are ultimately left to their own devices in reckoning with stories of child sex abuse.

In the particular contemporary setting of this project, I am still engaged, as were prior generations of anthropologists, in a journey to the unknown, traveling to Germany as well as a certain psychic distance to reach an understanding of an illegitimate desire difficult to fathom. But this journey is not to a radically different culture. It lacks the pathos of early pioneers in anthropology, who took it upon themselves to document indigenous peoples decimated in the imperial advances of the West. (That these pioneers named these peoples "savage" or "primitive" suggests the poverty of the language of the time but detracts neither from their noble efforts nor from the incredible advances to knowledge they made.) And it lacks what Susan Sontag described as the "exquisite, aristocratic version of neutrality" proposed by Claude Lévi-Strauss in his *technique de dépaysement*. Finally, my journey also lacks the conviction of more contemporary anthropologists, of either repatriating knowledge for the purposes of critiquing the West or of giving voice to the worlds' marginalized and abject populations in their unjust exclusions.

If I am neither engaged in any active estrangement from my country or the West generally, nor obligated to activism, folding my ends into those of the people I study, what, then, is the anthropological end of this book? For me, it remains approaching the truth, creating an accurate representation of this truth through its stories, and arriving at an understanding. The understanding I seek through generalizing and abstracting from empirical observations is permeated by introspection and empathic communication: to be there more fully, in the field and in the text, and to be able to communicate an understanding better, more self-reflexively, with Marquardt and Lemke and to my audiences.

Imprisonment and Therapy

In his first arrest, Marquardt was charged with the procuration of women, human trafficking in conjunction with pimping, aggravated battery, and unauthorized possession of a weapon. He sat in the detention center Moabit for close to ten months before the prosecutor accumulated enough evidence to go to trial. Ultimately, the evidence was insufficient, and Marquardt's skilled attorney got him off with a relatively light sentence of four years, plus a monetary penalty for nonpayment of taxes that took most of his savings. Marquardt was then transferred from the detention center to a minimum-security prison, which released him to work during the day.

Outside the prison, Marquardt continued his pimping business until it was discovered two years into his sentence. He was rearrested, sent back to the detention center, and charged with attempted murder. The prosecutor sought evidence to prove the worst of his crimes and to make an example of him. While he sat in the center another ten months awaiting trial, he turned suicidal and was introduced to therapy.

This second period of detention caused a crisis of self. Marquardt thought, "I'll spend the rest of my life here if I don't do something." His first prompt came from a social worker assigned to conduct a diagnostic interview. He found her sympathetic, he says, like a grandmother. She told him that she thought he was wounded and that deep down he was not actually so malevolent and tough as he presented himself to be. He broke down and cried.

When his lawyer came to talk, Marquardt told her of his mother's abuse. "She was," he says, "the very first person in whom I confided these facts." She then sought to find therapeutic help for him in the detention center. He subsequently also told Marion Erdmann. Marquardt was assigned to a psychologist, and in discussions with him—three times a week for six months—he began to explore his own history of sexual abuse. This was "not real therapy," explains Marquardt, but still helpful because the psychologist "sensed the pressure of a great deal of suffering."

The state prosecutor could not prove the charge of attempted murder in the second trial, so Marquardt was sentenced to the lesser charge of abetting aggravated battery. He was transferred from the detention center to the psychiatric wing of a maximum-security prison. There they heavily sedated him, but this did not make him less violent. After many scenes in which he demanded to speak with someone, he was assigned a psychiatrist. Marquardt terms those conversations "ridiculous," as the psychiatrist was skeptical of his history of abuse. Why, the psychiatrist asked him, did you not as a child just tell your grandparents what was happening? They were living down the hall in the same apartment, weren't they? Such questions drove Marquardt into a blind rage, making it impossible for him to respond to the questions. Now, he explains to me, I would say, "as a child I was incapable of resisting my mother's advances. But I did not have those words back then." After three months in the psychiatric wing, he was sent to the regular part of the prison to serve out his sentence.

If Marquardt had been charged with a sexual offense instead of a series of crimes focusing on various acts of violence, he would have likely been assigned a therapist from the start. Since 2002, in fact, German law mandates therapy for anyone serving a sentence longer than eighteen months for a sex crime. But since his conviction was for violence alone, he had to fight for therapy. In any event, most of the therapy in prison for sex offenders focuses on the delict alone and becoming conscious of the risks of repeating the offense. But Marquardt wanted to go deeper into his own experience. He had become a mystery to himself. But the prison therapists had insufficient time allocated to him for such treatment. Prison officials did eventually approve therapy once a week and assigned him to a series of therapists who, he says, began to "open the knots." One came from outside the prison for three months and even, he says proudly, "wrote her PhD about me." On her recommendation, he submitted written requests to find a therapist outside the prison, arguing that he needed to work on his difficult childhood to discover why he had such a profound propensity to violence.

After much hesitation on the part of prison authorities, his request was approved, and he called a number of therapists who had been suggested to him, including Jürgen Lemke. To see whether they both agreed that they could work together, Lemke insisted on three exploratory sessions. Thereafter, Marquardt began meeting Lemke twice a week for ninety-minute sessions, with another ninety minutes allocated for travel time.

Marquardt says the first several years were nothing new to him, just that the questions were deeper and more exacting about why he engaged in certain behaviors or felt certain ways. I asked him what ideas he had of therapy before entering prison. "Talk therapy? Ideas about it? Never, never, never, never! Totally virgin territory. On television I had seen weak people, children, lying on the sofa. Today I only think about it as food for thought." I ask him whether the gender of the therapist made a difference. "It's unimportant," he quickly replies, "but they must listen and give me a little prod about what I could change."

When Marquardt began therapy with Lemke at KiZ, the child abuse center, Lemke asked him whether an intern in training might sit in on their sessions. "I thought it was a bit odd," Marquardt explains, "but then I said, okay, I already have no problem talking, so perhaps I can help her progress in her training." As he explained this to me, I was unsure whether he meant this gesture of help ironically or actually had convinced himself that his therapy sessions might serve as teaching tools for young interns. At any rate, the intern did participate in most of the sessions. Her presence as a third person in the traditionally dyadic therapeutic sessions, and a woman at that, must have in some way influenced the dynamic of interaction. I ask both men about the intern. Lemke describes this intern to me as the very best of those he has worked with. He says that Marquardt called her "Tante," suggesting an older, undesirable woman, and yet he made frequent suggestive sexual innuendoes about what might have been possible if they had met before he entered prison. She would respond with a roll of the eyes and occasionally scoff at him. Marquardt now praises her work to me. She was easy to talk to, he says, about both his victim and perpetrator roles; she posed good questions, he thought, and reacted well and yet differently than Lemke.

Marquardt says that Lemke encouraged him to "use my own vocabulary, put things in my own words, not to use polite words to make things prettier. To be very direct." Lemke remarks that the intern was taken aback by some of Marquardt's word choices. Marquardt appeared to enjoy shocking her by describing his activities with such well-chosen words as *Fotze* (cunt), *blasen* (to suck a dick), *arschficken* (to fuck an ass), *anspritzen* (to cum on), and *anpissen* (to piss on). These words tend to be reserved for the company of men and were likely an attempt to intimidate and impress the young intern in the same way Marquardt used to recruit his prostitutes. Whatever the case, she obviously felt that she learned something from these sessions, as she continued attending and taking notes for nearly a year after her internship ended.

I ask whether the intern had not introduced an erotic element and some instability into the relationship between the therapist and his client, or changed something in their interaction. Both men dismiss the question. "I never had any thoughts about their relationship [between Lemke and his intern]," Marquardt explains, and he denies even being curious about her presence. "No, I concentrated on myself," he concludes. Marquardt's explanation of self-absorption is entirely consistent with his person. Nonetheless, he did change the presentation of himself during the initial year of the intern's presence, showing more of a flirtatious, macho self than he would have shown Lemke had the two men been alone with each other.

I ask Lemke whether he ever doubted that Marquardt was abused as a child. "Never," he says. "From my experience with such victims, I believed him immediately. In cases where a father abuses his daughter, everyone today believes the claim without evidence. In his case, people didn't want to believe him. They were skeptical." Ultimately, the most convincing case for the truth of Marquardt's account, says Lemke, lies in a detail that is difficult to explain away. In 2003 in therapy, Marquardt could still recite the lyrics from the musical *Hair* word for word without pause. For Marquardt, those tunes are subject to instant recall, unlike any other particular learned associations from his past. Lemke's decades of "experience with such victims" leads me to defer to his sensibility, at least initially. Over time, I have had my own experiences with Marquardt from which to assess his credibility, though these of course pale in depth and duration to those of Lemke.

An equally if not more significant reason why I should defer to Lemke here in assessing Marquardt's credibility is an unconscious communication that quickly developed into an affinity between them. Such communication is difficult to fake, as one cannot control the unconscious. Although the two men have very different motivations for talking and understanding, they share an experience of childhood abandonment by their mothers. That abandonment most likely resulted in an unconscious resentment toward the mother. Marquardt turned this resentment into aggression against women generally. Lemke, by contrast, was more conflicted about his loss and never made it conscious to himself. His emotion was complicated, in turn, by the guilt he felt in suspecting that he had somehow caused his mother to go away. Although he was told that his mother was killed in an accident and did not intentionally abandon him, this explanation did not lessen his aloneness nor did it make him feel any less responsible for her absence. The Jürgen Lemke whom I have known has a history of assuming responsibility for others, perhaps the legacy of the transformation of resentment at being abandoned and of the guilt assumed for that abandonment into a generalized need to engage in reparation. During our last visit with his brother, Lemke was confirmed in his unspoken hunch that his mother's death was a sacrifice to spare him and his brother from having to see her raped. This also confirmed his sense of his guilt.

"Did you ever correct his facts?," I ask Lemke about Marquardt's version of his own life. "Yes," he replies. "Marquardt would ask, 'How can you know that?' and I would say, first, logic leads me to certain conclusions, and then my own experience as a therapist alerts me to specific patterns." Lemke realized early on in the sessions that Marquardt responds well to pragmatic suggestions, so he encouraged him to think of his options for engaging in crime in terms of the costs and benefits. Although Marquardt has cut off contacts with his former milieu, many old acquaintances still come to him and work out in his sports studio. As might be expected, he receives occasional offers from them for illegal employment. Once, after being impressed with an interview he'd seen with Lemke on television, a former acquaintance of Marquardt even offered Lemke a job.

I ask both Lemke and Marquardt what their fantasies about each other were like and how they had changed. Marquardt denies altogether having had fantasies about Lemke, sexual or otherwise. Lemke, in turn, explains that Marquardt is for him an "antitype." He does not find him in the least physically attractive. Lemke says that he found interesting Marquardt's use of masculinity as a manic defense. He was attracted, he says, to this extreme masculinity as a therapeutic challenge. Also important for Lemke, I suspect, was the pull of a vitality issuing from a masculinity visibly wounded at its core, and Marquardt's appeal for his help to stabilize this masculinity to eventually secure release from prison.

"What was important for me," says Marquardt, "was that he guaranteed that I could talk openly, he would listen. I had no fear. I liked how he approached me, his pauses, allowing for time, posing questions. When he noticed I wasn't doing well, when I would sink into myself, he'd ask other questions, encourage me not to feel guilty, which took a heavy burden from my body. He helped to really build me up. The more I spoke, the more trust I had."

According to Lemke, Marquardt had occasionally tried to use the more familiar "Du" to address him, but Lemke maintained the distance. Now Marquardt finds this distance important also and uses the metaphor of a doctor and patient: "I don't know everything about my doctor, where he lives, what he does. My doctor helps me when I need help." Despite the formal way in which Marquardt and Lemke address each other, I observe an ease and familiarity that suggests intimacy at another, what I would call unconscious, level. "I always found it nice that the therapist knows everything about you but you know nothing about the therapist," explains Marquardt. "In retrospect, it is a bit odd. We did not become friends, ten years after, but I have the greatest respect for him and he for me. Actually, there is a friendship but not a real one. We have been together in many therapy sessions, many readings, we have travelled together for readings outside Berlin. Perhaps a friendship but not one that is daily."

Writing and Therapy

About two and a half years after he began therapy with Lemke, and after he had already been released from prison, Marquardt remarked to Lemke, "My theme is so interesting to people, one should write a book about me. It might also help people."

Lemke looked at him and replied, "I could imagine that. If you want to, you should start."

"I didn't understand his response," says Marquardt. "Three weeks later, he asked me if I had made any progress. 'No,' I said, 'I need someone to lead me through, who knows what he is doing. Perhaps you can help me.' I didn't know that he had already written three books. I thought he maybe had friends who were writers."

At that point, Lemke began to take notes himself during the sessions, and later even used a cassette recorder. He supplemented his own summaries and transcriptions with the extensive notes of the intern who had sat in the first several years of therapy. Writing the book, says Lemke, led him to clarify and analyze what went on in therapy sessions more than he would have otherwise. Throughout the process, Lemke remained, says Marquardt, "above all a therapist, not an author." After Lemke completed a draft of the manuscript, he wrote an exposé, contacted an agent, and secured a contract with a publishing house.

The manuscript took two years to complete, and the first reading aloud preceded publication by another two years. Before submitting to a publisher, Lemke read the entire work to Marquardt and Erdmann, over a couple of days. They deliberated for three weeks before making a decision to submit the text to a press. Their hesitation, explains Marquardt: "Would parents want to bring their kids to us, to our karate school, after they see what kind of asshole I had been?"

I ask Marquardt what it was like to hear his own words placed in carefully crafted passages for the first time.

My partner and I spoke about it. She took me in her arms and said she had not known that my life had been this difficult. We had always spoken about everything, but she did not know what I had said in therapy. What Lemke read was partly new to her, sometimes shocking. We had discussions for weeks, for months. She would ask questions, we would argue, and then we'd meet each other again. She also had therapy, but not over such a long period as I did. While I was in therapy she had been running our sports studio, eight hours a day. She had no time for therapy. While I had been changing, for the better, she had to swallow the entire shit. She developed another perspective on things. It wasn't easy, and she was often astonished, "Why did you do that? Or that?" she asked me. It was hard, really hard. With certain things, I said, we had our differences.

It was as if I was made to face a mirror, a mirror of my life was read before me. Lemke had brought it together. We debated whether it was correct, whether the words were mine, the feelings were right. But it was horrifying to hear how I had really lived. There were moments when I had to stop him from reading. I just couldn't take it any more. But he sensed that.

Marion took it better than I did. It was much worse for me. Lemke sensed when I was suffering, when something wasn't right in my experience of events. We read it once, corrected everything. Then read it once more, the entire manuscript. Both times it was a struggle for me. I began to shake. I was often near tears, often indeed crying. Lemke was very sensitive to my feelings. The room was oddly still.

Even today, Marquardt cannot read the book about his own life. "When I try [to bring myself to read], and I have tried, I begin to tremble. I get some unsettling inner feelings. I partly lose my voice, my eyes tear up, I need forty-five minutes to collect myself. I am not able to do it. It's like a mirror. I can talk about anything, that's what's unusual, about sexual abuse, about brutality to women, but I cannot read this."

In editing the book, Lemke had many disagreements with the publishing house. From the beginning, the publisher had assured him that although the book might sell well, there would be insufficient interest for a reading tour. Lemke had written three previous books, all with reading tours after publication. The theme of child sex abuse, and by a mother at that, the general editor said, was too distasteful for the general public.

In the middle of manuscript preparation, the two editors initially assigned left the press and were replaced by a single one who, in Lemke's opinion, was much less experienced in working with writers in addition to being uncomfortable with the content of the manuscript. The new editor returned to an early suggestion to recast the entire story as the history of a Berlin pimp, playing down the dimension of sex abuse. He wanted to remove many of the more provocative passages, especially those having to do with Marquardt's perverse sexual desires, claiming they were irrelevant to the story. These objections led Marquardt, in one meeting, to question the editors, "Who is the pimp here, you or me?" That is, he asked on what basis they claimed to know enough to make decisions about the manuscript's content. Lemke and Marquardt eventually relented and removed many passages, while still insisting on retaining several controversial episodes. The managing editor then called in a third party, a Bavarian writer familiar with the German prostitution scene. She defended Lemke's initial choices and surprised the editor by stating that her favorite chapter was one of those the new editor wanted to omit. Her suggested changes for the final version were merely organizational.

Since its publication, both Marquardt and Lemke have, in addition to readings, made many appearances on television talk shows to discuss the book and the issues it raises. After each event, it rises on the bestseller lists, several times reaching the rank of number one in Germany. In 2009, several years before Rosa von Praunheim began work on turning the book into a film script, another young film producer purchased the rights to the book. But after a year of work, the difficulties she had understanding the text and translating it into a film plot proved insurmountable. More recently, the book was made available as an e-book and translated into Braille for the blind. Lemke has been asked to sit on several high-profile commissions involving the sexual abuse of children. Marquardt has been the central figure in several documentary films made for television, and, for the work of his foundation Helping Makes You Strong, he was nominated in 2010 for the Laureus Medien award in the category "the social sport project."

Public Readings

The book's premiere reading was in January 2007, in a working-class bar-restaurant near Alexanderplatz in Berlin, in front of about seventy people, including friends of both men, a reporter for the *Bild* tabloid, a television crew, other therapists who work with Lemke, one of Marquardt's former therapists, Erdmann and Lemke's partner, regular patrons of the bar, and acquaintances from Marquardt's former underworld milieu. Most had been expressly invited. Marquardt recalls his experience, "I couldn't really hear Lemke speak, and [after only about three minutes] I started to tremble and began to cry like a baby. I thought about leaving the room, but I'm a fighter. My partner came to me, took my hand, and told me, 'You can do it, you can do it.' When it came time to speak, I did find my voice. But people could see that I struggled, and that won their respect. They saw that it wasn't going well, but that with the support of my partner and Lemke, I made it. Each time after that I became stronger. And today I can hear everything. With some passages, I feel kind of odd, but it's not as if I have to stand up and leave. I stay there, I listen, I get goose bumps, but I can talk immediately after. When I hear what is read, I am inside those words."

When Marquardt says he is "inside" the words on the page, he suggests that they contain or envelop him. The exercise of reading, as that of writing, should theoretically have been an exercise in externalization and symbolization, of creating a representation for what he had experienced that can contain the experience but is different from it. But Marquardt's relation to the words on the page has not yet attained much distance. He is, as he said earlier, incapable of speaking these words, of seeing them on the page and then uttering what he has read. When spoken aloud by someone else, however, the words inside him become tolerable to hear.

The question for Marquardt, then, is not whether the words describing his life belong to him, but under what condition he finds it possible to understand the words as symbols, as representations of his experiences, and how to place himself at a distance to them. As it is now, to read the words himself would place his pre- and post-therapy selves in an uncomfortable rivalry. Unable to read or speak them, he at most can listen to someone else read his story. The other's reading of his words permits him to remain with his posttherapy self. This struggle between reading and speaking is about establishing an authenticity of self, a Marquardt who owns his own traumatic history as a past for which he feels compelled to make amends. For Marquardt, these readings from the written book about his life are, as he says repeatedly, *Wiedergutmachung*. Not every member of the public trusts Marquardt's version of this struggle. At the premiere, the partner of another therapist asked Lemke whether that part of the performance when Marquardt broke down had been orchestrated. "Are you nuts?" Lemke replied, "He cannot sob on command."

The theatricality and emotional intensity of the premiere posed a challenge to Lemke's understanding of the readings as a continuation of therapy. At the moment when Marquardt broke down, Lemke asked himself whether he was taking advantage of his client. Perhaps Marquardt could not handle such a public airing of himself. Lemke stopped the reading to ask whether he should continue. Marquardt motioned for him to do so.

Subsequent readings certainly standardized the performance between therapist and client, but audience reactions still vary considerably from setting to setting. I am reminded in their reactions of what Thomas Mann said of "public activity." Based on his own experience reading and speaking in public, Mann said that public activity was "prone to take on a character of fantasy, dream and buffoonery" (cited in Juers 2011). Lemke thinks that the organizers of the readings largely determine the general atmosphere: how open, how enthused, how much effort is put into it. He himself was quite nervous the first few times, but as he had already done many readings for other books he has published, the readings for *Härte* also quickly became fairly routine. He usually reads the same passages, for about forty-five minutes: a section on Marquardt's abuse by his father, one on seduction and sexual abuse by his mother, another on his pimping, and a final one on his use of therapy. Marquardt says he would prefer "harder" passages, to confront listeners with the extent of the harm he had done, but Lemke says Marquardt only wants to shock the audience and that would not be productive.

Marquardt prepares himself for the readings, mentally and emotionally, like he did for karate competitions. He pays attention to the entire gestalt of the event and even makes suggestions to Lemke about length of presentation or appearance. Lemke, I notice, is generally resistant to these suggestions. Once Marquardt came with two pairs of white-rimmed glasses, and suggested they both wear them; Lemke said no. Once I even suggested that Lemke button his shirt cuffs, as they fluttered like bird wings when he gestured; Lemke did not button them. After the readings, Marquardt is also quick to praise Lemke for the clarity and wit of his responses, and for his support of Marquardt's project of reparation.

One question asked at each event is whether Marquardt can forgive his mother or whether his hate for her will forever accompany him. Marquardt's response: "Never. The hate is too much."

Most often, however, audience reactions are personal, likely stimulated by free associations made while listening to Lemke's voice and then drifting off to personal experiences of childhood or adolescence, of injuries, or of odd thoughts or transformative experiences:

· A man in his forties approached Marquardt and asked whether he could work for him as a pimp.

· A man who had seen Marquardt on television wanted information on how to become a pimp. "I did not answer," Marquardt explains to me, "but I could have told him what to do."

· A scantily dressed woman decked out in gold jewelry sat in the front row and ostentatiously flirted with Marquardt. After the reading she introduced herself to both men and told Marquardt that she would be interested in working for him on the street. Marquardt told her he was no longer in business.

· A woman introduced herself as one of the attendants at a gas station in Neukölln where Marquardt used to fill the tank of his Mercedes. She found him to be a very unpleasant person, she commented, and complained that in all those years he never once said hello.

· A man introduced himself, *"Ich bin Marquardt,"* and then explained that he had received more than a dozen telephone calls wishing him well with his new book. So he went out and bought the book and, on noticing there would be a reading, decided to meet this author who goes by the same name as his.

Frequently members of the audience identified themselves as victims of sexual abuse—by mothers, brothers, and fathers. After discussion ends, it is not uncommon for some individuals to approach either man for advice on therapists. Lemke himself is often asked whether he would take them on as patients.

In a reading to fourteen- to fifteen-year-old students in a school, the students questioned the presence of a police officer in uniform. Perhaps because Marquardt is a criminal, said one student, the policeman feels we need protection. Another student said that since Marquardt had already served his sentence, he should be allowed to speak without a police presence. The policeman said he came out of personal interest, not in a professional capacity, and would leave if the students so wished. In that case, the students agreed he could stay, and an open discussion, along with questions from the policeman, followed.

In a church, Lemke read only passages that had been omitted in the final edits. For example, he read a passage where Marquardt talks about the use of a candle in sex with a woman. She assumed that he wanted her to insert the candle in her vagina, whereas he wanted her to insert it in his anus. In response to a question, Marquardt explained his wish not in terms of homosexual desire but of a specific anal lust. The editor had rejected this passage as too ambiguous and provocative for readers. The church audience was ominously quiet, avoiding the usual questions provoked by free association. Instead, the discussion turned to morality and ethics: How could Marquardt have done this or that act? What are his ethical positions?

Readings in prison were initiated by Sister Angelika, a nun who through God had found her way out of drug addiction. While working in prison, she encountered many men who had been abused; some confided in her that they had been sexually abused, including four by their mothers. She thought the book might encourage prisoners to take therapy seriously as a way to facilitate changing themselves and ultimately securing their release from prison. In this, her goals coalesce with those of Marquardt on the efficacy of therapy and of Lemke on making amends: Get therapy if you do not want to spend most of your life in prison. Come to grips with your violent propensities and change yourself.

Before the first prison reading, Sister Angelika ordered copies of the book for the prisoners. Prison authorities who agree to stage these events are experimenting with how to construct free time so as to encourage the prisoners to reflect on their lives and deeds. In maximum-security prisons, space for such events is limited and controlled, so those wanting to attend must sign up well ahead. In one prison, the social worker in charge expected about twenty prisoners but instead more than one hundred signed up. The therapists employed in prisons tend to boycott these events, as they expect (correctly) that most prisoners will complain about the quality of therapy offered. In response to such complaints from prisoners, Marquardt and Lemke counter by arguing that the success of therapy depends on the investments of the prisoners more than the ability of the therapists.

At a reading in one prison where Marquardt had served time, another former pimp who had once competed with him questioned the credibility of the change he said he had undergone. At another, the audience included both the men and women who reside there: a woman spoke up that she had been a pimp and never had to resort to the extreme violence of Marquardt. She asked for a justification of such brutal measures. Two Polish women who had worked as prostitutes came forward to thank Lemke for his therapeutic work. And a large group of men approached him to ask whether he would be available for individual therapy.

I ask Marquardt whether he ever feels aggression in the questions of the audience. "Actually not," he says. "More curiosity. I see myself as offering information. Perhaps people become more reflexive, have a bit more courage to change. If I change a single person I think I have won, if I get them to choose a different path than criminality, or to not hit a child."

Both men have clearly come to enjoy the readings as public performances. Lemke receives recognition for his work as therapist, Marquardt for the work he has accomplished in his psyche, not, as in the past, for his physical strength and ability to overlook pain. Even in the most unexpected of locations, such as the proletarian golf club near Berlin or the upscale golf club near Munich, the two men complement each other while securing different satisfactions for the listeners. The public, in turn, appears to largely appreciate the ability of Marquardt to reflect deeply and in public, and they see this as an achievement possible only because of Lemke's unusual commitment to his client. They find it stimulating to see traces of a therapeutic session outside the private room where these sessions take place, and in this viewing of what is usually kept private they come to see therapy not as seeking an end or cure, but as an ongoing commitment to reflection and self-directed change.

Bringing these private reflections into the public sphere has its costs, however. Lemke risks disapproval by other therapists, who have various reasons for criticizing his unorthodox relationship to a client: publicizing details of a private life revealed in therapy; helping to raise money at charity events that inflate the ego of a man already suffering from a narcissistic personality disorder; focusing on a mother's sexual abuse when male abuse of children is much more frequent. It is a little like helping a Mafia hit man deal with his guilt. Beyond the individual issues, the same public that wants to see abused children helped is very ambivalent about helping the men who abused them or about helping men, like Marquardt, who turn their aggression against women instead. Therapeutic institutions that treat such men risk having their public funding withdrawn if there is ever much publicity about what they do.

The costs of these readings are much greater for Marquardt than for Lemke, and those costs complicate the idea that the readings are a simple continuation of therapy. After private therapy sessions, he says, he always felt lighter, precisely because the sessions brought him closer to the pain of his experiences and the feelings that he had not been able to acknowledge and express. In the secure setting of therapy, he was surprised to find things he could not control, ideas and impulses and patterns that he was unaware of, whereas in everyday life he was always the master of routine, the perfectionist in karate and in controlling his prostitutes, a man who also insisted on ironing his own shirts—because even that he could do better than women. In therapy sessions, he could yield control without feeling anxious or threatened. That experience of control and lightness is not part of the readings. In fact, the opposite occurs at readings. Anticipation of the public performance brings about nightmares a day or two before and usually for four days after every reading. These nightmares he cannot control. They burden him with a feeling of being followed and threatened, even killed, by *das Ding*.

The Public Sphere

Readings by Lemke of the story of Marquardt's sex abuse and self-transformation are a novel kind of intervention in the public sphere. That Marquardt was both victim of such abuse and victimizer (of women) creates for the public an uncomfortable and highly ambivalent dynamic of identification and estrangement. That Marquardt claims to have undergone a psychic change through therapy and to now dedicate his life to helping children tests the public's willingness to believe in the progressive narrative of human malleability and intentional change. Even those who want to believe are unsettled by the inimical mix of categories of persons involved in his story: mother instead of father as abuser, former pimp as victim, unmarried male as child protector. This mix challenges the purity of the distinctions between public and private, therapist and client, and victim and perpetrator, and the facile way in which these distinctions tend to work in our imaginations.

Large charity events are the other kind of intervention of Marquardt in the public sphere. Under the auspices of his foundation, *Helfen Macht Stark*, he organizes fundraisers to benefit institutions, like the one for which Lemke works, dedicated to therapy for abused children and offenders alike. I purchased a ticket for one such charity event in 2008 and was seated at a table with my partner, a script writer, a film producer, a (female) lawyer who specializes in defending sex offenders, and a young dentist who retired on a disability scam to a pension twice that of other high-end wage earners. The rest of the public was equally if not more diverse, reflecting the variegated residents of Neukölln who all feel in some way addressed by Marquardt's different selves—Turkish and Arabic bodybuilders, pious-appearing Muslim women in headscarves, the families of children who learn karate from Marquardt at his sports gym, students, fashionable upper-middle-class society ladies and businessmen, pimps, therapists, actors and actresses.

Two professional emcees hosted, and between songs and performances they took turns praising the greatness of "Andreas Marquardt" and his tireless efforts to help children in need. We worked through our four-course meal with hardly a pause in events: A lottery was held to provide a week-long vacation in the North Sea for a single mother and her child or children. (She later complained about the quality of the lodging.) Marquardt led the children from his sports studio in performing synchronized karate. The youngest, a two-year-old, received sustained applause. A prominent male television and stage actor and a brilliant actress from the Viennese stage, both longtime friends of Lemke's, movingly read selections from *Härte* (and later revealed to Lemke that they also both had been abused as children). Marquardt presented checks to several child therapy institutions. (One recipient later told me she felt uncomfortable accepting money from a man with such a record.) All of these happenings were projected onto a gigantic screen, making those on stage appear small in contrast to their oversized images on screen. I was undoubtedly not alone in finding it difficult to place myself in the audience. For the sake of sexually abused children, what exactly were we experiencing? Perhaps only a serendipitous carnivalesque could sustain an atmosphere indefinable enough to contain this public display of solemnity, saintliness, and burlesque, and bring so many West Berliners out of their provincial *Kiez* (neighborhood) to draw attention to an issue that under most circumstances they would prefer to avoid.

Today a steady stream of stories in the public media draws continuous attention to the issues of child sex abuse and the abuse of women. To be sure, such abuse desperately needs a hearing. But these stories also appeal to the paranoid side of the public, confirming fears of unforeseen predators on the loose. Those predators are invariably male, and the culprit is male sexuality gone amok. This discourse creates the impression of a single unit, WOMENANDCHILDREN, needing protection from male abuse. But as Marquardt's story informs us, this framing elides much of what is at stake.

In 2005 and 2007, several spectacular cases of brother-sister and father-daughter incest in Germany and Austria shocked the public about transgressions of sexual intimacy within families that have long been themes in novels and films. Sordid revelations of child abuse followed in 2010, first within the Jesuit, upper-class Canisius-Kolleg, a secondary school in Berlin, with cases dating back to the 1970s, and then also in secular elite schools in other cities, leading to even more publicity, high-level commissions of investigation, apologies, financial compensation for victims, and substantial changes in the laws relating to sexual abuse, including more federal money for research on the topic. In 2013, as I made final revisions in this manuscript, the issue of abuse entered the fight between political parties in Germany, decrying the position of the Green Party from the early 1980s when they argued for the decriminalization of pedophilia.

Media circulation of such stories and this new round of responses supports neither of the two regnant theories of the public sphere: neither Michel Foucault's theory of a disciplinary power that micromanages the body and redefines the family as a site of sexuality for state intervention, nor Jürgen Habermas's theory of a public sphere that mediates between the family and the state. In fact, widespread circulation of private, sensational disclosures coupled with more social and governmental attention to these issues points to some ongoing radical redefinitions of the family and the relation of intimacy to the public sphere.

The circulation of private scandals in the yellow press traces its German origin to the *B.Z. am Mittag* (Berliner Paper at Noon), first published in 1904. The most popular and most cited of the German tabloids in the period of the cold war was the Springer Verlag's *BILD*, which first appeared in 1952. What is novel today is the addition of the televisual to this earlier brew of print media, which increases the rapidity of and enlarges the audience for the circulation of revelations, pseudoconfessions, and exposés of intimate lives.

Although by the 1970s television programs about the private lives of celebrities had already cultivated loyal viewers, such revelations about noncelebrities were introduced first on a large scale in the 1990s, with the introduction of twenty-four-hour news on newly licensed cable networks. Intense competition for viewers among television networks has encouraged talk shows to dig deeper for intimate disclosures and to stage public humiliations in front of national audiences. The most prominent exemplar of this type of show was Bärbel Schäfer's *Explosiv—Das Magazin*, modeled on the U.S. shows of Jerry Springer and Oprah Winfrey. By drawing on the experience of intimacy and the most private of personal details that had largely been reserved for psychoanalytic sessions, an enlarged participatory public sphere has emerged. This participatory sphere makes it difficult to sustain the fiction of an independent private life to be protected from public scrutiny. Even after private persons reveal intimacies before the camera, the public always seems to want more.

One way to conceive of this contemporary development is, to use terms developed by Habermas in other work, as a "colonization of the lifeworld" by the capitalist "system." That is, the public sphere increasingly operates within the systemic logic of market differentiation, cannibalizing everything personal, including the language of psychoanalysis, so as to appropriate the power of lived experience and the mysteries of the psyche for the goals of capital itself. The instrumental logic of the market vitiates, Habermas argues, the communicative goals of everyday experience. Such goals create experience as meaningful according to different local logics. Under the conditions of a market logic, however, only that which can be commodified and exchanged is given value—and survives.

The success of the readings of Marquardt's repackaged life and the publicity events for his foundation would seem to be a result of this market logic, but that understanding of cause and effect is too facile. It fails to consider that the marketing of his life in the public sphere responds to a deeper need present in audiences, which is to bring them into an experience of unconscious proximity with something dark, powerful, mysterious, indefinable, wanted and not wanted at the same time. The proximity created is with the double-sided nature of the experience of abuse. Audiences are presented with the opportunity to think abuse and intimacy in a novel way. Perhaps the most controversial and important taboo Marquardt's story reveals is the importance and power of the mother's seduction of her children. Without such early seduction, children develop a limited capacity for emotional growth and vulnerable attachments to others. Yet, the mother's seduction must give way to that of others. If the process of separation is not adequately managed, the damage to the child is even greater. These complex dynamics rarely find their way into public discussion, however, except as framed by child sex abuse at the hands of men. The revelations of abuse in elite German schools, mentioned above, focused solely on abuse by males of a particular generation who grew up in the prudish atmosphere of the 1950s and early 1960s. Today's more open sexual atmosphere makes it unlikely that those particular patterns of abuse will be repeated, and, in fact, all studies confirm a steady decline or leveling off in the last three decades of child sex abuse patterns in Germany. As it is, far too little attention is given to the systemic and enduring effects of forms of child abuse that are nonsexual, such as neglect, particularly in poorer families with little access to social resources, which in today's Germany includes many first- and second-generation immigrant families from outside Europe.

Child Sex Abuse

Marquardt's mother obviously transgressed the necessary seduction of her child by extending erotic play into her son's adolescence and sexual coming of age, thereby denying him as he grew up any autonomy over his body and erotic imagination. Rather than create a holding environment in which he felt secure to change, she undermined or threatened his every attempt to separate himself from her desire. Although I am unable, or perhaps simply unwilling, to approach this mother with empathy, I can nonetheless offer a plausible interpretation of her motives.

As her photos clearly show, she was a beautiful, sensual woman, whose father convinced her to divorce her husband after he nearly killed their son. The temptation to fill the absence created by the divorce with a new pact with her son must have been great. She appeared unable to, or disinterested in, finding another person, a substitute lover, to whom she might direct her erotic interests. One must infer that she failed to find another erotic partner, in part, because of the responsiveness of her son to her attention.

Marquardt's responsiveness to his mother's desire, about which he was initially proud, also later created in him a sense of shame, a feeling that overwhelmed and blocked him from understanding why the renunciation of desire was not his but his mother's responsibility. As a child and youth, his ability to win and then retain the heart of his mother, his sole parent, was undoubtedly extremely important for his self-esteem, his sense that he was worthy of love. As a consequence, he was unable to develop a perspective independent of hers. When I asked Marquardt about the dynamic of seduction, he bristled—the only time he reacted in this way in our conversations. I suspect that he thought I assumed a mutuality of interest and responsibility for the sex with his mother. Nothing could be further from my thoughts, I said.

The reaction of Marquardt to this transgression, and to the shame he felt for having loved his mother and yielded to her needs, was to weaponize himself, to become more masculine and tougher than other boys. First it was through the full-contact karate his grandfather had encouraged him to learn. Then he turned these weapons on other women, whose victimization came to symbolize retribution in the form of reparations for the aggrieved child in him. In this, he reproduces in his own narcissistic use of others his mother's narcissistic use of him. Through therapy, in particular through the empathic communication with Lemke and the other therapists who preceded him, he brought these aggressions into speech, even, with the help of Lemke, into writing. This speech helped him change, but it did not take away all his symptoms, and certainly not all the underlying triggers, the initial wounds. Despite the psychic distance traveled by Marquardt from his earlier self, his inability to read about that self on the pages of *Härte* implies a fear of recognizing the presence of those earlier desires and a fear of rage at the consequences of that recognition, which remain, in every sense of the word, too intimate and inexpressible. There is no language for, and no subject who can explain, desire for a sexually abusive mother.

All of this psychic work is supposed to enable an authentic voice to emerge distinct from his mother's. One of the things this new voice does is displace Marquardt's aggressions, his rage, his sadistic urges, into projects of *Wiedergutmachung*. Nonetheless, Erdmann says to me that Marquardt remains "massively preoccupied" with his mother. She complains that although he has discussed this preoccupation in therapy, he "cannot discuss it" with her. The aggressions are still there but more latent now, and some of them, she says, are directed against her in the form of turning away, silence, evacuating himself at emotionally laden moments in communication. Even after turning away, and in sleep, however, Marquardt says he cannot dream, cannot do the unconscious work that might access his fears at their source.

Erdmann says that she has always encouraged Marquardt to forgive his parents and to go see his father again before he dies. Once, as we sat in the courtyard outside the sports studio, I turned off the recording machine in anticipation of leaving, but Marion kept on talking. She had agreed to talk to me and to let me tape our conversations, after I assured her I was interested only in her interpretation of Marquardt's story. Knowing that she had been and still is an integral part of that story, journalists and TV producers have often asked her for interviews. In those, journalists often shift the focus to her life instead of Marquardt's. She preferred, she said, to leave the public nature of Marquardt's work to him. Yet, as I prepared to leave, not wanting to take up more of her time, she suddenly wanted to tell me more, a situation I have often experienced in ethnographic research, of the sudden arousal of an affect and a pressing need to share something else with me, the listener, during the narration of personal history.

Erdmann says that the reckoning with her own father's abuse brought her to the unexpected realization that she herself is a product of incest. She had always suspected something, as she does not physically resemble any of her siblings, who resemble her father. Instead, she says, "I am the image of my grandfather." She confronted her mother directly in her final months with the question of whether her grandfather was in fact her biological father. Her mother refused to answer. Erdmann interprets that as an acknowledgment. With the help of a therapist, she has found her peace with this knowledge and with the experience of her own abuse. Ultimately, she reasons, her grandfather was a loving man to her, unlike her own uncaring and abusive father, so, she concludes, it is perhaps better to think of him as her father than to have to carry around the image of herself as the child of the man her mother had married who also had sexually abused her.

To be asked to contain the other's emotion, in Erdmann's case to share with me a reckoning with intense pain, is one of the incredibly disturbing experiences of fieldwork for which I am also grateful. Such experience takes me outside myself and my own cultural references, increasing the scope and complexity of my world. It took me some time to begin to register Erdmann's last-minute disclosure. Perhaps I am still registering it. Her abuse, or rape, and history of such abuse, now appear to me as part of a larger set of disclosures, an entire cultural landscape of memories extending over generations; and I begin to sense why Lemke entrusted me to enter into the set of relationships and facts in which he as therapist, author, and public figure was embedded. In his relations with Marquardt in therapy, and with Marquardt and Erdmann in various public events, Lemke always appears unperturbed, in full control of his emotions. Yet hearing the facts of child sexual abuse, which he does daily in his work, and participating in such an intimate way with the continuing saga of Marquardt's abuse, must produce an experience of bewildering inundation, with effects that linger long after he has listened to the stories, written them up, or read them in public. Perhaps by inviting me in, Lemke would no longer be alone in being asked to contain these emotions.

Despite being gravely wounded and split at his core in his private life, Marquardt is able to present a public self who is confident and continuous. In his public interventions with Lemke, his former therapist, he does for the understanding of child sex abuse, of its personal effects social consequences, what nobody else has been able to do. The staged public readings bring listeners close to the truth, parts of which most people would prefer to keep as taboo deeply sequestered in their imagination. He creates an opportunity for not merely informing oneself but for knowledgeability.

Authenticity

Marquardt praises Lemke as an "authentic person." Of himself, he says,

> I try to be truthful, to talk authentically, to be authentic. I will not prettify myself. I answer all questions honestly, including critical and difficult questions.

I answer them all. And they notice that I am honest, that I want to help children, that I don't look around to see what they think before talking, before writing this book, that I go to the public. For me that is a kind of *Wiedergut-machung*, to explain how this happened. I won't exculpate myself; everything I did was shit. No, there are two ways and I chose the false way, and I regret it, still today, really very much. I can't help the people I hurt, I can't help the women, I can't torment myself, I can't make things good again. I can only try to turn things around, help the prisoners, help the young boys find another way. I say to them, "Kids, I am one of you! I came from the same pot, I sat on the same stool as you. I was in prison eight years and four months." Today my life is much better, I do many beautiful things, much better than spreading fear, making money. That can't be the sense of things. I offer something else.

As a child, Marquardt trusted his grandfather, perhaps his grandmother, but no one else. Even with this trust, he never told his grandfather of how his mother abused him. That would have, I suspect, made conscious to him another betrayal: that of his grandfather to him. He claims to have had no friends until after his first imprisonment, when he began to confide in Erd-mann. Instead of trust, he created fear in others, threatened them with merciless brutality, dominated them with his money. He developed his body as protective armor and weapon, showing no weakness, permitting no one to near him. He always had doubts about the authenticity of that person. He says, "I knew everything wasn't 100% with me. When I was alone, I thought about myself, but I always repressed some things." In other words, since his childhood, Marquardt made some things unavailable to himself in part by creating another self for the public to view. That other self protected him from recognizing who he was and prevented anyone else who might be curious from knowing who he was or what he was experiencing. Of all his experiences, that of the sex abuse by his mother was the one he needed most to hide.

Today he cultivates what he calls a "normal" self, one who has a partner with whom he shares meals; goes to movies, concerts, the ballet; strolls in the park; shares an occasional glass of wine (he never drank before). And he reaches out to children, teaches them how to defend themselves, to have values, to be punctual, to be clean, to say no. He wants the children he works with to respect adults but not to fear them. He claims that helping children learn to defend themselves—the youngest is three—gives him tremendous energy, when they look at him with eyes like "little mice," when they call him by his name, "Andy" or "Meister Marquardt."

Since his imprisonment, he has, he says,

retrieved the normal Andy. But the other Andy is still there. I am not a good person. I do have more control of my impulses than before. But if I see a child being beaten, and I say to stop, and he doesn't stop, I'll hit him. I can very quickly retrieve this hard person. It would be totally normal for me to activate the brutal Andy in certain situations.

The other Andy is still there, quiet but not dead; he is tranquil. But he is not authentic. Now I don't have to play games.

Memory

Only recently did Lemke begin to ask about the small child who has no memory of his mother but who witnessed her murder as she defended herself from sexual assault. He says to me, "Odd, I sometimes think of that child and have pity on him."

What actually happened to the "child" whom Lemke has begun to pity and the one whom Marquardt has tried to retrieve? Where was the "normal Andy" during all those years Marquardt worked as a pimp? Can therapy transform the self of the child molester and rehabiliate him to allow a reintegration into social life? And, finally, in what way does therapy and imprisonment enable the sex offender to assume responsibility for the harm done to the child? I begin to address these questions in the next chapters, remaining with the ethnographer's voice.

ONE

The Phenomenon of Child Molestation

Child Sex Offenders

In every culture intimacy between adults and children is subject to regulation, but it is not always regulated by modern law. Most often it is a taboo, subject to unwritten rules that lack the enforcement power of the state. In the last half century in most of the Western world, such taboos have become explicit objects for legal regulation. The ambivalence of the taboo is replaced by the certainty of a crime. New criminal types have emerged, one of which is the child molester, a figure of abjection who evokes a visceral reaction of loathing and repulsion. The mother who abused her son in the Prolegomenon escaped this loathing; only in her last years did she confront repulsion, and that only because of her son's belated recognition of what had happened to him and his private confrontation with her. Marquardt's mother is neither a statistically typical molester nor a new criminal type. That person is a male who has sexually abused a young girl to whom he is no stranger. And he appears in two guises: the incest abuser and the pedophile. It is common today to describe a child molester as the epitome of evil, a "sexual predator" outside the moral limits of the human. More is at stake in this loathing than the identification of evil.[1] He shares with the "Islamic terrorist" the designation of a major security risk. Confounded by such an evil, the public unites in a general sentiment that of all criminal types he is the least assimilable, the least deserving of empathy, unredeemable (cf. Berkel 2006; Meyer 2007). In legal jargon, he risks becoming a recidivist, doomed to repeat his crime; in psychiatric jargon, he is accursed by a psychic disorder, a "paraphilia" that makes him virtually incapable of change (Dannecker 2001).

Paraphilias (from Greek, meaning "beside affectionate regard") are problems of impulse control, characterized by recurrent, intense, and unusual (variously called "perverse," "abnormal," "anomalous," or "deviant") sexual fantasies and desires. Not until the late nineteenth century did psychiatrists and psychologists begin to classify nonnormative sexual interests. A century later, in 1980, the authoritative guide of the American Psychiatric Association, the *Diagnostic and Statistical Manual of Mental Disorders* (DSM-III), explicitly dubbed such interests "paraphilia"—after testing these classifications on three patients. Despite more than thirty years of effort, however, and the translation of these classifications into German and twenty-one other languages, experts have been unable to agree on what to include in the classification of paraphilia, a category that now, depending on the expert, includes well over five hundred kinds of interests and behaviors. Even more disagreement is found over the proper etiologies and treatments for the diagnosis of paraphilia. Although the DSM does not classify all paraphilias as "disorders" or "disturbances," adult sexual interest in children has always been on the list of such psychic disorders since there is nearly universal consensus that this interest, irrespective of the form of its expression, deviates from normal relations with and undoubtedly harms the child.

For legal purposes in Germany, anyone under the age of eighteen can be a victim of child sex abuse. Technically, a person under the age of fourteen is not yet capable of exercising a "right of sexual self-determination" (*Recht auf sexuelle Selbstbestimmung*), a legal concept explicitly developed in West Germany in 1973 to empower women and homosexuals by legalizing the pursuit of those sexual desires not defined in terms of heterosexual male desire. The concept has since increasingly been applied to children. Therefore, in Germany any sex before fourteen with someone older than fourteen is a statutory offense (other European states set this age of consent between twelve and eighteen) (§176 StGB). Youths, those between fourteen and seventeen, can be, like children, subject to the same abuse by adults, except that they enjoy a positive right to sexual self-determination (based on a 2003 decision by the European Court of Human Rights, which German courts respect). If anyone under seventeen is remunerated for sex, monetarily or otherwise, or if an adult has in some way taken advantage of the youth, then the right to sexual self-determination is nullified (§182 StGB). Adults who engage in "sex" with anyone under the age of eighteen can be charged with sex abuse, and on that basis are classified as paraphilic and subject to sentences from six months to eleven and a half years, depending on the severity of the offense.

Today the common treatments for paraphilias include hormone injections, cognitive behavioral therapy (CBT), psychotherapy, psychopharmacology, and psychiatry. The most controversial and ethically contestable of these has been castration. Since the 1960s in most Western countries, medical doctors and psychiatrists in the growing field of criminal endocrinology have been experimenting with chemical castration for child sex offenders—pharmacological intervention most commonly administered in the form of selective serotonin reuptake inhibitors (SSRI) or antihormonal substances in either testosterone-lowering medications (TLM) or androgen deprivation treatment (ADT) (Turner, Basdekis-Jozsa, and Briken 2013). Such treatments ostensibly increase voluntary control over sexual arousal at the stage of fantasy. For many men, however, they not only eliminate the sex drive but sometimes also the desire to experience aliveness. In those cases where the will to live is weak, the offenders usually take some type of amphetamine or antidepressant to counter the effect of the depressant.[2]

ADT was initially developed for the treatment of cancer and discovered to be highly effective for prostate cancer. The major side effect, loss of interest in sex, was considered negligible because pharmacological use for cancer treatment is temporary. Paraphilias are chronic, however, requiring long-term if not permanent attention. If used over years, ADT has additional major side effects, similar to those of the other pharmacological medications, including increasing the likelihood of mood disturbance and depression, cardiovascular problems, diabetes, and, perhaps most seriously, of rapid bone loss "comparable to the depletion of skeletal integrity in women after surgical ovariectomy or early menopause" (Gooren 2011, 3632–33).

In the last decade many courts have endorsed or prescribed the most invasive of these psychopharmacological measures as a preferred mode of treatment for particular sex offenders, in European countries not limited to those in traditionally conservative Catholic places like Estonia, Moldova, Poland, Portugal, and Spain, but also in Denmark, Sweden, and the United Kingdom. Surgical castration (removal of the man's testicles) is the most extreme of them, but only a few European countries still permit it. The Council of Europe's antitorture committee has condemned surgical castration as a "mutilating, irreversible intervention [that] cannot be considered a medical necessity in the context of the treatment of sexual offenders" and recommended it be discontinued (CPT/Inf 2012, 58–60). Nonetheless, the practice continues, with the Czech Republic resorting to it in approximately ten cases a year, Germany in approximately five. In all countries that permit castration (chemical or physical), it is employed only under a rigorous protocol, including the offender being older than twenty-five and formally volunteering ("informed consent"). In Germany sex offenders (not only child molesters) are most commonly prescribed SSRI or ADT treatments.[3] How voluntary such treatments are is unclear, as the conditions under which men are asked to agree are hardly noncoercive; agreement usually facilitates (although does not guarantee) either a shorter sentence, less surveillance during probation, or actual release from prison rather than indefinite incarceration.

Legal and medical authorities tend to converge in diagnoses of child sex offenders: They are said to suffer from a paraphilic disorder with a high risk factor. To produce this diagnosis, classifications with different assumptions about etiology and treatment are brought to bear at the same time on the same subject to arrive at a prognosis: to predict the sex offender's future. This harmonization of classifications to create a consensus diagnosis obscures contradictions in forms of legitimation offered by the two fields of expertise: if an object of medical treatment, child sex abuse is an illness, and hence requires healing; if an object of law, child sex abuse is an intended crime, and hence deserves punishment. Medicine is about health and illness, law about innocence and guilt. Child sex offenders have become, then, simultaneous or alternating objects of medicine—afflicted by a "paraphilic disorder"—and of law—individuals who intend to commit or have committed a crime, subject to the claims of expertise in both fields.

In much of the West, however, the focus has been shifting from healing and punishment to "rehabilitation" of the child molester. In Germany treatment has become in fact a legal right and duty. There are two proposals for treatment that try to maintain a critical distance to this medical-legal harmonization, each proceeding from radically different premises. On the one side is the emerging field of neuroscience, which maintains that "problems of the mind" or psyche should instead be identified and analyzed as "brain problems," doing away with legal and social concepts of guilt, blame, responsibility, and volition. Brain problems can be addressed with pharmacological interventions. The most optimistic of neuroscientists suggest treatment even before the commission of an offense. Although such proposals are increasingly common, the field of neuroscience is still in its infancy, and its proposals for assessment and prognosis of criminality are still largely theoretical.[4]

On the other side are forms of therapy that seek to effect a change of self through reflection and introspection. In much of Australia, New Zealand, North America, and Western Europe, major efforts are made to "rehabilitate" the child molester through therapy. Rehabilitation (*Rehabilitierung*) is, strictly speaking, neither a cure nor a punishment but a therapeutic transformation, though it is still subject to the evaluations of both medical and legal experts. In the process of rehab, legal experts employ therapists to bring about the self-transformation of the child molester that might enable an accurate prognosis.

This book is an anthropological account of the attempt to rehabilitate child sex offenders through therapy, often accompanied by short-term imprisonment. Using select exemplary case studies from ethnographic research in Berlin, Germany, the book follows offenders through the process of ritual rehab: from accusation to arrest, admission of culpability, trial, imprisonment, treatment, release from prison, and social reincorporation or indefinite surveillance. It gives a descriptive account of, and tries to account for, the potential grievous harm to the child alongside the potential for self-transformation of the offender. These insights are placed within the contemporary social context and public sphere in which rehabilitation takes place.

This is also a book of that curious genre of activity called theorization, abstraction and generalization from the empirical, about which there is today considerable disagreement (and confusion) despite its widespread popularity. In addition to a detailed depiction of what the rehabilitation of child sex offenders entails, which is itself one form of theory, I try to theorize rehabilitation as a secular ritual. In this endeavor, descriptions begin not with theory (e.g. theories of evil, exclusion, abuse, the mind, child ontology, ritual), or worse, with a theorist (e.g., Sigmund Freud, Karl Marx, Walter Benjamin), but with an object—child sex offenders in Berlin, Germany—and follow this object, which is also a subject, in its relation to children, families, and prisons, and as it experiences incarceration, therapy, and rehabilitation. The promise of theory here is to generate questions and frames to understand some contemporary changes: in adult-child relations, male sexuality, self-transformation, secular ritual, and psychic change.

I began this research in 2008 and selected two ethnographic sites, one therapeutic (*Kind im Zentrum, or KiZ,* literally "child in the center"), the other legal (*offener Strafvollzug,* a minimum-security, open prison), to probe in depth the process of rehabilitation.[5] From 2008 to 2009, I sat in on four weekly therapy groups at KiZ, Berlin's largest center for therapy for both offenders and abused children, best known for specializing in group therapy for offenders. Using an eclectic mix of systematic techniques, some Anglo-American inspired, therapists currently divide offenders into five groups: youth offenders (under age seventeen), young adult offenders (ages seventeen to mid- to late twenties), adult *Pädosexueller,* adult incest abusers, and mentally handicapped abusers.[6] In my initial year of fieldwork, I attended one session weekly of youth offenders, one weekly of incest abusers, and two weekly of pedophiles. In those groups, I listened to thirty-five men and boys between the ages of thirteen and sixty-two as they were asked to talk about themselves and what they did, sharing in front of one another and two therapists, a man and a woman. The talk I listened to was obligatory, under the threat of legal prosecution for those not yet tried, under the threat of *Sicherungsverwahrung* (compulsory detention for reasons of security) for those who had already served their sentences, or under the threat of *Führungsaufsicht* (special conditions of supervised release, such as surveillance) for those already released from prison. Therapists also occasionally told me of individual case histories of men or women in the past or present, which I did not have the opportunity to observe; one such case I recount in the penultimate chapter.

In the group therapy sessions, the men and boys (the youngest was thirteen) sat in a semicircle facing the therapists, while I sat in a corner of the room behind them, taking notes, which I filled in and elaborated later that evening or the following morning. In several groups a young therapist-apprentice sat next to me. She also took notes, which she at times shared with me. Except for initial sessions when I introduced myself and asked for permission to sit in and observe, I intervened only once in a group—at the request of a female therapist (as the male therapist had suddenly fallen ill).

Despite these circumstances I did have a presence. My spatial location was classically paranoid—behind, observant, withholding—and twice led clients to invoke me as an excuse for resistance in their conflicts with the therapists. All in all, however, I remained relatively insignificant to the therapeutic function of the group. I did not ask to observe individual therapy sessions, which rely more on the direct transference between therapist and clients; my presence might have disturbed this dynamic and made the therapist's job much more difficult. The men in the group were more concerned with one another's comments, criticisms, and corroborations, which the therapists elicited to serve as reliable reality checks on the relative truth of statements made. The more significant transference involving me was with the therapists themselves since I was actually evaluating them as professionals and at the same time was depending on their granting me access to the actual process of treatment. Throughout the process our relations were always mediated by the clients, the male sex offenders, who had a presence in our relations even when not physically there. I remained in contact with the therapists from KiZ during the writing of this book, and for an additional four years after my initial year of observation they informed me of their progress or problems with clients until those clients I had observed left therapy. In August 2013, I gave a final presentation of my findings before the group of therapists working at KiZ (several with whom I worked had since left or had retired, and some of those present had begun working at KiZ after my period of observation).

During the same period of my initial observations at KiZ, in 2008 and 2009, one day a week I visited a minimum-security prison, where some of the men were serving or had served time. There I worked with a psychologist responsible for evaluations of the offenders as to their security risk and suitability for this prison, for therapy specifically, and even for placement with a particular therapeutic institution or therapist. The Berlin Senatsverwaltung für Justiz also granted me access to the archives of all convicted sex offenders from the years 2001 to 2008 who had applied to serve time in this minimum-security prison rather than in a maximum-security one (some of these men had in fact already served time in a maximum security prison before being transferred out). From the approximately 200 archival cases of sex offenders in Berlin that I examined, out of a total of some 1,200 crimes of sexual violence in Germany, I selected for analysis the cases of 50 adult men convicted of child sex abuse. Files of these cases were then shipped from various locations to the minimal-security prison and stored in the corner of an office for my use. When I visited, I was given a key to a separate office in one of the prison dorms, where I could take the documents that I had requested to read them and take notes. I occasionally talked with prisoners and other prison officials, and I attended several staff meetings.

Ritual Rehabilitation, Incest, Parricide

Rehabilitation of sex offenders is a ritual process that unfolds in many of the different spaces and scenes that make up the contemporary public sphere: local, national, and international. It begins formally with the accusation or discovery of an illegal sexual transgression, usually disputed by the suspect, and often follows with the arrest of a suspected offender. In most cases, the arrest leads to a sequence of events: detention, admission of culpability, treatment, release from prison, and either social reincorporation or indefinite surveillance. If a particular case offers any sensational details, televisual and print media quickly seize on it to increase their audiences. These outlets publicize pictures of the offender that portray him in the most unflattering light and divulge intimate revelations from the interrogation and trial. If the release of the offender is made public knowledge, communities at times organize to prevent him from residing in their midst. Throughout the ritual process, images and stories of offenders circulate between countries, as does the knowledge from the various sciences involved in evaluating and processing offenders.

Psychological and legal professionals, prison officials, medical doctors, psychologists, psychiatrists, prosecutors, judges, and journalists drive the ritual process through their expertise. In Germany, and in much of the West, they are charged with reconstructing the initial act as a violent criminal one of sexual transgression, leading to the punishment and public humiliation of the offender—or of resisting this reconstruction (on the history of rehabilitation in Germany, see Rosenblum 2008). Since the child molester is usually diagnosed as the subject of a paraphilic disorder, he is also obligated to enroll in therapy to facilitate, minimally, abstention from criminal behavior, and maximally, a proactive change in his self (Jung 1987). A 2002 German federal law (which went into effect on January 1, 2003) mandates that individuals sentenced under §§174–183 StGB of the German Penal Code to more than two years of imprisonment for sex abuse have not only a duty but also a right to *Behandlung*, therapy or treatment. Consequently the key to the rehabilitation of such offenders has become therapy, now seen as the primary means for the *Aufarbeitung der Tat*, reckoning with the act or deed.[7]

Rehabilitation follows the definitive sequence of rituals—separation, transition (or liminal), and incorporation—initially identified in 1908 by Arnold van Gennep. Drawing from studies of preindustrial Western and what he called "least advanced cultures" of non-Western societies, Van Gennep examined rituals that mark transitions from one stage to another, calling them *rites de passages*. He was particularly interested in the sequence for a male subject of "birth, social puberty, marriage, fatherhood, advancement to a higher class, occupational specialization, and death." This life course sequence shares with other initiation rites "magico-religious foundations" and is part of the "sacred sphere" (1960, 2, 3).

Much of the structure that van Gennep identified for magico-religious rites in premodern societies a century ago holds for the secular ritual of rehabilitation in complex Western societies today (Borneman 2010). But unlike these life stage rituals—birth, coming of age, marriage, death—modern rehab rituals rely on expertise that not only depicts the cultural codes and life stages of the normatively approved *person* but also accesses and unsettles the interiority of that person, the *self* that is never fully under conscious control. This represents a dramatic break in the function of rituals elaborated by Victor Turner (1967, 92) in "small-scale, relatively stable and cyclical societies." Generalizing from ethnographic work with Ndembu ritual in Zambia, Turner developed a processual framework that stressed the cosmological and ontological significance of transformation during the liminal period. That framework has oriented several generations of anthropologists and is useful in identifying the prison and the therapeutic session as liminal sites, where the prisoner or client is separated from the social for a limited time. During this separation, the sex offender is subject to processes that might teach him to act as a person who will obey the law on release. But that is it. Medical and legal authorities are oriented to changes in behavior alone, not to transformations of the self in the register of experiences embedded in cosmological and ontological structures.

Moreover, while Turner sought to open up the liminal stage and understand the potential of liminality for change even outside the confines of ritual, he nonetheless saw the subject of ritual as moving through stages that are "relatively fixed or stable condition(s)" (1967, 93). This movement through stages does not require that we ask about changes in the self, which may in fact remain unchanged through the imprisonment and treatment of rehab while the person who appears in public will present himself as conforming to social norms.[8] Indeed, most offenders retain aspects of the liminal stage—marked by separation and stigma, never considered fully human—even after rehabilitation is judged to be successful. That is, their history as child sex offenders follows them in their intimate lives and into relationships at work, even if they have undergone a radical transformation of self. They remain liminal, marginal to society, and can rarely regain the structural stability granted to the normative person in modern societies.

The idea that many secular rituals are no longer about the reproduction of social arrangements but attempts to engineer social change was first suggested by Sally Moore and Barbara Myerhoff (1977) in their path-breaking edited volume on secular ritual.[9] They argued against van Gennep's contention that in modern societies the secular necessarily dominates the religious. Instead, they emphasized that secular and religious ritual alike dramatize "social/moral imperatives" and address an essential quality of the sacred, its "unquestionability" (Moore and Myerhoff 1977, 3). In the case of child molesters, the significance of their rehabilitation ritual rests on the specific contemporary libidinal investments of Western cultures in the child, who is ascribed a source of unambiguous sacred power and therefore set apart from the social while at the same time embodying the vitality and future of the social.[10] A rethinking of the distinction between the contemporary secular and traditional religious ritual leads to a departure from the Durkheimian frame of how rituals reflect and perform social relationships to a concern with how modern rituals, as Moore and Myerhoff put it, "attempt to structure the way people think about social life" (4). In other words, modern rehabilitation rituals attempt to effect a transformation in the interiority of the offender, with the aid of the knowledge industry and the apparatus of the state.

At the time Moore and Myerhoff were writing, the Marxist-inspired socialist projects of the planned transformation of nature, both human and nonhuman, had revealed themselves to be overconfident in their goals and unable to account for unintended effects. "Perversion"—the act of turning something to a wrong use, producing opposite effects to those intended—was indeed a key concept for many fields from the 1950s to the 1970s. The legacy of many such projects—for example, building large highway networks, nuclear energy development, massive rerouting of waterways, medical experiments—rests as much on their achievements as on how destructive they were of local differences and what perverse effects they had (Buck-Morss 2002). Moore and Myerhoff (1977) saw clearly the limits of planned approaches to social change, which of course characterized not only socialist designs but also the twentieth-century Big Science projects in the democratic, capitalist West. The socialist experiments in the former Soviet bloc of Eastern Europe, as well as those in parts of postcolonial Africa, Asia, and the Middle East, were the most exemplary of attempts to remake both the human and nature itself. In the former Soviet Union, the attempt to reverse the direction of Siberian rivers was perhaps the most dramatic reversal of nature; the building of collectives at all levels of the social had the larger goal of producing a specifically new type of "Soviet Man" in a new kind of society.

The rehabilitation of child sex offenders follows in this modern secular tradition of orchestrated change, with one major addition. The object of this change is not society itself, however, but the self of the individual. This individual still goes through stages to become a normative person, in a process similar to that detailed by van Gennep, but he also has a recognized interiority, a psyche, which is neither essentially good nor bad but malleable. The secular rehab ritual seeks to alter precisely that interiority, the partly unconscious activity of desiring and dreaming, to effect a psychic change.

Awareness of the limits of projects that plan change can result in modification of such projects, perhaps stopping them altogether, but it also can lead to the denial of limits and a stubborn, persistent, dogmatic pursuit of the original goals. Despite the grave problems and perverse effects resulting from rational, planned change, what Max Horkheimer and Theodor Adorno ([1944] 1972) identified as imminent effects of the dialectic of the Enlightenment, modern secular rituals are nonetheless driven by an essential human quality: belief in change and experimentation. Excessive confidence and ambition may even be one of the conditions necessary for experimentation of any sort. Utopian visions—symbolized, dreamlike images of the future—appear to be integral to the human species, sustaining the hope and vitality necessary to fight the appearance of immutability, stasis, the frustration and despair imminent in the everyday.

Rehabilitation is the work of what we might call a modern utopian dream. It is now, in the post–Cold War world, applied to a very broad range of ritual transformations across cultures and continents. A cursory review of German everyday use of the term, in speech and newspapers during the period of this research, includes incredibly disparate objects to be rehabilitated: for example, addicts (*Süchtige*), orphans (*Heimkinder*), gay men and lesbians (*Schwulen und Lesben*), victims of the East German Socialist Party (*SED-Opfer*), war resisters (*Kriegsdienstverweigerer*), fascists (*Fascisten*), hospitals (*Krankenhäuser*), and brain functions (*Gehirnfunktionen*). As the idea spreads outside the West, it is taken up for unusual objects in radically different social contexts. One of the more peculiar recent attempts at rehab is in Saudi Arabia, where, in 2009, the government set up a center to rehabilitate (*i'adat ta'hil*) jihadis to "the true Islam," including former Guantanamo captives.[11] To conceive of rehabilitating present and former states of being, injuries, sexual identities, and even buildings and mental functions, is part of a belief in the possibility of intentionally changing our worlds or at least changing our place in the world. Rehabilitation rituals are infinitely expansive and inclusive, with no clear limit as to their subjects or how to change them, including, for many sex offenders, experiments with the dosage to be administered.[12]

Because changing child sex offenders is usually assumed to be impossible, their rehabilitation, and the therapist's task, puts this promise of self-transformation to an extreme test, one that can be framed in terms of status change of the person in the rituals examined in classic ritual theory. The offender possesses some of the power classically ascribed to the criminal, representing a sacred source of negativity outside society capable of turning the social upside down if not contained. The child possesses a sacred source of positivity similar to "holiness," an innocence and indeterminacy symbolizing the power of life and liveliness. The therapist fills the essential role normally assigned a religious specialist, to guide the child sex offender through a process that transforms him into a person capable of reintegration in the social. The public participates in an everyday language that frames the offender in neither legal nor psychological but explicitly moral terms that originated in Abrahamic religious ritual and centered around the work of evil, the taking of souls, and the possibility of redemption. It is not as if the public first seeks to understand sex offenders and then decide whether they are good or bad. Rather, the first public classification is of moral abjection, and from that follows an understanding of the sex offender as polluting, intrinsically dangerous, beyond the pale of humanness—a point emphasized theoretically by Mary Douglas (1966) in her studies of dirt and impurity. Imprisonment seeks to contain the danger posed by the person who molests children. But rehabilitation goes further, presenting the hope of a self-transformation of the offender while at the same time not demanding belief, maintaining doubt about how, exactly, the ritual can be so efficacious.

The degree of self-transformation of sex offenders desired, or demanded, or even possible, varies greatly. Those offenders who repeatedly molest preadolescent children are perhaps the least capable of changing their unconscious fantasies (the younger the child-object the more fixed the erotic image), and thus those I observed in treatment remained largely unchanged even after months of therapy. Although few of them were able to make significant changes in the self, most nonetheless developed both more impulse control and a better understanding of their own ethical relation to others (e.g., developed a more elaborate superego—the moralizing, judging part of the self).

Those offenders who repeatedly molest youths are, in turn, more flexible with their fantasies regarding the youthfulness of those they desire. Two of the men in the course of therapy that I observed began dating (one even married) Thai and Filipino women, respectively, as it was the image of youth (small and pubescent looking) that was erotically important to them, and not the actual age of the women. Those who had consumed Internet pornography pose an entirely different question about self-transformation. The legal system assumes that children in pornographic images did not (and legally cannot) consent to the use of their images; hence it tends to prosecute those who abuse children through use of their pictures in the same way it does those who physically abuse a child. For many pornography users, however, the fantasy world of viewing images is a reprieve from the empirical world of face-to-face encounters with actual people. The image, in their mind, is divorced from the actual child in a photo. If the cost of avoiding jail is to renounce the visual consumption of published images, then most try to comply: some successfully, many not. Refraining from the consumption of pornographic images does not itself indicate a changed self, however. Fantasies cannot be turned on and off like light switches; they emerge in thought mysteriously, often out of unconscious associations resistant to conscious control. Nonetheless, it is possible, if not likely, that the link of erotic fantasy to children or youths for men who view child pornography persists beyond therapy but still changes some over time. Such fantasies would therefore perhaps look different over a much longer period of time than this study allows for.

Among these different men, there is a large group whose motivation for molestation is not to be found in any sort of "sexuality," and often not even in the desire for a particular gendered object, but in diverse other experiences or relations having to do with death and aliveness. In the time period of my observation, these included the loss of someone close (and hence a turn to the vitality of the child as a escape from this death), adult betrayal (and thus a turn to children as the only human creatures one can trust), and experiences of personal abuse as children (and thus a desire for the sensation of aliveness that often turns into sadomasochistic longings). This last group of men is often classified as the most "perverse" of the child molesters, meaning that it is difficult to understand their desires with reference to any normal or typical subject.

What makes the rehabilitation of child sex offenders distinctively contemporary among rituals that mark transitions is something else, however: the force and consciousness of sexual desire as it relates to incest and parricide, the two arguably universal human taboos (Bolin and Whelehan 1999). To be sure, every universal has some exceptions. But not only in the West do these deeds still evoke particularly disturbing horrific associations, despite extensive changes in family structures and households. As the ethnographic record attests, the horror is even more pronounced outside the Western world, where the Oedipal complex does not at all conform to the nuclear family model of late-nineteenth-century bourgeois Europe.

Anthropologists have devoted considerably more attention to the incest taboo than to parricide, and then interpreted this taboo as forbidding sexual intercourse among certain degrees of relatives for the purpose of marital regulation and group exchange. Research that followed this insight about the function of incest taboos reached its apogee in Claude Lévi-Strauss's magisterial *The Elementary Structures of Kinship*, published in 1949, which generated what is called alliance theory. That theory stresses the functions of kinship and social organization in regulating horizontal relations of alliance and exchange between groups. It ignores the ontology of desire, and it largely neglects vertical relations of descent, the other foci of kinship theory and that to which British scholars of Africa made the primary contributions. In their defense, alliance theorists argued that marital alliances—lateral relations between siblings or age groups—were more integral to relations between groups, as they generate the motivation to fantasize within discrete yet interchangeable social units. Hence, marriage is key to the differentiation between and identity of groups, of social order itself, whereas relations of descent may be primarily oriented to in-group hierarchies over time. On the other hand, by presenting marriage and its prescriptions and prohibitions as a resolution of the incest taboo, alliance theorists elided the purely sexual function of the taboo, its importance specifically for regulating the deleterious effects of child-adult incest on human development. Moreover, scholars of both foci in kinship theory paid little attention to sex and aggression and the desire to experience aliveness and change, which traverses and informs relations of both alliance and descent (see the critique by Spiro 1979).

My concern with actual incest and its criminalization, rather than with the taboo against it, generally turns attention to vertical relations and sex between generations rather than to lateral relations and marital alliances. Today most accusations of abuse that result in legal complaints are not of sibling or cousin but of parental or neighbor abuse, in any case of familiar adults becoming too sexually intimate with persons not yet able to legally consent. Cases of child sex abuse dramatize some of the problems inherent in vertical relations. In its everyday use, such abuse is a very broad category that includes many kinds of relationships and improper behaviors. Incest is still the prototypical kind of such abuse, and, as Jean La Fontaine (1998, 5) astutely pointed out in one of the first major ethnographic studies of actual incest in the West, the popular use of incest tends to be restricted to the act of sexual intercourse alone in the regulation of improper relations within kinship groups, households, or families.

To restrict the term "incest" to sexual intercourse is in part recognizing that not all adult sexual advances or improper overtures have the same effect on children. For example, in law and in therapy a distinction is made between "aggravated sexual assault" and "sexual assault," the former involving nonconsensual penetration with a sexual organ of an orifice (e.g., anus, mouth, vagina) of another person or causing the sexual organ of another person to contact or to penetrate an orifice of one's own. The experience of incest as aggravated sexual assault is particularly debilitating with lifelong effects for most victims. In my own observation, and in comments made by therapists to me, these effects include a tendency to regress to a childlike state when a certain register of affect is triggered, feeblemindedness especially when asked to reflect on experience, and a general inability to ever clearly articulate what one has experienced. In sum, incest with a child that is an aggravated assault should be distinguished from other types of child sex abuse in which victims often can in fact articulate their injuries and minimize the duration of their deleterious effects.

Theoretically, the two horror scenarios of incest and parricide depict inverse relations within the Oedipus complex: In incest the parent kills the child; in parricide the child kills the parent. The fact that these murders usually occur only in the imagination does not make them any less significant, for, as Freud was the first to argue, already in 1913, the taboos against incest and parricide are biologically necessary to manage the human transition to adulthood. Therefore, they both appear to be part of a mythical or "archaic" unconscious. More recently, in a comprehensive study of the ethnographic record, Allen Johnson and Douglass Price-Williams (1996, 99) have demonstrated that the Oedipal conflict is present in all world folk literature and varies from one society to another only in its strength, outcome, and degree of explicitness.

In short the taboos against incest and parricide are necessary for the development of human sociality as we know it but are also related to the (socially constructed) sacred and the forbidden.[13] Freud most clearly identified the critical elements of the taboo: As a prohibition of something "capable of enjoyment," it relates to something "sacred, consecrated; but on the other hand . . . uncanny, dangerous, forbidden and unclean" (Freud 1913, 31, 26). The universality of the incest taboo does not mean that the Oedipus complex is unchanging or carries the exact same meaning and significance for each individual today as it has in the past. This is obviously not the case. In the West, factors such as the changing significations of male and female; the radical reduction in family and household size; and increases in divorce and single parenting, serial monogamy, and same-sex parents situate today's children and youths in an experience of an Oedipal conflict of alternative configurations, intensities, and duration. Add to this set of factors the increased legal regulation of the taboo, and we have an intimate configuration that differs substantially from that about which Freud wrote a century ago. Especially important for Germany and much of Western Europe is the oft-stated belief in a "demographic crisis." The symbolic value of the child increases as his or her numbers decrease, reinforcing a belief that the child is a source of sacred power and vitality for the social. Despite the temporal and cultural contingency of the Oedipal, we should, however, keep in mind a point made a half century ago by Meyer Fortes ([1959] 1984) in drawing from work in African societies: In the case of incest and parricide, biological processes impose themselves on social occasions as much as individuals also impose interpretations on biological processes.

As for the relation to the child to the sacred, incest and parricide are also acts that refer us back to our mythical origins, a quality Mircea Eliade (1957) identified as central to the sacred. In this unknowable origin, incest and parricide reference a fundamental ambivalence and mystery in the relation of children to adults. This relation builds on the powerfully uncanny presence of the child, who is both uncomfortably strange and comfortably familiar. There is the fundamental indeterminacy of the child while he or she acquires language. The child is filled with unrepressed impulses difficult to understand or often to satisfy. The child itself, as well as the adult, does not know how it will "turn out." And there is the fact that every adult has been an infant but cannot remember the experiences of infancy, which are nonetheless formative in human development. The child's own ignorance about its origins and orientation permits adults to shield themselves from its ambiguous nature, to act, in the contemporary West, as if children are intrinsically innocent and good. But the child learns from the adult by mimicking what is projected onto and into him or her, a mimicry that no adult can trust, often done only to please or deceive the adult, and not really an expression of who the child is or what the child wants to do or will become.

Enter the child sex offender: He takes advantage of the child's mimetic capacity and his or her lack of repression by entering into a sexual relationship that preys on the child's unformedness. In one sense, the offender seeks a union with the child in the maternal register, halting the process of separation from the mother by lapsing back into a nondifferentiated state.[14] This is, of course, the adult's view of things, not the child's. But since the child is inadequately prepared to deal with adult sexual stimulation, this stimulation exposes it to repression. Adult sexual desires are in any event difficult to translate, even for other adults. An added complication is that the child is used to having its own desire translated by the mother or female caregivers, or perhaps by siblings, but rarely by adult men. If the specific desire to be translated is adult male sexual desire for the child, then the child is confronted with a fully alien desire, one outside his or her budding self that the child cannot easily situate. Moreover, in the act of violation the adult male mimics the initial erasure of childhood memory due to the lack of language. The adult sex offender is said to rob the child of childhood itself, of precisely those experiences that cannot or "should not" be remembered yet are formative. This thought is uncanny. It is hard to bear. It is unthinkable.

Hence the raising of a child brings into play an aporia, what Jean Laplanche (1989) has called "the fundamental anthropological situation" of the human being: primal seduction. As I elaborate in many of the case studies that follow, adult seduction of the child is enigmatic and necessary—how else does the adult keep the child's attention despite its growing autonomy needs? And child seduction of the adult is a necessary part of its humanization—how else does the child learn how to attract and keep the attention of others? This seduction is always asymmetrical and dangerous because adult sexual obsessions insufficiently repressed or inhibited risk becoming untranslatable psychotic delusions for the child recipient.

The supreme importance of the incest taboo, from this perspective, is not how it might regulate marriage or exchange between groups—the primary interpretive focus of anthropologists for more than a century—but how it regulates the relation of adults to children. The infant's first relations (and transgressions) are experienced with unmarked adults because, without language, the infant has not yet learned kinship terms (Laplanche 2009). Along these lines, the incest taboo is first learned as a taboo on sexual intimacy between adults and children generally, and only later specified with respect to kinship categories such as mother, father, brother, sister, cousin, and so on. Kinship categorization, therefore, does not found the incest taboo but is derived from and elaborates it. Maurice Godelier (2004, 459) drew a similar conclusion in an erudite comparative study of kinship

> The most extreme permissiveness in matters of sex, the case in which individuals are socially permitted to fulfill their every desire, must stop at the "family" door, that is to say at the door of the groups which, in a society, are directly connected with child-raising, and in most cases with procreation. To cross these limits would be for those who make up these families to commit what is known as incest.

From the perspective of the individual psyche, incest damages the integrity of the child, making it extremely difficult to overcome an initial dependence on the parents to become an adult in one's own right. Parricide is, on the other hand, a necessary murder. Without eliminating the parent as parent, the child also never assumes the roles of adulthood, remaining a child forever. When we hear of actual murders of either the child (through adult sexual imposition) or the parent (by its children), the reaction of horror has less to do with the specific information of any particular case of violation, with its banal or prurient details, than with an intense aversion to knowing something that we should not know but have already fantasized. A feigned disinterestedness in the act is often coupled with a protective feeling, with empathy for the victim if not a direct identification with the innocent child as oneself. To not know while simultaneously empathizing allows us to recoil at the thought of an intimacy with the child that has already been imagined.

Knowledgeability

At the outset, and throughout this book, I feel compelled to address the question of knowledgeability, by which I mean the condition of knowing something well. My focus on understanding the offense and the offender asks of readers to overcome repulsion of the act—to overcome a sense that the act of child sex abuse is truly alien to oneself—in order to empathize with the offender's rehabilitation. To empathize, as I am using the term, is to mobilize curiosity to reach an understanding of something other, in this case of an antipathy, by making present the feelings of that other. It does not mean being in the same place as offenders or inhabiting and duplicating their feelings.

Repulsion, like curiosity, is often sparked by an antipathy. By contrast, repulsion converts an antipathy into an aversion; it empowers one to protect oneself from possible affective contamination by the other. Repulsion would seem to foreclose empathy, to lead one to turn away from understanding. But the act of physically distancing oneself from the subject is betrayed by the intense affect attached to "child sex abuse," betrayed by the excitement aroused by a topic that remains so central to our being. That affect does not lessen but intensifies through repulsion. The process of creating distance inadvertently brings one closer to the sex abuse one wishes to avoid. Repulsion also increases the distance to travel to become knowledgeable.

Engaging with the child sex offender brings readers in the proximity of the power of a social evil that, unlike the international or "foreign" terrorist, is intimate and familial, hence likely to provoke an extreme fear of contamination. Such fear will block curiosity and understanding, which in any event is unlikely to be the primary goal of readers. The goal of readers is more likely to be about bringing them in the proximity of the power of a social good: confirming an affinity with the victimized child, condemning the offender. If, on the other hand, readers seek to understand and become knowledgeable, they will be caught between repulsion and empathy. To prevail over this repulsion, the capacity to empathize must be mobilized to understand the offender's attempt at rehabilitation. That does not mean one need accept or approve the offender but only be strongly motivated to know well and better.

The initial position of listeners or readers is shaped both by a flood of information and a motivated ignorance about child sexuality as well as our early experiences of sex. The difficulties we encounter in thinking of child sex have much to do with infantile sexuality being inclined to transgression, a fact that makes us uncomfortable because we have all been there. Children are not yet in a position to set limits precisely because they have no experience and therefore cannot yet know what these limits might be. Indeed, our first attachments—to our own body and to a maternal caregiver—were without limits, without renunciations. To complicate matters further, in thinking about the mother, we are, as Freud wrote, also forced to think about our first seductress and our first encounter with limits (Freud 1931). The necessity and ambiguity of that seduction—initially an experience of attachment and withdrawal of the nipple, milk, the breast, as Melanie Klein ([1937] 1975) was the first to systematically theorize—is the basis for the initial renunciation of the incest taboo, on which all other sexual taboos are built.

If we permit ourselves to think about this mélange of power and evil and the sacred and sex, we are able to narrow our visceral distance to child sex offenders. But such thoughts are most unpleasant, repulsive. They are usually made possible only by thinking about the tragedy within hope, the unrecuperable loss within redemption, the evil within goodness. The seriousness with which we approach the child expresses a strong wish for unadulterated innocence rather than an acknowledgment of the ambiguous animality of the child. The excess of humanity attributed to the child is abstracted from the lack of humanity attributed to the offender, a normative perspective reinforced by what Roger Lancaster (2011, 13) called the "routinization of panic" and to which offenders often turn to judge themselves.[15] To further a formal interest in recognizing fully the harm done to the child, irony, joking, humor, and teasing are fully banned.

The demand for an unambiguous, condemnatory response to the child sex offender arises in the context of a contemporary European, indeed Western, sexual landscape that, in the last four decades, has rapidly and dramatically changed: increased taboos on touching, elimination of coming-of-age rituals for boys, effacing of distinctions between children and youth, sexualization of young girls and children (or youth) generally, criminalization of some forms of male sexuality, decriminalization of prostitution and homosexuality, decrease in size of households, historic decline in rates and status of physical reproduction, disproportionately large aging populations, and a movement toward equality between same- and cross-sex intimacies coupled with a frequent withdrawal of men from the responsibility for raising children (though this responsibility was rarely ever fairly or evenly distributed anyhow in prior ages).

Many of the best contemporary novels, films, and television serials depict aspects of this unsettled state, and many of the most popular of these even focus on aggression, sex, and evil—attributes that the child by definition is said to lack. They can be read and viewed without troubling our strong identification with ourselves as people who wish for ourselves and others only goodness, contentment, solace, happiness, peace. By contrast, thinking about the rehabilitation of sex offenders brings forth a range of unconscious affects that threatens to derange these identifications. Rehabilitation may create opportunities to transform the offender, but outcomes are as uncertain as life itself. And rehabilitation does not do away with the harm done to the child; it does not make things good again for the victims of sex abuse. Its meager offering to the public is hope for nonrepetition of the offense.

About these matters we—readers, listeners, bystanders, and those individuals who themselves suffered abuse—are in a position similar to child sex offenders themselves while in therapy: We already know a great deal, but we do not want to know too much more. To leave that state of ignorance is to become informed, but information alone does not suffice to make us knowledgeable. To leave the state of ignorance and become knowledgeable about child sex abuse requires thinking through highly charged information and the affect attached to each and every trace such information deposits in us. We must allow an analytic imagination of something already in the imagination, the deed of child sex abuse. Only then, after we have humbled our resistances to the active forms of sustaining motivated ignorance, can we begin to appreciate the potential of rituals of rehabilitation. Aware of our own points of resistance—through denial, repression, dissimulation, and delusion—we might mitigate the effects of being informed but still not want to become knowledgeable.

Knowledgeability, in turn, requires the cultivation of curiosity beyond the usual investment of interests, a kind of critical thinking that is thoroughly mediated by introspection and empathic communication but nonetheless does not avoid the difficult task of assessment and verification. If we seek to understand how others conceive of themselves in their own contexts, the ethical doctrine of cultural relativism developed by anthropologists must remain our initial position. But this doctrine, which entails an analytic imagination of and with those one studies, is, as I argue in the final chapter, neither a dogma nor the goal of an inquiry. That goal is neither to relativize ethical qualms about our subjects, child sex offenders, nor to absent ourselves from the problems entailed in standing in proximity to them, but to be there more fully to communicate better an understanding to ourselves and to others (Borneman 2009, 237–58).

Real Abuse and the Phantasmatic

Today, as in the past, we confront emotional impediments when imagining sexual intimacy with children. But unlike in times past or in many other parts of the world, we in the West are very well informed about child sex and child sex abuse. The public sphere is flooded with stories of such abuse. It is no longer a mystery. We know, for example, that child sex abuse is not something modern, nor is it a product of the nuclear family or of the sexual permissiveness of the 1960s. We know that the sexual desire for children can be either for the same or opposite sex, but that this desire resembles neither homosexuality nor heterosexuality and has little to do with the difference between these two normative types. We know that, despite considerable shifts over time in the categories used to describe it, child sex abuse has always been a theme integral to the suspense in many traditional folktales.

For at least a century, child sex abuse has been a recurrent trope in Western literature and art. In film, its initial appearance was in Fritz Lang's first sound film, *M*, screened in 1931. Featuring Peter Lorre as Hans Beckert, a former mental patient who stalks and murders young girls for erotic satisfaction, *M* does not represent the acts of abuse on screen, though it clearly implies sexual molestation. And as the film nears its climax, the focus shifts from the story of catching a child molester and threat of mob violence to an affirmation of justice through the rule of law.

Toward the end of the film, Beckert, surrounded by an enraged crowd intent on lynching him, cries out, "Who knows what it's like to be me?" Indeed, what it is like to be Beckert in the 1930s was a complete mystery, even to Beckert, and was to remain so for another half century. Two years after the film opened in the United States, the *New York Times* criticized Lang for wasting his talents on a crime "too hideous to contemplate." Nonetheless, as Estelle Freedman (1987, 83) has written, the "reviewer's distaste for the public discussion of sexual crimes" did not suppress popular interest in them, which instead subsequently grew, leading the *New York Times* in 1937 "to create a new index category, 'Sex Crimes,' to encompass the 143 articles it published on the subject that year."

Although we are today well informed about what it's like to be *M*'s Beckert, the thought of the child molester still evokes a phantasmatic reaction of rage and often incites something similar to the mob that sought to lynch Beckert. To see *M* today one cannot but be impressed at how Lang, who never intended to make a film about child sex abuse, presciently brings to the screen conflicts that today's public still finds "too hideous to contemplate." In linking Beckert's ignorance of the nature of his desire to public repulsion of it, however, Lang, despite his disavowal, made some progress at least in depicting the problem.

One of the social functions of films such as *M* is to control the fantasy associated with a taboo through its depiction. For the last half century, the media, films, and music have publicized the issue of child sex abuse and depicted it with ever less circumlocution. At least since the late 1990s, television crime serials, such as *Tatort* in Germany and *Hill Street Blue Streets* in the United States, along with many crime series in other European countries lacking wide audiences beyond their national borders, have taken up the graphic violence of sex crimes, introducing a victim-oriented view with the same titillation as the most sensational stories of sexual predators disseminated by the tabloid press. In these very popular serials today, catching the molester of children is perhaps the most powerful plot for attracting audiences. What was considered so obviously heinous that it was unworthy of serious thought or representation less than a century ago is now spoken about and portrayed endlessly. But while giving the fantasies and fears form might be expected to disempower the phantasmatic aspects of abuse for the public, it also reinforces certain clichés about male desire gone amok and, in this way, introduces another set of phantasms.

One recent example is the 2009 award-winning film *The Lovely Bones* (translated into German as *In Meinem Himmel*), adapted from the 2002 novel of the same name by Alice Sebold. The story is similar to Lang's *M* in that sex abuse is implied but not addressed in the serial murder of young girls, and the molester is unfathomable; with no biography presented, he is reduced to his crime. What is new is the narration from the perspective of the victim. One of the girls who is already dead narrates, motivating the revenge of her family. More specifically, she has the power to activate her father, who seeks the justice that in *M* was sought by a mob. The story maintains a redemptive or reparative promise, unlike *M*, but not for the rehabilitation of the offender. It is the girl victims who are rewarded for their horrible murders by an afterlife in a surreal netherworld that they reach by detaching themselves from their families, thus freeing them of the burden of their families' loss.

In a review of the categories and classifications of child abuse in Anglo-American texts since the late 1970s, Ian Hacking (1991, 284) noted some prior changes in the three decades 1960 to 1990: The categories that used to arouse public sentiment, like "cruelty to children" or the "battered baby syndrome," have been replaced with the more generic term "child abuse." "Concerned pediatricians and radical feminists" were, he wrote, responsible for "molding" this discourse; etiological and epidemiological questions have seized control of ways of framing it (286).

During the later twentieth century, then, the focus on physical abuse shifted to sex abuse, and the concern for prepubescent children expanded to include youths up to the age of eighteen. Hacking wrote, "many unrelated kinds of harms to children [have been lumped] under one unreflective but powerful emblem" (1991, 276, 284–86). My research confirms his assumption that most cases of child sex abuse have indeed become "powerful emblem[s]" to refer to a wide array of "unrelated" interactions between children and adults, most of which do not involve intercourse but are concerned with improper touching. When it is assumed the consequences are bad, touching becomes molestation. Although immediate consequences are usually detectable only in cases of repetitive and severe abuse, or in cases of fondling by adults who are in some way inappropriately and intimately close to the child, adult anticipation of negative consequences frequently leads to intervention and, at times, prosecution of the offender.

As a result of an elastic definition and increased publicity and sensitivity, from the late 1960s through 1993 in the West, the number of reported cases of child molestation increased exponentially. In the 1980s, at the time Hacking was writing his article, a wave of cases of "moral panic" drew public attention to alleged Satanic rites and pedophile murder rings, and to accusations of abuse within families and in institutions (see La Fontaine 1998). "Child abuse" had become, Hacking concluded, a "normalizing" instead of a "thick moral" concept," and "in the power struggle over who owns child abuse, the doctors triumphed" (1991, 286–87).

While Hacking found most of his evidence for panics in the United States and Great Britain, one can easily supplement them with examples from continental Europe. Such waves are cyclical, as I suggest in chapter 2; they position law to take up the space of sorcery in "naming the witch," a phenomenon that James Siegel (2006) has theorized using ethnographic material from Indonesia and the Americas. Those accused of sorcery—in this case, accused of child sex abuse—often succumb, at least initially, to the power of the social in finding ways to agree to their assigned guilt. This recent period of "moral panics" began with the discovery, or often invention, of cases, which through publicity spread from country to country, uniting the West as the assumed center of a moral and moralizing universe. Many of these panics were driven by what is called "false memory syndrome," memory of a traumatic sexual experience that is objectively false yet strongly believed in and resistant to correction. In Germany, the most publicized case was that of Tillman Fürniß, head of Jugendpsychiatrie in Münster, who between 1983 and 1991 led the charge of perverse sex abuse of sixty-three children against teachers in two Montessori schools. The German court found all parties innocent (Friedrichsen and Mauz 1993). Innocence was also the verdict in the most publicized and sensational cases of panic from the 1970s and 1980s in Great Britain and the United States (Jenkins 1992; La Fontaine 1998).

Be that as it may, much has changed since Hacking's assessment, written in the midst of a wave of sex panics and published in 1991. Above all, there have been few similar panics, and there has been a dramatic decline in reported cases of all sex crimes, including sex abuse of children. In Germany, this decline was from more than thirty legal complaints per 100,000 residents between 1955 to 1965, to fifteen to twenty legal complaints per

100,000 residents in the 1990s, to fewer than fifteen per 100,000 residents by 2009 (Bundesministerium des Inneren 2009).

This decline has also been noted in most other Western countries that do such reporting. The most intense tracking has been in the United States. There the decline was 40 percent from 1992 to 2000, and an additional 20 percent from 2000 to 2010 (Finkelhor, Jones, and Shattuck 2011; Finkelhor, Turner, Omrod, and Hamby 2010; Finkelhor and Jones 2004). Although multiple factors as yet not well understood undoubtedly influenced this decline, Finkelhor, Jones, and Shattuck (2011) argued that it is a real reduction (not merely a statistical artifact), due at least in part to increased prevention efforts, including more prosecution and incarceration of offenders. Drawing from recent empirical data, two important factors concerning prevention stand out: All Western countries have enacted laws strengthening the rights of children, and in most such countries it is now a legal requirement for health care workers and teachers to report suspected child abuse to authorities.

Today men commit an estimated 95 percent of all sex crimes, and half of all sexual offenders were already involved in some other type of crime as youths. Beyond this generalization, research is conclusive in suggesting we revise several commonplace prejudices about sexual criminals: They do not share the same etiology, most do not suffer from fixed perversions, recidivism rates among child sex offenders are much lower than other kinds of crimes, and treatment of sex offenders does in fact reduce the likelihood of repetition of the crime.[16]

Classification of sex crimes has remained constant since West German legal reforms after 1969, when female prostitution and homosexuality were largely decriminalized. In 1998 another set of reforms lengthened minimum penalties and criminalized specific acts that brought more attention to child sex abuse. Criminological discourse today tends to classify the sex abuse of children as a crime against sexual self-determination, rape as a crime of violence, and pornography as an economic delict. Over the last several decades, the number of sexual delicts has remained constant while public reporting of them has increased manyfold, radically disproportionate to their numerical significance, and the public focus has been on the most spectacular cases. In 2002, for example, of the more than six million criminal acts in Germany, only 0.8 percent were of sex crimes (PKS 2002, tab. 1, cited in Stolte 2005, 174). In 2003 those sentenced for child sexual abuse, rape, and sexual assault comprised 1 percent (7,333 of 736,297) of all sexual delicts, 0.4 percent of all crimes (Günter 2005, 62–64). Between 1960 and 1985 "pedosexual crimes" declined and have since remained relatively constant, with a very slight increase after 1987. Police-reported rape increased in the 1950s and then remained constant until the 1980s before again declining. While it is unclear what exact effect public sensitivity and awareness has on the commission of such criminal acts, increased sensitivity has surely led to increased willingness to report and prosecute (Urbaniok 2005).

In 2011 in Germany the sex abuse of children accounted for 0.3 percent of all criminal offenses. By comparison, the largest category of crime was that against property, comprising 46.4 percent of all criminal acts (Statista 2013). Although one must assume a considerable underreporting of abuse, the numbers are by any statistical measure relatively insignificant compared to other crimes. Yet the social significance of child sex abuse far exceeds its empirical incidence. The topic of sex abuse and the figure of the sexual predator continue to appear nearly daily in an enlarged, mediatized public sphere, indexing to some extent the waning and waxing of orchestrated moral panics. On the other hand, unlike in the 1970s and 1980s, the allegations in the more recent spectacular cases from around Europe that come to light with a disturbing regularity have proven shockingly true, in both familial and institutional settings, and most of those accused and still alive have been convicted and imprisoned.

For example, in 2008 and 2009 two cases of extraordinary transgressions of sexual intimacy within Germany and Austrian families received widespread international publicity. In Germany Patrick Stübing had been convicted already in 2002 of incest with his sister Susan Karolewski; after being set free, he committed the same act in 2005. If the act occurs before the age of eighteen, relatives of any degree, including siblings, are not punished for incest (though they may be prosecuted on other charges, such as rape, assault, or child abuse). But Stübing and Karolewski were already adults during the first prosecution. The case reached the German Constitutional Court in 2008. It ruled that brother-sister incest "endangered the order of the family," and it confirmed the prison sentence of two years given to Stübing. In Austria in 2009 Josef Fritzl, who had imprisoned his daughter along with three of their children (the daughter had seven in all and one miscarriage) in the family's basement for twenty-four years, was convicted of repeated incest with his daughter and sentenced to life in a psychiatric ward.

One year later, in 2010, sordid revelations of child abuse in German institutions followed, first within the Jesuit, upper-class Canisius-Kolleg, a secondary school in Berlin, and then in the secular elite Berlin Odenwaldschule, with offenses dating back to the 1960s. Revelations followed from secular schools in other German cities, with offenses dating from the same period. Unlike the United States, where public debate has focused on priests and the

Catholic Church, in Germany it turned especially critical of secular schools. In the case of the Odenwaldschule, Gerold Becker, its former director, had apparently been simultaneously sexually abusing some of his students as he formulated the internationally acclaimed "reform pedagogy" for secondary school education. Because many of the graduates of the Odenwald school came from elite German families, those who had been abused led the public face of investigations, which found up to 132 victims of abuse in that school alone. Individual revelations led to extended and ongoing publicity, resulting in high-level local and federal commissions of investigation. There was a flurry of apologies, documentary films, and substantial changes in the laws relating to sex abuse, including, for example, more federal money specifically earmarked for research on the topic, a national monetary compensation fund (*Hilfsfond*) for all past and future child victims of sexual abuse, and extension of the statute of limitations to lodge a civil complaint from three to thirty years for civil cases.

Despite the constant threat of moral panic in this atmosphere, the sum of accusations has not yet coalesced in an all-out witch-hunt.[17] The reaction of the relevant institutions has been swift and precise. Victims were granted immediate credibility and publicity. Three federal ministers—of education and research, of justice, and of family, seniors, women, and youth—cooperated in 2010 to create a round table (Runder Tisch Sexueller Kindesmissbrauch) for "child sex abuse in dependency and power relations in private and public institutions and in the sphere of the family" (Bundesregierung 2010, 1). The round table resulted in some of the programs and laws mentioned above. Governmental institutions acted immediately to realize these programs. What distinguishes these events from the scandals and panics of other periods is the factor of class in the peculiar voice of the victims. Most were well-to-do men who had become successful in their careers and were capable of marshaling the support of politicians for redress and the media for publicity.

In sum we are dealing here with phenomena both real and phantasmatic, both known and not known, which elicit repulsion. We are dealing with a topic that is omnipresent in the public sphere (despite an actual decline in reported cases of sex abuse), yet most publics resist becoming knowledgeable. It is important to underline that the 2010 revelations of cases of abuse in Germany involved offenses that had occurred several decades ago, in institutions; they express problems in regulating adult-child relations of a generation before the decline in cases of real abuse. Still to be explained is why the decline in cases of real abuse has no effect on the phantasmatic investment in abuse, and in what way this relation between the real and the phantasm affects the empirical nature of abuse and its frequency. That investment is important for this study because it frames the public context in which adult sex offenders experience the ritual of rehabilitation.

Two obvious contributing factors keep the sex offender in the public eye. One is the prominence given to victims, in this case children, for whom adults are eager and willing to speak and with whom the public is eager to identify.[18] The United States was prominent in changing the rules whereby victims who sought a legal remedy were subject to procedures in the trial of sex offenders that frequently had the effect of punishing the victim a second time. Germany has followed the United States in this regard, granting more rights to claims of abuse and victimization, and acknowledging the distinct qualities of traumatic experience. Today in both countries the accusation of sex abuse alone can compel legal authorities to investigate and arrest the suspect. Granting victims an initial assumption of credibility in their charges signals a progressive change. However, this often also means that an initial assumption of guilt for the accused is envisaged even though disavowed.

In fact, during my research two male therapists were accused of pedophile abuse in an anonymous letter, resulting for one of them in an investigation and a threat of suspension from work. The anonymous accuser submitted a second letter, but he was ultimately never identified. Nonetheless, the letters set in motion the ritual process described in this book, truncated in this case only because the charges proved completely preposterous. What is significant here is not the veracity of the accusation but the mechanical automaticity with which it is brought into a public sphere, where new laws and protocols and a group of highly invested individuals in institutional settings endowed with a renewed sense of moral purpose are also legally obliged to act as if anonymous accusations are all plausible if not true. A principle of "assumed true until proven false" now counterbalances that of "innocent until proven guilty," and codirects, if not leads, the protocol of discovery following an accusation of sex abuse. This shift in protocol might in the future facilitate witch-hunts and moral panics, though, as mentioned, such panics were avoided in the period of this research in Germany.

The other factor is the tendency of the contemporary media to sensationalize by resorting to tabloid description of surface realities. Description usually begins before there is sufficient information to tell an accurate story, and once there is sufficient information, the stories are often so messy and confusing that they are no longer deemed "newsworthy." Through the use of distorted images (silhouettes, angry faces, frames of faces partially anonymized) and repetition of key affective terms (e.g., *Kinderschänder* and *Pädophil*), depictions distance offenders from the human relationships and contexts that have motivated possible transgressions. In this way, they reinforce the power of social taboos and encourage distancing from the empirical or phenomenal by flight into the phantasmatic. Irene Berkel (2006) has trenchantly explicated the role of media in creating abuse as a phantasm in Germany and the modern West, demonstrating with respect to publicity that Germany is not much different from other countries in the West. Both print and visual media everywhere, not only in the yellow press and not only in Britain (where it appears most extreme), will report anything to increase their market share. Popular media invariably magnifies the harm and evil of the offender, but also plays to the titillating attraction of the taboo surrounding the experience of sex of the innocent child (for the United States, see Levine 2002; Berlant 1997; Ivy 1993).

Increased public awareness of this age-old taboo likely contributes to the decline in violations, but it does not automatically translate into a "state of heightened consciousness," as Hacking concluded in 1991. Consciousness would imply enlightenment, or the absence of repression. The public is informed, aware, but it is not knowledgeable. Something remains repressed, even though, if we stick to the German case, new laws have been passed, national hotlines have been initiated, more money has been allocated for research, and the government plans monetary compensation for all victims of child sex abuse past and present. There remains a taboo on the thought of childhood sex, but one that does not operate, if it ever did, simply to uphold a prohibition. An explicit cultural turn to an unapologetic sexualization of children and pubescent youths contradicts the idea of an effective prohibition. There is little if any objection to the increased use of very young girls in the advertising of lingerie, for example, and organized opposition to the traffic in children in world sex tourism for Western consumers has had limited effects.

Part of the explanation for why today the taboo retains its power is that it is useful for the new and rapidly changing field of information flow and knowledge. That sexual taboos can be productive and not merely repressive has been a standard assumption in the academic field at least since the publication of Michel Foucault's ([1976] 1978) study of sexuality in the Victorian Age. There he demonstrated how a repression of sex is accompanied, paradoxically, and even superseded in significance by a proliferation of discourse on the topic, a fine gradation of types of sex, and the creation of pathological and normal distinctions as well as distinct sexual identities. This is the line of inquiry Hacking also pursues: discourse accumulates, identifies, marks, demarcates, reconstitutes. Where this approach fails is in its ability to account for the persistence of repression despite the proliferating, disseminating discourses. If sex is a product, or a determination, of the discourse around it, then there is no reality of child sexual abuse with a force of its own independent of the discourse. To be sure, children learn about what they have experienced in cases of abuse through the discursive elaboration of what happened. At the same time, child sex with adults, the deed, does often have a materiality that escapes or exceeds discursive attempts to contain it, returning in mysterious symptoms without or perhaps despite not having been spoken about.

Because Hacking remains within the categories of expert discourse, he restricts his purview to aspects of the identification and naming of sex abuse, what Foucault called the "truth of sex." Other than to question the plausibility of the claims of sex abuse, Hacking has no means to evaluate the actual veracity of the claims and whether these have, in turn, any reciprocal effects on the process of categorization and classification of offenders. He assumes that classifications have automatic effects and therefore makes no attempt to understand how identification with categories actually works for the individuals, victims and offenders alike, who are objects of these classifications. Hacking's omissions are also a result of the occlusion of psychoanalytic theory characteristic of the Foucauldian-inspired discourse approach he takes.

Freud himself outlined an amazingly prescient and controversial position on child sexuality. He hypothesized, for instance, that adult genital stimulation of children will return to them later in life as a memory and produce a release of sexuality stronger than at the time of the initial stimulation, partly because it is a memory attached to excitation of abandoned sexual zones. That hypothesis might lead us to conclude that because the early sexual zones, abandoned with age and maturity, preexist language, their function and effects cannot be attributed to discourse alone. The outcome of such memories, Freud argues, will be not pleasure but unpleasure (*Unlust*) and a feeling analogous to disgust (Freud 1985, 279–80; Freud 1915, 195). Many child and even youth victims of sex abuse report their experience in terms congruent to Freud's hypothesis. That stated, what Freud neglected in his account is the social context of this memory recall, the presence and effects of the transference in interactions with others—parents, friends, partners, colleagues—at the moment of this release of sexuality, which powerfully influence the manner in which unpleasure manifests itself (Laplanche 1999).

In the years since Freud's seminal work, all of these questions and more have been addressed, if not answered or resolved, in a growing field of research on child sex abuse—by psychotherapists, psychologists, psychiatrists, social workers, criminologists, anthropologists, and sociologists—that is critical of the accuracy of the classifications and diagnoses of medical and psychiatric experts. The accelerated pace of scientific production of empirical knowledge about child sex abuse—its motivations, frequency, and effects—has made it possible for scholars to be more specific in addressing not only the social construction of events of abuse and scandal but also the "true" motivations, frequency, and effects of the actual phenomena of abuse in its various social contexts.

To consider one poignant example: contemporary research has changed the status of the term "soul murder." Taken from the myth of Kasper Hauser, soul murder was popularized by Leonard Shengold in his important research on the traumatic effects of early childhood sexualization and abuse. Shengold (1991, 16–17) argued that soul murder characterizes "instances of chronic and repetitive overstimulation, alternating with deprivation, that are brought about by another individual." The term effaces an important distinction, however. Kasper Hauser suffered physical abuse and neglect, not sex abuse. Physical abuse overwhelms the senses of the child; deprivation or neglect starves those senses. The two forms of child abuse should not be confused with each other, even though some of the effects might be similar, because the possible therapies would not be the same. And while the most recent studies suggest a decline in the incidence of child sex abuse, they also suggest that child physical abuse has remained constant or increased. It has not been established that "soul murder" results from all cases of child sex abuse unless also accompanied by neglect or other kinds of violence. In his more recent work, Shengold (1999) himself introduced many caveats and distinctions into understanding the effects of child abuse.

The long-term effects of childhood sexual victimization are, in other words, not equally pernicious for all children. One of the best early studies, consistently confirmed by others since, remains the research by Judith Herman, Diana Russell, and Karen Trocki (1986), which concluded, first, that about half of a community sample of child sexual victims claimed to have recovered well from abuse; second, that recovery from such abuse is closely related to the type of abuse (e.g., duration, level of intimacy, degree of force); and third, that abuse by a father or stepfather was more likely to produce long-term effects than abuse by other males. David Finkelhor (1984) further specified that such abuse does not produce the same particular effects from case to case, and thus suggests limits to the generalizability of the model of posttraumatic stress disorder (PTSD). A variety of immediate psychological effects may be observable, but behavioral changes appear to be only secondary results. These behavioral changes are dependent in large part on the experiences of individuals subsequent to the abuse. Likewise, Paul Mullen and

Jillian Fleming (1998) confirmed a series of behavioral changes—limited capacity for trust or intimacy, lowered self-esteem, and disruption of sexual development—but they also argue that many of the mental health problems associated with abuse are second-order effects. Overall, rates of child sex abuse are estimated to be two to four times higher for girls than boys, and the risk of psychiatric disorder is two to four times higher for those sexually abused than those not abused (Fergusson and Mullen 1999; Mullen, King, and Tonge 2000, 6, 9).

The many analyses that seek to collate the results of some of the more than one hundred studies over the last thirty years have reached very similar conclusions. Although most of these studies suffer from a self-reporting bias, they are nonetheless remarkably consistent in confirming the findings outlined above.[19] Where the data is most problematic is when conglomerate categories lump together children with youths; incest with nonincestuous abuse; physically intrusive contact (e.g., brutal sexual assaults, intercourse) with improper suggestions or touching, exhibitionism, and pornographic viewing; or a single instance with repeated, long-term abuse. For example, what we know is that the effects of abuse on prepubescent children is exponentially greater than on youths who are already sexually active; forced sexual contact with a trusted intimate is psychologically more devastating than with a stranger; sexual intercourse with children is a physical invasion and leaves scars more difficult if not impossible to redress than being forced to submit to fondling; and abuse over many years creates mental and physical disturbances of a different order than one-time abuse. In a review of the literature, Paul Mullen and colleagues (2000, 3) concluded that, "from a research perspective, there is nothing called CSA [child sex abuse] but a variety of acts, situations, and relationships that can reasonably be considered to be part of such a construct."

Touching and Therapy

Among the range of acts that constitute child sex abuse as an identifiable experience, the most frequent is improper touching. What is remarkable today is the extent to which, in the West generally, most touching has come to be defined as a sexual act, even when not involving genitalia and even when between adults. Yet the sensation of touch is also considered a primal activity, one of the five senses for which the others cannot substitute (Montagu 1971). It is central to the psychological development of not only humans but all primates. Without being touched or, more specifically, without the creation of a holding environment that includes touching by a primary caregiver in early infancy, the child is likely to grow up with permanent insecurities and anxieties with regards to the external environment (Bowlby 1973; Winnicott 1960). On the other hand, as described above, if the child interprets adult touch as "sexual," then this experience of touch becomes a violation of the child's integrity, potentially hindering the development of a capacity for intimacy and trust.

Given that the need for touch is primal while at the same time having ambiguous if not diametrically opposed effects, it should be no surprise that its cultural coding is extremely variable. There is no place in recorded human history where touch is unregulated, yet the regulations differ radically about who can touch whom and what constitutes improper touching. There are entire cultures, or classes or statuses within cultures, where people are encouraged to touch a lot, and cultures where they are strongly discouraged from most touching. Whether encouraged or discouraged, touch is especially sensitive when it comes to relations between adults and children or men and women. For our purposes here, it is important to note the special phenomenal quality of a child's skin, often theorized as an evolutionary device to attract adult touching. Adults across cultures repeat versions of the telling line, "You're so cute I could eat you," suggesting not just the attraction of touch or kiss but a metaphor of ingestion evocative of a cannibalistic desire.

The Brothers Grimm folktale of *Hansel and Gretel*, published in 1812, in fact introduced a cannibalistic witch to resolve the tension between the oral needs (in this case, initially hunger) of two children and their parents. I will return to this tale in a discussion of seduction and empathy in chapter 5. For our purposes now, the moral is not that the witch is successful in seducing the children into her gingerbread house but that she is ultimately unsuccessful in eating them (the children set her on fire and escape with her wealth): Children taste good and must be wary of abandonment by their parents. In a sign of the primal appeal of this tale, a private foundation named *Hänsel + Gretel* was created in 1997 to help abused children by raising awareness of children's needs, *Kinderbewusstsein*.

Cannibalism is the most extreme and unambiguous attempt at oral incorporation. Touch, by comparison, would seem innocuous and unproblematic—but it is not. Perhaps the best-known example in the ethnographic record of the cultural coding of touch is in the context of ritual status in India, which developed an elaborate set of transactions between persons and objects, frequently petrifying into violent hierarchical distinctions between groups. In India, adult fondling, kissing, and licking of babies and children is very common and relatively unregulated by taboos. By contrast, oral contact and touch between adults is highly regulated if not often forbidden—witness the public rioting and warrant for the arrest in 2007 of Richard Gere for kissing Bollywood star Shilba Shetty at an AIDS campaign event.

These taboos on contact and intimate exchange originated in ancient and medieval India in the ritual relations of the four varnas (social ranks) that form the functional divisions of labor in Hindu society. Brahmins, being the ritual specialists closest to divinity, stand at the apex of the varna system (at least according to Brahmin theories), while Untouchables (Dalits) are conceptualized along the lines of a group altogether outside the varna system, and thus outside society proper. The Brahmin and Dalit are radically separated by many taboos, including those around touch. While the basis for any systematicity in caste hierarchies is disputed, it is nonetheless useful to think about touchability through this conceptual frame. As theorized by Louis Dumont ([1966] 1970), these taboos revolve around a conceptual link between the purity of the Brahmin, or those highest in the varna, and the pollution of those lower in caste system, especially the Dalits, who are conceptualized as outside the varna system proper. Purity and pollution taboos involve both the prohibition on touching—Untouchables or Dalits cannot touch or be touched by others—and avoidance of being touched—Brahmins are allowed to touch other varnas, but not to be touched by those of lower status. For the purpose of my comparison, what is most important to understand is how the Dalits become the caste responsible for disposing of the remains of the upper castes. As Gopal Guru (2012, 213) has remarked, "The untouchable is forced to become the repository of the impurities of the touchable."[20]

From this perspective, the contemporary child sex offender in the West has touched the untouchable, the member of society considered most pure. An adult has polluted the pure state of the child, which is pure because it is assumed to be without sexuality. That violation makes the offender an untouchable of the impurest sort, impure because of sexual intention, the genital intention behind the touch. That touch places the offender outside the social order. The conceptualization of the child without sexuality becomes all the more important and difficult to sustain to the extent it is contradicted by the reality of contemporary children, that is, their explicit sexualization.

Obviously, the child sex offender has not been forced to become the repository of the impurities of the touchable, as in the operation of the Indian caste system. The offender has, for reasons to be explicated in later chapters, chosen to act out a set of primal phantasies that are considered impure. He indulges in these impure thoughts, which he may share with others but which are collectively disavowed, by acting on them. Only after choosing to act does he become a repository of impurities and thereby makes himself an untouchable. And unlike in the caste system, in reality no one is consciously forbidden to touch the offender—though he elicits visceral repulsion, and for this reason others avoid touching him.

And in contrast to the Hindu theory of relationality, everything in the West today is cast as voluntary. Unlike the Indian Dalit, the sex offender's status can change if he is fully rehabilitated in the eyes of the law and the community in which he lives.[21] Yet for the public, even after rehabilitation the child sex offender remains a repulsive figure. Repulsive because his "truth" is sex, the desire for children assumed not to have a sexuality. Touching the offender—emotional, cognitive, physical, even imaginative proximity—puts one at risk of contamination. Yet his difficulty of touch must be overcome to make possible rehabilitation and reintegration into society. Touch bears directly on the obstacles to intimate proximity with the child molester and to the possibility of therapy.

Disgust in the Transference

I remember my first encounters with child sex offenders in the two places I worked, in the prison and in the therapy groups at KiZ in Berlin. Up to that point, offenders for me were merely the clients, defendants, or subjects of people I knew. And they were the object of documents, figures of my imagination. The prison is a *Selbststellermodel* (self-administered model), where prisoners voluntarily admit themselves into prison, then cook and clean for themselves, check out for work during the day and check back in at night. There are only two such prisons in Berlin, and they are still considered experimental. People often compare them to a country club. They place as much everyday responsibility on the offender as possible in a system of incarceration. I entered the prison with an employee involved in the evaluation of offenders. Everyone knew and, I assume, feared her. Those present watched us as she took me for a tour around the grounds. She did not introduce me to any of the offenders whom we passed in the hallways and courtyards. After that, I was as uncertain about how to approach them as they were about approaching me. At most I shook the hands of a few employees now and then, and had a few brief conversations with them. I physically touched no one, nor did they me. In any event, most of my work in prison was reading the documents that detail some of the cases elaborated in this book.

At the treatment center KiZ, I asked for permission to observe the therapy groups at the beginning of every ten-week session. The therapists then introduced me to the men in the groups collectively. They were not introduced to me individually. After that I was left alone with the offenders during a coffee break. Forbidden to have contact with each other outside the group, they obviously found it awkward to make small talk with each other during breaks, much less with me, whom they identified unambiguously with the therapists. To switch registers from the intimate and embarrassing or shameful details of their lives to something less charged was difficult. I sometimes ran into them on the U-Bahn, underground, as they returned either to the prison or from the therapy center. At those times I avoided mentioning therapy sessions and instead engaged them about such quotidian matters as train schedules and the weather. I usually shook their hands before one of us left the underground, as is custom among the Germans I know. In doing so, I was fully aware of how artificial it must have seemed to them to engage someone of my status and background who tried to treat them as equal. To treat the people one studies as equal is a methodological and ethical injunction of contemporary ethnographic fieldwork. This equality existed, obviously, only in my eyes. The crimes these men had committed made everyone else morally superior, even in their own eyes.

At the same time, moving out of their world—of therapy and prison—into mine was radically disjunctive for me. It was as if I had been in another moral universe and now returned. I had to work hard to redirect my thoughts away from what had been disclosed to us in the small therapy room. I had to quit thinking about histories of abuse and violation, and, for those who had completed their prison sentences, about problems with social reintegration, in order to open myself to happenings in more relaxed social situations in the city. They, by contrast, were left alone with these thoughts. Living in a prison that was boring instead of, as in the United States, a crime preparation laboratory, brought some if not most of these men to think critically about themselves, which I in turn observed during group sessions (Rhodes 2004; Western 2007; Wacquant 2000).

Therapy groups met in the late afternoon or early evening to accommodate the men who were on regular work schedules and had to return to the prison in the evening. Often I was struck by the stink of the room as these sweaty men, most who were returning from blue-collar jobs, took their seats. Someone would frequently open a window, but as Berliners tend to be sensitive to drafts, someone would shut it fairly soon afterward. I kept busy in sessions in my role as scribe, observing details of dress, listening to changes in voice, tone, and locution, to how clients reacted to each other and to the therapists as someone spoke. Only after the two-hour sessions and as I reconstructed my notes the next morning was I able to begin to assess what had gone on in the sessions.

Of the five groups into which therapists divide their clients, I attended two pedophile groups, one incest group, and one youth group. Initially I had wanted to focus on incest abusers alone, as the theorization of the incest taboo has been so important to anthropology and social theory generally. But only one such group was active. One therapist told me that the incest abusers were uninteresting compared to the pedophiles. A colleague in the prison said their problem was simple: They were fundamentally lazy (*faul*), not motivated to make themselves attractive enough for a partner outside their marital spouse or immediate kin group. By contrast, their own children were easy prey. I was initially suspicious of these claims, but ultimately I found them confirmed and somewhat accurate. And I broadened my scope.

I also noticed a certain amount of burnout by therapists during my five years of work with them. Most therapists simply could not bring the same amount of energy and enthusiasm to each session, or to each client. When their investment was minimal, so was that of their clients. Sessions lagged, distracted clients mumbled, everybody appeared bored. Some therapists developed a repugnance to particular clients, which they glossed more as a form of indifference, but the clients were not fooled. This clearly affected the efficacy of the therapy, as it blocked any positive emotional transference between them and their clients. When that transference was acknowledged and directed, clients who had formerly been lethargic and resistant became more alert and began reflecting more critically and in more detail on experiences that they had withheld.

In several cases that I observed, therapists began to show disappointment in clients who came in with the same complaints every week or who appeared unable or unwilling to engage in a minimal amount of introspection about their own improper behavior (instead repeating stock phrases about culpability they learned from others in the group). Or alternatively, therapists began devoting more attention to clients who took an active interest in exploring their own pasts. Some of these men were classic narcissists, simply using the opportunity to speak to be the center of attention. For others, however, this attention was not what they sought. Once, after a therapist left the group and was replaced by another, two of the more reticent members suddenly began to open up and offer insights into their motivations. It is clear that working with sustained emotional transference, which in part is based on the client's sense that the therapist understands him emotionally, facilitates trust and leads to more disclosure and less self-deception. On the other hand, however, some clients were simply incapable of therapy because they could never grasp what it was about. In the course of the year's therapy that I observed, they never revealed in either word or bodily expression an understanding of the difference between chatting and introspection, or the difference between a self and the image of themselves they presented in public appearances, or of how they might objectivize the self through critical reflection. In what follows, I focus on cases of men who were challenged substantively by therapy but nonetheless demonstrated they were capable of grasping what therapy offered them.

Although the transference makes therapeutic success more likely, therapists frequently had a difficult time dealing with it, precisely because it entailed *emotional* transference *with child molesters.* I observed them struggle with this transference as an introject of the disgust attached to the person of the molester (Reinert 2010). This disgust functions as defense and protection in its original sense, as Mathias Hirsch (2010, 109) argued, "to prevent the absorption of harmful substances." The proximity of the therapists at KiZ to the stigma of their clients—the pollution of the abject— forces them to become, much like those they treated, untouchable. But also the therapists were put in the position of proximity to the child who was sexually abused. The touchable, that which can touch but must not be touched, is, in this case, not the Brahman but the child. The child's impurities are, in turn, not the remains of the upper castes that Dalits are to dispose of, but those adult thoughts concerning children that are unthinkable. Those thoughts are about the dynamics of child seduction and child sexuality.

Whereas therapists who treat child molesters, such as those at KiZ, deserve respect for the extremely difficult work they do, instead the public is skeptical that they can avoid the disgust they are assumed to contain from the transference of their work. They have an even more difficult time defending themselves from this contamination to the extent they think of their clients as incorrigible, incapable of self-transformation—which many do. To defend themselves in interinstitutional settings, when they enter public forums to talk about their work or to inform or train other therapists, they often find it necessary to foreground their treatment of abused children, whom they can represent as unambiguously innocent, rather than emphasize the work they do as therapists for child sex offenders, which potentially contaminates them with the evil offenders represent.

In talks I have given about this research, I have also felt this projection of impurity onto me. The topic itself tends to divide audiences. For example, in one German academic setting a female professor said that she did not recognize Germany in what I reported and asked me where I got my material from, whereupon a male colleague sitting next to her questioned her bias. In one British setting, I received an e-mail after a talk asking that I refrain from publishing material I presented, as the child whom I cited (who talked of her abuse in a recording with a psychologist, which was then introduced in the trial of her uncle and was in his prison file) had not agreed to this. In one US professional setting, an anthropologist commented after my talk that I had unsettled him, implying it was not the material but my own disclosure of it that disturbed him. In the event of a moral panic in the future, male therapists are just as likely as their clients to be named "pedophile," initiating a social process of "naming the witch" to resolve the tensions inherent in contemporary identifications with children.

Treatment and Efficacy

Therapists who work with sex offenders employ many different models for assessment and treatment, most of which are situated between two alternatives. One is minimalist and less demanding, and focused on risk assessment and behavioral change in the person alone. The other incorporates the goal of behavioral change into a more ambitious attempt to understand what factors motivate the person attending therapy and aims to bring about a "psychic change" in the self. The behavioral change model reassesses what has been done (the wrongful sexual act) without necessarily trying to change the hidden motives and unconscious drives behind the act (desiring illegal sexual acts). It requires that the offender only refrain from the act, agree to no longer engage in wrongful behavior. Therapists call this delict-centered therapy, and it is the kind of treatment followed by therapists in nearly all German prisons.

To be treated according to the second alternative usually requires obtaining therapy outside prison. Therapy aimed at psychic change makes greater demands on both the therapist and the offender. Rather than simply obtaining the offender's assent to avoid the violation in the future, it locates the motivations for such behavior in the particular biographies of clients to offer to them something akin to what Tony Ward has called a "Good Lives Model" (Ward and Maruna 2007). While the risk assessment model emphasizes community security and protections, the Good Lives Model places the affirmation of "human dignity" or a "human-rights based practice" at the center of therapy. Ward and Connolly (2008, 88) defined this approach as "entitlements to non-interference in the affairs of the agent or for the provision of specific human goods that are seen as being owed to the person concerned (e.g. health, education, water, food, etc.)." As an ideal, this Good Lives Model is comparable to the basis for treatments in Germany generally, though there are many empirical differences between institutions and regional differences in approaches to forms of imprisonment. Ward, Gannon, and Birgden (2007, 205) argued that this philosophy of treatment is not only more ethical but also has pragmatic effects in facilitating the process of rehabilitation by "providing [offenders] with the learning experiences and resources to develop regard for the interests of others."

Therapists at KiZ, similar to others working outside the prisons, do not restrict themselves to cognitive behavioral approaches but employ an eclectic mix of techniques through four modules. In these modules, offenders explore (1) the sequence of events leading to the act (often called crime cycle), (2) empathy for the victim and apology, (3) personal biography, and (4) relapse prevention.[22] I shall elaborate them in the course of analyzing specific cases in other chapters. It suffices to say at this point that the approach of KiZ operates somewhere between behavioral modification and psychic change. Whether self-transformation is an end in itself depends largely on the particular client's wishes and how much he invests in the therapy. While I did hear complaints by offenders serving time in prison about the quality of therapists to whom they had access, I also heard stories of men who fought with officials to obtain access to more therapy hours than they were allotted or to go outside the prison to employ a therapist of their own choosing. German law guarantees access to treatment, and ultimately choice is usually available for those who persist.

Despite inherent problems in measuring the effectiveness of therapy for sex offenders, studies uniformly confirm that, regardless of the model used, treatment decreases recidivism (Ward, Gannon, and Yates 2008; Mandeville-Norden and Beech 2004; Matson 2002).[23] In a general assessment and summary of recidivism rates in different studies in different countries, Günter (2005, 69, 77) concluded that treatment programs reduce the recidivism rate of sex offenders generally by up to 50 percent. Research conducted already in the 1980s in the United Kingdom comparing the effects of therapy (restricted to cognitive behavioral) versus mere supervision found lower recidivism rates for treated offenders in both institution-based and community-based programs (Marshall, Jones, Ward, Johnston, and Barbaree 1991). With additional relapse prevention treatment, recidivism rates declined to less than 5 percent over the four years of follow-up study (Marshall, Hudson, and Ward 1992; Marshall, Eccles, and Barbaree 1993). In an analysis of seventy-nine treatment outcome studies, comprising almost 11,000 offenders convicted for many different forms of sexual offending, Alexander (1999) found that treatment lowered recidivism across type of offense, with the exception of adult rapists. Offenders enrolled in relapse prevention programs were

10 percent less likely to reoffend than their untreated counterparts. Overall, recidivism rates for treated offenders declined in the 1990s, to below 11 percent for all categories of offender, except for rapists and child molesters who had abused boys.

While nearly all statistical studies of therapeutic and educational interventions in sex offender treatment in different places and times conclude that such interventions are effective in reducing recidivism, rates vary considerably by the type of sexual abuse (e.g., exhibitionism, rape, assault, child abuse, and prostitution). Consideration of each type separately would probably lead to divergent prognoses, but as these types are constructed for reasons specific to certain kinds of expertise and institutional logics (penal, juridical, criminological), there are inherent problems in comparisons. A study by the US Bureau of Justice Statistics (Langan, Schmitt, and Durose 2003, 2) on US offenders, which compared the rearrest rates of sex offenders with those of other types of offenders for any time of crime (not only that of sexual abuse), concluded: "Compared to non-sex offenders released from State prison, sex offenders had a lower overall rearrest rate," and only 3.5 percent were reconvicted for a sex crime within the three-year follow-up period of the study. In German prisons, sex offenders have a lower recidivism rate, 10 to 25 percent, than most of the other offenders (Dünkel and Maelicke 2004, 132). In a study collating different countries and programs, Günter (2005, 68, 76) estimated that 35 to 40 percent of all sex offenders commit a similar offense, 10 to 20 percent commit the same offense. Some studies show that child sex offenders tend to have a higher relapse rate than other types of offenders, and the more severe the crime the less likely a repetition of the offense.

Recidivism studies aim to arrive at an accurate assessment of individual risk, which then can be used to orient sentencing and treatment programs. Criminologists use intuitive, statistical, and clinical information to take into account factors such as dependence on specific contexts, duration of time in which the offender engaged in abuse, and the frequency and extent of abuse (Nedopil 2000). But these factors are not sufficient to assess psychic change. That assessment necessarily includes both intrapsychic and intersubjective processes of self-formation that are largely unconscious and not accessible through the question and answer methods used by criminologists (Hollan 1992; Spiro 1993). In any event, the question of psychic change for child sex offenders is about what sexual renunciation means for the self, and what kind of self-transformation is possible through therapy, assuming the metric of change will be specific to each individual. It is important, then, to know whether the reduction in recidivism rates means a renunciation of sex altogether, a renunciation of specific kinds of interaction considered sexual, or a reorientation in sexual object choice.

Ethnographic case studies, supplemented by a close reading of legal documentation and expert reports, can come closest to assessments of psychic change. They are limited, in turn, in that they can respond only to the question of *how* or *why* treatment can be successful, not to the frequency of success or failure. And while the representations produced through ethnographic studies can serve as initial orientations about general variability, they cannot be subject to the validity controls of standard statistical methods to produce numerical measurements.

The following chapters address these different kinds of renunciations and reorientations, as well as the larger theoretical questions I have elaborated here. Each presents a different empirical perspective on the rehabilitation of child sex offenders through one or several specific case studies, often told in different voices, and each theorizes and contextualizes these perspectives.

TWO

Incest, the Child, and the Despotic Father

From the publication of *Das Mutterrecht* by anthropologist and classicist Johann Jakob Bachhofen in 1861 to the 1970s, the incest taboo has fascinated anthropologists much more than has real incest. The taboo was about the celebrated social institution of marriage and the regulation of sociality, real incest about the ambiguous and murky thing we call endogamous sex. Yet, as Michel Foucault ([1976] 1978, 148) was the first to theorize, there had already been a marked shift in the eighteenth century in the West from a "symbolics of blood to an analytics of sexuality," from regulation of the social through the incest taboo, which controls marriages and alliances, to the identification of sex as an interior truth. Nonetheless, because of the increased importance of what he called "the family cell" for the deployment of sexuality, Foucault argued for the continued significance of incest, as an "object of obsession and attraction, a dreadful secret and indispensable pivot" (109; cf. Borneman 1996).

To uncover what Foucault called the "immense apparatus (*dispositif*) around sex for producing truth"—the interior truth of sex and the sites for its production and regulation—anthropologists have largely followed his suggestions to examine surface intersections of power and knowledge and to investigate the biopolitics of populations and the imagination of bodies and pleasures (48). Yet the accumulated expert knowledge on child sexuality and incest offers more nuanced explanations of the experience of incestuous sex than one that reduces it to an effect of the institutions producing the discourse about it. Moreover, the numerous and shifting sites of this more modern sexual analytics have had a way of circling back to incorporate and redefine incest and the older symbolics of blood. Incest involving relations between adults and children or youths, as the prohibited sex that involves certain subcategories of Oedipal desires, is one of the most significant of such sites today.

In contemporary North American and European societies, sensational cases of real incest have become regular items in the news. Its publicity has been increasingly restricted to "a form of sexual abuse perpetrated by men," which, wrote feminist theoretician Vikki Bell (1993, 2), "no longer finds its place as a social rule requiring explanation as to its origin and function, but has been identified as an abuse practice, located as a social problem to be uncovered and measured." As real incest is narrowed and subsumed into the discourse of child sex abuse, it has become part of an imaginary complex[1] that includes the figures of the child, adult male relatives, and the pedophile. While contemporary research in many fields confirms that most children subject to coercive intimate acts by close relatives suffer long-term psychological harm, the phenomenon of such sex is also subject to phantasmic investments that exaggerate the frequency and severity of the threat to society.[2]

This chapter examines two paradigmatic cases—one taken largely from archival data, the other of a participant in the group therapy I attended and observed—in which real incest is brought under the penumbra of law, when this violation of a rule is made into an illegality. It then uses these cases to theorize at a higher level of abstraction about this imaginary complex, including about the use of myth by the unconscious, the meanings of incest, the relation between taboos and law, the nature of male and female attachments to the child, gender conflict, and changes in the position of the father in the symbolic order of the West.[3]

The Incest Taboo and the Oedipus Myth

Two interpretations of the Oedipus myth have oriented conflicts about the nature of the symbolic order of the West. Bachofen (1861) published one: early human groups depended far more on female than on male reproductivity; hence most early gods were indeed female, and inheritance was matrilineal. At some unspecified time, men expropriated women's power, creating other myths (e.g., of parthenogenesis) that celebrated male labor while obscuring the actual contributions of women in physical and social reproduction. For Bachofen, *Patriarchat* replaced *Mutterrecht* and instituted a new system of lineage and gender demarcation. The incest taboo was the central mechanism for this replacement, as it forbid the sexual relations of mothers with their children, in particular with their sons, minimizing women's control over inheritance while forcing children into a complicated reidentification with a newly empowered social father. According to this version of the myth, the first renunciation was that of the mother, resulting in a denial and redirection of desire.

Darwin (1871) developed the second interpretation, which Freud (1913) combined with William Robertson Smith's insights on sacrifice and elaborated more fully some forty years later: A father resolves his competition for authority with (Darwin's) primitive brother horde by driving his sons out of the social order to secure or maintain a monopoly on power as well as on the sexual access to women in the group. After the sons rebel and kill the father, they vow allegiance both to a totem representing him and to a principle of renunciation regarding their own desires.

Situating the incest taboo within the Oedipus myth yields powerful alternative interpretations of the two renunciations (of patricide and a sexual monopoly on women) considered foundational for human culture, law, and civilization. For anthropologists, more specifically, this taboo not only has come to stand for marital exchange and exogamous relations, as Claude Lévi-Strauss (1971) most famously explicated, but also is said to regulate the entire symbolic order, marking the transition from nature to culture and orienting relations between generations and between males and females. It is the one human universal on which most anthropologists would concur.[4]

Renunciation and Verbal Prohibition

Incest is always subject to regulation, but it is not always regulated by modern law. It is most often subject to unwritten rules that lack the enforcement power of the state.[5] The tension between the incest taboo as the "rule of all rules" and modern law rests in part on the fact that the taboo should not be spoken while law requires articulation.[6] Hence, people find it very important to affirm the female and male renunciations of incest and patricide, not by referring to their legal status but by refusing to verbalize them.

The fact that renunciation is affirmed through a verbal prohibition— renouncing incest by refusing to bring it into speech—is a key aspect of the practice of incest. Moreover, the difficulty of bringing incestuous desire into speech is often so great that an internal censor is activated to make the desire itself inaccessible to consciousness.[7] In most places in the world it is very important to deny vehemently that one even thinks about incest, that, in fact, one has ever felt a sexual desire for a close relative. As the very integrity of the self seems at stake when thinking the thought of incestuous desire, the obstacles are great for speaking about what this experience might be in fantasy or had been in practice. This impediment to thinking explains, in part, why the incest taboo can be frequently violated, everywhere, and not just in dreams, and why these violations are not usually treated as illegalities. In Berlin, an average of fewer than twenty men are convicted of incest each year, and in Germany fewer than one hundred, though surely the number of actual violations is anywhere from twenty to a hundredfold greater, depending on one's definition of sexual behavior and endogamous sex.[8] Most frequently, however, violations of the incest taboo are never acknowledged, privately or publicly. When prosecuted, offenders are usually indicted under other, substitute laws—for example, laws against coercion, rape, the exploitation of a dependency relationship, or laws protecting the "right of self-determination," which are increasingly used to regulate relations of adults to children generally.[9]

Evidence of Crime: The Case of Uncle Bodo

How does a violation of the prohibition against incest become not merely a wrong but an illegality? Or, to paraphrase Foucault ([1975] 1977, 89), how do we make sense of this new administration and redistribution of illegalities? The first step is to produce evidence that counts in court.[10] The following is a summary of a case of the production of such evidence, Uncle Bodo's abuse of his five-year-old niece, Juliet. It illustrates how the mother's desire and the child's identification with her is integral to transforming acts into sex acts, which in turn are classified for legal purposes as sex abuse and for the purposes of therapy as incest.[11] This summary of the two charges (Sachverhalt) is taken from a psychological profile of the victim written in December 2001, ordered by the court (Landgericht Berlin) to determine the capability and believability (Zeugentüchtigkeit und Glaubwürdigkeit) of the child's testimony.

1   On an evening in February 2001 in the bedroom of his apartment, with Juliet after he had brought her to bed, he called on her to have intercourse with the words "I want to fuck you!" He had induced her to take off her pajamas, whereby he also took off his pants, lied down next to the child and inserted one of his fingers, moistened with spit, into the vagina of the girl, after which he lied on his back, placed Juliet facing backwards on his naked lower body and penetrated his genital organ [Geschlechtsteil] a little into her vagina. In the course of this, he held the child firmly in the area under her ribs. Because it was not possible to completely penetrate the vagina, he desisted and let her go.

2   On the next day, he watched a porno film together with Juliet and a friend.

Few discussions of the incest taboo begin with its transgression, with a depiction of what actually went on.[12] Reading this transgression in such detail requires "containment" of the emotional experience of the child and her uncle, a difficult processing of a potentially destructive and deadening experience (Bion [1967] 1984). Incest and child sex abuse awaken affect in ways unlike most other crimes. In presenting this material in public, I have often sensed that some members of the audience experienced the listening as an entrance into a nightmare and, feeling overwhelmed by their thoughts and associations, were inclined to project onto me the emotional ambivalence, or repulsion, that these stories awaken. That is to say, to think through incest today, as in the past, demands high levels of cognitive and emotional work to become intimate with unsettling experiences while at the same time critically distancing oneself from an imaginary complex.

Perhaps the major obstacle to the legal regulation of sex abuse is the difficulty inherent in defining the act (*die Tat*). Uncle Bodo, as Juliet calls him, denied the accusations of his niece up to the time of the trial, in which he then agreed to all charges to spare Juliet from testifying in court. Disclosure of the act began eight days after the event, when Juliet uttered the word *ficken* ("to fuck") in a fight with her thirteen-year-old brother about how one begets children. Her brother said it happens when a man sleeps together with a woman. Juliet disagreed; that is called *ficken*. Her mother was shocked, as she herself had never uttered this word nor heard it used by Juliet. She asked Juliet where she had learned it, and Juliet replied, "Uncle Bodo said it to me, he wanted to do it with me!" This happened while Juliet was spending a few days with her father—her parents are divorced—who is more relaxed and lenient than her mother. The mother asked, had she told her Papa? Juliet said, yes.

Thereupon, the mother called her ex-husband, who denied having been told anything and insisted it could not have happened. Meanwhile, the mother could not put aside her own experience as a victim-witness. Based on her testimony some twenty years earlier, her father was sentenced to two years in prison for sexually abusing her. She reports since suffering from massive guilt feelings, and during her youth twice tried to commit suicide. In other words, the mother fears for her daughter precisely what incest usually entails: the inheritance of a familial dynamic that reproduces over generations analogous links between sex, guilt, and death.

By coincidence, the mother had received a recording machine as a gift from her mother to record the children's songs that she sang with Juliet. The machine was in fact recording while Juliet and her brother had argued about procreation, and the tape was later introduced in court as evidence.

Three days after this initial conversation, on February 18, with the recording machine on, she asked Juliet again about the events while the child was in the bathtub. Juliet protested, it was all embarrassing, she didn't want to talk, she wanted nobody else to hear about it.

As the mother dried Juliet with a towel, she asked again how Uncle Bodo had held her. Juliet said, "No, not on the ribs but otherwise," and turned her mother around and held her hands firmly. "Did Uncle Bodo set you backwards on his belly?" Juliet nodded yes. "Did he move you back and forth as you sat on his belly?" Juliet said no. Did Uncle Bodo hurt you? Juliet nodded yes and pointed to her vagina. Did he try to insert his penis in your body? Juliet nodded yes, but, she said, he didn't enter and he quit after trying. When the mother later decided to press charges, Juliet surprised her by making a statement to the police even more detailed than what she had already told her.

Uncovering Incest

Two factors steered the uncovering of incest and the way Juliet refigured her experience: first, the desires of her mother as they entered into an unconscious transference in the relationship between mother and daughter, in which the daughter was under pressure to act out her mother's unconscious; and second, the production of Juliet's account facilitated by the psychologist, who conducted three psychodiagnostic interviews with Juliet nine months after the act.

Juliet showed no signs whatsoever of problems stemming from what had taken place until six months after the act, in the summer of 2001, after her brother returned from an orphanage, where he had been for several years, to live with her and her mother again. Then Juliet began stealing and hiding things from her mother. This conspicuous behavior coincided both with the return home of Juliet's brother and with the mother's separation from her then-partner around the end of August. He had called Juliet "my Princess," but after the separation he suddenly distanced himself. The mother herself felt psychically overwhelmed and had nightmares. Juliet's brother became physically abusive and so difficult to control that in November the mother sent him back to the orphanage. Also contributing to Juliet's behavior was that her mother initially had the visiting rights of Juliet's father revoked; she later relented to Juliet's demands to visit him, and this quieted the situation at home.

Meanwhile, the psychologist informed the mother that Uncle Bodo would be released from prison if Juliet refused to make additional statements. The mother then scheduled the interviews with the psychologist, in which Juliet vehemently resisted talking about the events, making statements like, "You read what I said to the police, to the court, and then I don't have to go there again, and also I don't have to tell the story again! This is all too embarrassing to me!" Ultimately, however, Juliet responded with a very nuanced use of words and was able to make connections between events. The psychologist concluded that Juliet was linguistically and intellectually very capable and believable as a witness to Uncle Bodo's actions.

Protecting Children from Sex Abuse: An Interpretation

To make Juliet's account reliable and consistent for the court, a large group of professionals asked her in a series of interviews to repeat statements, to clarify the sequence of acts, and to create verbal representations for legal purposes. Juliet was clearly and consistently responding—confused, identifying, resisting, cooperating—to her mother's desire to protect her from the repetition of a dynamic of incest; the mother saw in her daughter's experience with Uncle Bodo the same act that she had experienced as a girl with her own father. This pressure to tell made Juliet bring into language what she knew sensually or knew only in fragments of experience, what Bion ([1961] 1984, 7) would call "undigested facts" or "beta elements." To become conscious required translation of the new sensations, "dirty words," and unmentionable things in what had happened into therapeutic and adult, legal languages themselves full of elisions, ambiguous phrases, conceptual and legal abstractions, euphemisms. This work transforms Juliet's experience into evidence of the phenomenon of "child sex abuse," an illegal act and, above all for her, an act to be judged as shameful.

For Juliet, shame and repression of the act are strengthened, if not indeed initiated, *nachträglich*, that is, after adults intervene to make infantile sex into a fully discursive experience of sex. In this, the professional psychologist succumbed to the pressures of the legal community in its standards of causality, proof, and precision, to arrive at a narrative of sequenced events that can be construed as an act of motivated sex abuse. Paradoxically, the entire psychological and legal terminology is oriented to protect children— "innocent beings" (*unschuldiges Wesen*)—from the adult world of male desires, but to secure the punishment of offenders that is assumed essential to their protection, children must enter this world as precocious witnesses and participants.

The expert opinion for the court noted that the mother disliked naming the sex organs or acts, especially the male sex organ. She taught Juliet to use the same word, *Pipiloch*, for both male and female genitals. Nonetheless,

Juliet seemed to sense much more complexity in human anatomy and even made a distinction between words her mother intended to share with her and those not intended for hearing.[13] She seemed quite capable of distinguishing *ficken* as intercourse (*Beischlaf, Geschlechtsverkehr*), what she had seen in film scenes of the beach and the bedroom, from what she had experienced, which was, at the prompting of her uncle, that she sat on his belly and simulated riding him. What she did not immediately describe, but later revealed to the psychologist, was her own enigmatic experience of this: that it was odd (*"War irgendwie komisch"*) and alternately fun (*"Irgendwie hat es mir spaß gemacht"*) and disgusting (*"Eeeeee"*).

Social and legal attention to the child's experience as it is incorporated into the world of adult sexual representations also repositions the males in the family. Juliet's father and men other than her uncle are reduced to objects about whom the "truth of sex" is produced, though they are of course not absent as subjects, in particular as men with aggressive drives. Before this abuse, Juliet had had a good relationship with her biological father; with her mother's last boyfriend, before they separated; and even with the uncle who abused her. However, after the work to uncover abuse, men enter into the truth of sex neither as genitors with permanent rights nor as a structuring device in a conflictual complementarity to women but as the origin of a desire, genital sexuality, that needs stricter regulation, even criminalization, to protect women and children.[14]

The assumption that women and children need legal protection from men suggests a major cultural-legal transformation in the relation of the father to the family. Taking the long view, the doctrine of *patria potestas* in Roman family law identified the father as having authority not only over his wife and own children, whom he could decide to adopt or not, but also over more remote descendants in the male lineage. He controlled the inalienable rights to their persons and property, including the right to take their lives. Since Roman times, however, this basis of law in male authority, specifically the authority of the father, has been radically transformed, in a very uneven history with geographical differences within Europe between north and south and between east and west. Some of the most extensive changes followed the delegitimation of the order of the father following the devastations of the two world wars (Borneman 2004). Also integral to the transformation of familial and social order have been the creation of a large middle class and the relatively successful propagation of a bourgeois model of the mother, which delegated to her increased authority over and responsibility for children (Gebhardt 2009; Perrot 1990; Weber-Kellermann 1977). This new model did not by any means eliminate the sources of male power and authority, especially in the economic and political spheres, but it did, importantly, solidify a trend of granting women equal access to the authority of laws regulating intimacy. With regard to the domestic unit, however, women have obtained much power through divorce and control of reproduction, and, since the many legal reforms in the 1970s, they have obtained a virtual monopoly over and responsibility for the psychodynamic processes of child formation, from early child care through primary education and adolescence, with quite different effects on male and female child sexuality.

Much attention has been directed to the liberation of female sexuality and homosexuality from Victorian era norms but much less to changes in the regulation of male heterosexuality. Among these neglected changes is the criminalization of specific forms of male sexual behavior, especially those having to do with touching women and children. Symptomatic is both the heightened sensitivity to male sexual violence and the elimination of the elaborate and violent male initiation rituals that have been central to anthropological theorizing of masculinity and the social.[15] In the West, such rituals exist only as survivals: the hazing rituals of school fraternities or right-wing cults, military boot camps, the play of New Age Men's groups, learning soccer, obtaining an individual identity card (*Personalausweis*) or driver's license (*Führerschein*) to enter the culture of the automobile. Most of these contemporary rituals are understood as voluntaristic, matters of individual choice, and therefore transformative processes that can be reversed.

The dominant explanation for rituals of initiation has been either that girls can become women without the need of ritual elaboration or such rituals occur for them later in life, tied to coupling and reproduction; their identification with the mother and the feminine is continuous and, whatever problems this may present for the development of female autonomy, it evolves without much open resistance (cf. Chodorow 1978). The process of making boys into men is more socially fraught (Greenson 1968, 370–74; cf. Klein [1937] 1975, 306–43). The boy's separation from his mother and initiation into a male-identified order relies heavily, as Michael Diamond (2006, 1122) put it, "on the aversive power of shame to shape acceptable male behavior." The boy loses not only his dyadic relationship with the mother but is also pressured to "repudiate what he has lost."

That leads us to the other side of the gender question: What kind of man is Juliet's brother supposed to be? The legal archive tells us much less about him. Nonetheless, we know that he is a sullen, unhappy child in contrast to his lively, playful sister, and that his destructive behavior has led his mother to send him out of the family to an orphanage. He seems to have no relationship to his father. Ultimately, his mother feels compelled to sacrifice him a second time, along with her most recent boyfriend (i.e., a father substitute for the daughter), to enable her to sustain a protective and caring relationship with her daughter. The masculinity of the brother appears to offer nothing of significance to his mother or sister; if anything, he is reduced to the role of disturbing the relationship between mother and daughter.

In this case, granting the biological father visiting rights to his daughter is unlikely to weaken the mother-child bond because the mother controls the terms of these visits. But the mother's goal here appears to be to unite in herself the roles of both father and mother: source of authority, protector, and caregiver. Her efforts rest on the premise that the parents are exchangeable, as are—so she teachers her daughter—their genitals. A ban on naming the male genitals can only contribute to a negative cathexis with the penis, the consequences of which are more drastic for the brother's self-image than for his sister. For the young boy in this family, it means that the pressure in puberty to disavow identification with his mother is coupled with increased shame about his gender difference. He likely interprets the mother's refusal to acknowledge his genital difference from her as a negative identification with male difference generally.[16] A negative identification with either male or female genitals, especially in puberty while the adolescent struggles with self-identification, surely has a detrimental effect on the self-esteem of the child. In Germany, there are particularly compelling historical reasons for this specific negative identification, not least the collective defeats in two world wars initiated to defend a patriarchal order.[17]

To be sure, the mother's pre-Oedipal fantasy of nondivision with her daughter remains merely an ideal, impossible to realize even if desired. Given her own history of abuse and the discovery of Bodo's transgression, her heightened interest in protecting her daughter from male abuse seems warranted. But for the purposes of phantasmatic investment, the child is to be protected—kept innocent—by the mother from all father figures. Uniting the roles of both parents within the mother gives an unusual twist to Mitscherlich and Mitscherlich's (1965) term, *vaterlose Gesellschaft*. It is not the father's physical absence, as in the first postwar German generation, that is the issue here but the way the mother negatively identifies with the adult male figures with whom her daughter plays (Dammasch 2008b, 237–54; Metzger 2008, 91–106). Adding to this the ways in which the maternal has been strengthened in postwar law, it now appears that the mother-child dyad has replaced the father function and its responsibilities, which has been a defining feature of European law since early Roman times. Indeed, it is the mother-child dyad—and not the household, the heterosexual couple, or the extended or nuclear family—that best represents the modular domestic unit with a claim to legal protection and care.[18] This, however, does not spell the end of the marital couple or the nuclear family, configurations of intimacy to which I will return below. Nor does the modularity of the mother-child dyad in law necessarily enable the mother to protect the child in practice, as the two case studies presented here suggest.

On a larger historical scale, the criminalization of forms of male sexual behavior can be seen as part of the long struggle of women against patriarchy and of feminism specifically. From the fifteenth to the seventeenth century in Europe, this struggle erupted in ritual witch-hunts, with women often identified as the perpetrators of child abuse. A historical account of the eruption of periodic witch-hunts and criminalizations—now dubbed "moral panics"—in the intervening years is beyond the scope of this book. Suffice it to say that in the early 1970s, such accusations were reversed and directed against men, most sensationally against fathers and teachers. A decade later, German women in groups such as Wildwasser, founded in 1982, began initiatives to protect girls from sex abuse. In 1986 Kind im Zentrum was founded to treat both girls and boys who are victims of such abuse, and such treatment was later extended to the offenders. One interpretation of the imprisonment of Uncle Bodo, then, is as a repetitive resurrection of the historical truth of Bachofen's myth of *Mutterrecht*, as revenge for an initial renunciation and disempowerment, and as three Trojan horse-type victories: over a compulsively repetitive male sexuality, over male irresponsibility in families, and over arbitrarily exercised forms of male authority.[19]

For the public in much of Europe and North America, this struggle emerged again in the late 1970s and crystallized in the dual threats that incest and pedophilia are said to pose to the child and to the security of the social order. The media obsesses about these threats and circulates them as phantasms, which, as Berkel (2006, 27) has brilliantly demonstrated, creates an identification with the child that renews the adult subject's "primary narcissism and fantasies of omnipotence." Important for these phantasms is the dissolution of childhood, accompanied by both increased pressure for parents to monitor the behavior of their children and the increased autonomy of youth culture and the incitement to sex of and with youth generally (Erdheim 1995; Foucault [1976] 1978; Postman 1982). Children are frequently treated as sexualized mini-adults with the power to make rational decisions about their own interests (true especially for activities labeled "consumption"), while adults are increasingly overstimulated by and encouraged to identify with the innocence of childhood/youth.

Calls for protecting children from experience itself express an anxiety about policing what Géza Róheim called "neoteny": adult pleasures and desires for a youth-state or state of innocence (1950, 400–402). Capitalist advertising preys on these anxieties by attaching subliminal desires for sex to all commodity forms (Haug 1987). And, as the kinship systems and prohibitions that structure and delimit the flow of desires in collective life are dissolved into more diffuse and voluntaristic systems of relatedness, individual meaning is increasingly construed as "self-determination" and further specified as the freedom to pursue one's own "well-being" and "pleasure." One reaction to this extension of "free will" is to generalize the model of child protection and consent to any relation of inequality, but especially to those who are supposed to know (teachers, employers, men) and their dependents (students, employees, and women).

In this way actual sex abuse becomes difficult to distinguish from the phantasmatic pull of the phenomenon of child abuse, and the ideal of legal "self-determination" for children is linked to the sense that children need more security and protection.[20] This linkage has resulted, on the one hand, in an unconscious unable to confront, much less resist, the sources for the sexualization of children in the media and popular culture and, on the other, in strong popular support for lengthening prison sentences for crimes of male sexual transgressions, independent of questions of cost, efficiency, or the likelihood of recidivism (Bernstein 2010; Böllinger 2007; Dünkel 2005; Seifert 2007).[21]

The court sentenced Bodo to two years and six months in prison. The concept of incest does not enter the case until Bodo goes to therapy, where it is used to classify his type of abuse, as the counterpole to what in Germany is called *Pädosexualität*, in other words, sex that occurs because of a particular familial situation and not because of a fixed object choice.[22] As convicted child offenders occupy the lowest rung of the prison hierarchies, the prison where Bodo served his sentence provides a separate facility for their own protection to prevent contact with other types of criminals. The official goal of the German penal system, as stated in the Penal Code amended on March 16, 1976, is "to enable the prisoners to live a life of social responsibility in the future without illegalities; it should also serve to protect the general public from further criminal acts." A 2002 federal law (which went into effect on January 1, 2003) mandates that individuals sentenced for sex abuse to more than two years of imprisonment have not only a duty but also a right to *Behandlung*, therapy/treatment. *Die Aufarbeitung der Tat* (reckoning with the act) is the key to a prisoner's rehabilitation and, ultimately, a condition of his release. That part of the act that he was unwilling or unable to acknowledge becomes what must be recovered and reconstructed as the crime of sex abuse, and, for the purposes of therapy, it is diagnosed as the symptom of a possible personality disturbance (Sigusch 2001). Bodo participated in therapy while serving slightly more than two-thirds of his time before being released on probation, with the stipulation that he remain in therapy until his probation officer/social worker (*Bewährungshilfer*) and judge decide otherwise.

Reckoning with the Act in the Unconscious

In cases like those of Uncle Bodo, determining the motivations for incest in order to renounce this behavior, if not the desire motivating it, is the legal goal of the *Aufarbeitung*. Questions of individual motivation and desire are precisely what the anthropological resolution of the incest taboo proposed by Lévi-Strauss—the requirement of exogamy or marriage outside the most intimate group in the interests of maintaining or enlarging social affiliations—elides. To be sure, Lévi-Strauss's more abstract and formal definition still carries considerable explanatory power and some ideological weight, for instance, in the legal reasoning of the Bundesverfassungsgericht (German Constitutional Court) in its decision to uphold a conviction of brother-sister incest on February 28, 2008 (2 BvR 392/07).[23] The public response to this decision is noteworthy, however, in that there was little reaction. It seems that the German public, however disturbed by the idea of brother-sister incest, would have accepted and even perhaps preferred an innocent verdict. After all, the brother and sister were adults in love, and in Germany today protection of the free exercise of consensual sex in a couple usually trumps protecting a particular image of the nuclear family.

This mild reaction contrasts sharply with the public uproar over the 2009 Fritzl case in Austria, where, after a four-day trial, Josef Fritzl pleaded guilty to incest, rape, false imprisonment, enslavement, coercion, and murder, by neglect, for confining his daughter, along with three children he fathered with her, in a windowless cellar under his home for twenty-four years. In this case, public outrage, not only in Austria and Germany, was directed against incestuous sex that clearly began with child sex abuse (when Fritzl's daughter was eleven). To be sure, the other coercive aspects of this case, in particular imprisonment in a cellar, appealed to traumatic registers in German and Austrian history, such as the common experience of hiding in bunkers during WWII, and also contributed to the outrage.

To understand the reasoning of the Constitutional Court and the public, one must engage several questions that the structuralist solution to the incest taboo avoids. First there are the epistemological foreclosures due to the structuralist method. As André Green (2005, 281) has argued, it is based on a "dual obsession": first, to divorce the representation "from any reference to the signified in its conception of the unconscious, [and second], to avoid any possibility of anthropology being reduced to a natural discipline." As to the first point, divorcing the representation (e.g., the incest taboo, the Oedipus myth, rules for exogamy) from the signified makes it unnecessary to account for intimate acts, actual incest, or actual sexual desire as part of conscious and unconscious processual dynamics; as to the second, in the interest of affirming a distinction between nature and human culture, Lévi-Strauss, although denying an absolute distinction, fully severs the link between them.

One way to acknowledge the signified and affirm the conceptual distinction between nature and culture without severing the link between them was suggested by Georges Bataille (1957), in a very positive critique of *The Elementary Structures of Kinship*. Lévi-Strauss, he wrote, moves to a level of formal abstraction that evades the erotic, the sensual, the experiential. By characterizing the transition from animal to human as an abstract move from nature to culture, he avoids the question of how humans manage to negate their "animalistic needs"—needs that psychoanalysis has taken up as of archaic or instinctual nature and hence more subject to unconscious repetition. The incest taboo as a norm is an attempt to prevent the aggression that people would act out should their "animalistic" behavior be subject solely to the power of sex drives.

Concerning substantive foreclosures, it is important to defend an idea of the unconscious whose content is more precisely circumscribed than the linguistic unconscious (structure) posited by Lévi-Strauss, which is timeless, a language of relational oppositions, and a reservoir of myths. It is important to also ask about the mechanisms of repression and censorship, whereby the unconscious obtains a content from lived experience that is nonetheless normally unavailable to consciousness; and it is important to ask in what speech settings a bringing to consciousness changes the signified—for example, in psychological interviews as in the first case study, television talk shows, police interrogations, or group therapy sessions, as I discuss in the second case study below.

With these criticisms in mind, we might, following (and slightly modifying) Green (2005, 227–35; 2008), pay particular attention to several characteristics of the unconscious: It is made possible through the natural functions of language, through symbolization and narration, but its content is also resistant to ordered syntax (contrary to some readings of Jacques Lacan), that which language is unable to structure; it aims to stop time and repeat or rework conflicts from the past; and, it is meaningful in either hindering or reordering consciousness for each individual in a particular social context. A theory of the unconscious that addresses these three characteristics—linguistic inadequacy, temporality, and individual meaning—is particularly important to understand how the two myths of renunciation with which I began this chapter are deployed by incest offenders.

The Case of Alex's Incest

In this last section, I examine the case of Alex, a man who has been in therapy at KiZ since January 2006. When I met him in August 2008, he was serving a sentence of three and one-half years in a minimum-security prison for the crime of "aggravated child sex abuse" of his daughter Karola. At a meeting of Alex's therapy group in February 2009, the therapist noted that for four of the seven men present, including Alex, it would be interesting to know why their wives decided to let them stay in the family after the discovery of incest. Alex responded, "My wife said I am the exact type of man (*der Typ*) who she wants. I have been this type of man already for twenty years."

The incest began in 2001, when Karola was thirteen, and accelerated over eighteen months from kissing and petting to masturbation and intercourse, until his wife noticed, whereupon she threatened him with a separation if he did not immediately stop. Karola was then given her own bathroom to avoid running into her father in any half-naked state, and Alex agreed to submit to certain rules of contact, in his words, "I left Karola alone (*Ich habe sie in Ruhe gelassen*)."

This arrangement continued for slightly more than a year without incident, except that Karola was not happy simply to ignore what had happened. She tried to open up a discussion, but neither her father nor her mother responded. She sent a text message to a school friend, announcing she wanted to commit suicide; this message was passed on from friend to friend, and even to her primary teacher and her sports trainer. Yet nobody reacted. In February 2003, during a regular exam by a pediatrician, Karola shared her story of incest. The doctor told Karola that she would have to report this to the police and gave her the choice of going to a home for girls instead of returning home. Karola chose the home for girls and has not lived with her parents since.

Asked in therapy why Karola and not he had to leave the family, Alex explains, "Karola was sixteen by then, and it was a good time [for her to leave]. My wife said that Karola was old enough to go. We still have two children to raise [one is severely disabled and requires twenty-four-hour care]. The family needs me."

There are three usual configurations of intimacy in response to the uncovering of incest, and all point to the classic tensions between the mother-child dyad, the nuclear family, and the couple. In the case of Juliet, the mother, already divorced, stayed with her daughter but ended relationships with Juliet's biological father, the abusive uncle, and her boyfriend; in addition, she sacrificed the adolescent brother to stabilize the situation with her daughter. The most common response, by contrast, is to repress the revelation of incest and keep the nuclear family together. A third alternative is that the wife stays with her husband, in which case her role as mother is compromised, and the abused child usually must leave the family to save the couple.

In the case of Alex, his wife initially kept both daughter and husband in one household. She tried to maintain the nuclear family. But holding the family together became an unbearable solution for the abused daughter, eventually leading to the daughter's sacrifice (she left the family) while the couple remained together.

Alex had been in therapy for two and one-half years before I encountered him. Despite being incarcerated at night, he was extremely busy during the day, traveling long distances to different parts of the city: He drove an hour to work outside the prison in the morning and stopped off at home in the late afternoon to spend a few hours caring for his handicapped son and seeing his wife and younger daughter before returning to prison to spend the night. Petitions to visit his family on weekends were usually approved, and in the fall of 2008 he even obtained approval for a three-week vacation with his wife. His father is a Lutheran minister, and Alex is the only one in the group who reports going to church and praying regularly. The entire family knows of his crime and that he spent time in prison, although it is never mentioned. They appear to stigmatize and avoid him, but they do not exclude him from their activities. He talks often of their many reunions and birthdays. For example, once he celebrated the fifty-fifth wedding anniversary of his wife's parents and attended the eightieth birthday of his father, which took place in a hotel with a "wellness pool"; he joined his sister for her fiftieth birthday; and he planned a trip with her to a "wellness weekend" and to use the occasion to go over family history. Karola, the daughter he abused, is usually present at these events and often travels to them with him and his wife. When they stay in hotels, she spends the night with her cousins. On a recent trip, she indicated she would like to return to the family after the weekend, but the mother ruled this out.

Alex describes conversations with his daughter and the rest of the family as nervous, hesitant at best, but he does think that a kind of reconciliation with them is taking place. Recently Karola told him about her current boyfriend and gave him a hug in departing. And for the first time in five years, his nephew shook his hand at a family gathering. The rest of the family, he reports, are also giving him more attention than usual.

At the end of September 2008, Alex's petition for release on probation, after having served two-thirds of his sentence, was rejected. The majority of incest offenders are indeed released on probation at that point. He complains bitterly. *Die Aufarbeitung,* reckoning with the act, is the key to a prisoner's rehabilitation, and the court-appointed psychologist had ignored the evaluation of KiZ therapists and instead gave him a very negative evaluation of his. The therapists told Alex they were not surprised by this evaluation. They advised him to take the evaluation seriously and compare his position back then with that today. On July 6, 2009, Alex was set free, having served his full sentence, but at the same time placed on probation for five years, under supervision with special security measures (*Führungsaufsicht*). For now, he must continue therapy. In his first therapy session after he had obtained his freedom (and the final one I attended), Alex said his wife greeted his return with mixed emotions; she insisted that she keep the larger bedroom upstairs for herself and that he move into the smaller bedroom downstairs. His children were excited, however, and Karola came by to do her washing.

It is not as if therapy has not changed the way Alex thinks of himself and his crime, but he seems to miss the point of most questions, and he often falls into a position of shame and self-pity. His own diagnosis of himself is that his abuse does not indicate a "sickness" because, he says, he never was interested in children outside of Karola. He turned to her only because, at the time, he says, "I was often not satisfied sexually, so I tried it, so to speak."

In different therapy sessions he repeats frequently one sentence, which strikes him as particularly explanatory. Karola testified at his trial that she permitted his sexual advances because "Papa was always in a better mood after." He protests, "That is an error she makes." She may have thought what she did was necessary to create a positive atmosphere in the family, but, Alex insists, he was only more friendly to her than to the others in the family. "Perhaps we didn't really understand Karola," he laments.

In one session he offers the explanation that he was trying to establish a "pact" with Karola, so that together they would have a positive influence on the atmosphere in the family. He blames his wife for refusing to allow any discussion about conflicts in the family, for making all suggestions and criticisms herself so that nothing he said made any difference.

Another time, he suggests that Karola never had many friends, that she was a loner, and that when she went out with friends they used her. Her loner behavior was not a response to his abuse, he contends, as neither he nor his wife had much influence on her. Asked if he was angry at her for reporting the abuse, his voice becomes defensive, betraying his response, "No. I don't have any reason to be." Even after two and a half years of therapy, he still maintains that his daughter enjoyed sex with him. He thought of it as a shared hobby; Karola didn't have any hobbies of her own.

In therapy, Alex is able to recall a number of key experiences from the past and can now interpret them in a different light. He remembers that after what he calls his "visits" to Karola's bedroom, she often asked him when he would come again. At the time he interpreted her question as a sign that she was looking forward to his visits, whereas now he recognizes that it indicated fear of his return.

He remembers a "scene building sand castes" at the beach with Karola and her younger sister. Karola had been screaming, which she apparently often did, and he penalized her by locking her in the car. He recalls that he in fact often locked her up, which he now interprets as preventing her from being a child.

He remembers that during the eighteen months of incest, Karola left her room messy and neglected herself. At the time he thought this was an expression of too much energy, perhaps attention deficit disorder, and of inadequate recognition from her classmates. Now he interprets this behavior as an attempt "to make herself unseemly." He says he is angry that everyone decides what Karola should do but nobody asks her what she wants.

His relation to his youngest daughter is different, he says. When Karola entered puberty, he took no note, but now he is aware of the changes in his younger daughter. When Karola was at that age, he was strict with her about returning home at night, while his wife allowed her more freedom. Karola was often angry about these restrictions, but the younger daughter does not object much. Today he and his wife are more united in their approach to the younger daughter than they were with Karola. When he spent the evenings in prison, his visits with his younger daughter during the day resulted in hugs; she told him explicitly how much she enjoyed having him around. He notes these differences between his two daughters without being able to point to the jealousy he must have felt for Karola when she went out with her friends.

Along these lines, in response to the question whether it was important for him to think of himself as "the first" to have sex with Karola, he says no, although he adds that he did think about being the first for the "harmless things" such as stroking and petting. Did he do anything against her wishes? He admits that he was always the active one, but "yes, actually, she wanted to do it with me, she was aroused. That's how I understood her." But wasn't it your actions that aroused her? "Yes, you can say that. She was aroused, she was wet, and she went along."

Did you ever look at her to see her reaction during sex? He is silent. What did you conclude from what you saw? "I kept doing it," he says meekly, and as he hears himself, he is appalled. He begins to whimper softly.

The fantasy to sleep with your daughter, it doesn't come out of nowhere, says the therapist. Where did your fantasies come from? "I don't know. She was very loving. I don't know if I have many fantasies." Alex pauses before adding, "I fantasized only about what I wanted to do with the girl. That's probably true."

And the harm you were inflicting? "It was nice, that's why I did it so often."

Another time, he concludes, "But it was love, a false love, she couldn't do anything to resist me. I always went to her, she didn't come to me. I thought she was curious, also about sex. The sex with my wife then was not satisfying. Living without talking about any conflict with each other, I wasn't able to take it any longer."

Now Alex's relation with his wife lacks this tension it had in the past. After she had discovered his incest with Karola, she never talked about it because, he says, "Nobody wanted to talk about it." Even today, this has not changed. His wife has refused offers from KiZ to have some joint therapy sessions with her husband. Early on, she did agree to one session, where she said that she did not want to know any details about what went on between her husband and daughter. That is something Alex must deal with on his own, she insists. The experience of therapy is one part of Alex's reckoning; the other part is the experience of imprisonment and, with his release, the fear of returning to prison.

For Alex, reflecting on his past in therapy is like another trial. He is resigned to therapy but frequently cantankerous and glum in the group. Most often he responds to queries with statements like, "I don't know that anymore." Or he is simply silent. If he feels cornered by a question, he collapses into himself, shoulders rounded, head bowed, avoiding any eye contact with the others. His conflicted internal experience begs silence, while the external pressures of the group demand that he speak. When the tension between them becomes unmanageable, Alex looks like an admonished child.

Saying is doing in such therapy sessions, and the illocutionary force of saying is painful. For Alex to say what he has done is to externalize the act, to make it more fully conscious so he can inspect it from multiple vantage points, and to give not only the therapists and the other clients in the group the means to judge him but also the means for him to judge himself. He fears making a mistake in describing his transgression, and this, along with the feeling of shame, often paralyzes him. His silence is not the result of refusing to think but of an overstimulated mind. He is working too hard, and failing—unable to convert his psychic elements into language, unable to symbolize what had gone on.

A focus on the *inability* to symbolize and its relation to temporality might provide a second way out of the impasse reached by the structuralist solution to the incest taboo. Alex fails to symbolize in three temporalities of experience—of timelessness, development, and regression. First, there is the timelessness of Alex's lived experience as it worked in his unconscious, largely unavailable to conscious reassessment. Second, this timeless unconscious is under assault in therapy, as Alex is pressured in each session to reframe his experience as a sequence of impositions and the development of a desire for a particular object (his pubescent daughter). And finally, in treatment, Alex comes to give voice to a third temporality, regression to an infantile sexuality, which prevents him from engaging the interventions of the therapists and the other clients in the group but also opens him to empathy with his victim. Developing empathy is one of the most important factors leading to a transformation of his desire. Whether he has changed psychically and his rehabilitation has been efficacious is indexed by his growing appreciation—symbolization, one might say—of the intentions and feelings of his daughter and of her transformation as he coerced her into sex.

Above, I argued that Lévi-Strauss was unconcerned with the mechanisms by which experience becomes part of the unconscious and that in his explication of the role of incest in the transition from nature to culture, he ignored the necessity of a continual negation of the animalistic in time. Freud, in his second topography, dubbed this chaotic reservoir of libidinal drives the "id," out of which, he further argued, humans develop the instrument of judgment, the superego. This conflict between id and superego is posed acutely in Alex's case of incest, in that shame for his sexual desire for his daughter precisely blocked any self-reflection on his desire and what it was doing to her. Self-absorption in shame immunized him to other voices, other perspectives and assessments, meaning that his conscious self, his "I," was insufficiently constrained or bound by an internalized judging, condemning voice that might not only control his impulses but also acknowledge the voice of and assume responsibility for the child's experience (see Schore 1991).

The reasons men in therapy groups give for incestuous desire are extremely varied, as are their personal histories, although they tend to attribute their behavior to a response to specific familial configurations rather than to a drive (see Hirsch 1999). Unconsciously, however, what unites them above all is a desire for the young. Such incestuous desire across generations is fully human and not merely occasional or accidental. The ethnographic record and the clinical material of psychoanalysts provide us with sufficient evidence to conclude that the revulsion of incest usually results from the mere thought that one has "unwittingly" slept with a prohibited category of kin. Such category errors rarely provoke the same degree of horror today, in an age that heralds freedom of thought and association and "self-fulfillment." An explanation for why Alex committed incest with his child, then, must account for why he did not perceive this category error as horror.

Seduction of the child begins, as Freud said, with the mother, and her power to seduce is initially tied to what her breast and care provide. It is a unique pleasure she obtains from this power, as it is for the child. Without this early seduction, children develop a limited capacity for emotional growth and vulnerable attachments to others (Bowlby 1973; Laplanche 1989). But in the development of the child's relationship with her, the mother's seduction should also be coupled with love for the child's own development. In weaning the child from her, she must manage its first separations: the loss through the cutting of the umbilical cord and the loss of the breast.

By contrast, adult male desire for children must overcome an initial separation and establish an alien closeness to the child. In the case of Alex, he appears to identify his daughter with an oral phase from which he has already departed—appreciation of her skin, smell, innocence, perfection. He regresses to a sexuality we might associate with infantile narcissism, fixated on his own pleasure, intent on reception alone, and wishing to retain full control over the object of his desire.

Alex's identification with his child is dissociated from his public self, and that dissociated part of himself, relegated largely to his unconscious, does not get older. It yields to the timelessness and freedom of the unconscious. At the same time, his identification with his public self, the one who does get older and will eventually die, becomes less meaningful, less enjoyable, more alien. Alex's relationship with his thirteen-year-old daughter, then, as against that with his wife, makes him feel alive, younger, and reinforces his dissociated image of himself, his largely unconscious subjectivity, as someone who can reverse the aging process and stop time. Even if he is no longer so sexually potent or active as in his youth, this former potency retains its power in the unconscious, in memory traces of what has been, and from there is a source to sustain the illusion that the phenomenal and biologically determined experience of time can be subverted and generational differentiation nullified.

The point here is that Alex does not begin a relationship with Karola, his daughter, from a position of unity to be taken apart, as does her mother, but from a difference to be effaced. Put another way, the desire of the Other, the Other that is the source of Alex's desire for his daughter, is an introjected child (Ferenczi [1933] 1955; Freud [1914] 1957).[24] That is, the source of incestuous desire is internal to the subject, and Alex projects this internal subject onto an external object—his real daughter. In this, Alex regresses back to an oral moment in his own desire, wanting to ingest the innocence of little Karola, but his sexuality has obviously also gone beyond orality. He is already an adult man and appears so to his daughter. Indeed he is a father, with a visible genital sexuality, a man who has already lost his innocence.[25]

Herein lies the fundamental moral transgression of the male incest offender: the inability to distinguish between the meaning of his own desires and the infantile sexuality of the child. The mother initially also must struggle with her difference from the child, but she is confronted early on with managing the child's separations and autonomy needs as well as with her own. If she holds on to the moment of *jouissance*, of unity with the child, she is also likely to severely stunt the child's emotional development, but her closeness is rarely criminalized.[26]

Indeed, that is one of the paradoxes with which I began, that throughout the world transgression of the incest taboo, however it is defined, tends not to be criminalized. In most places and times one is usually prohibited from even speaking about such transgressions. That is because the raising of a child brings into play an aporia, what Laplanche (1989) has called the fundamental anthropological situation of the human being: primal seduction. Adult seduction of the child is enigmatic and necessary—how else does the adult keep the child's attention despite its growing autonomy needs?[27] And child seduction of the adult is a necessary part of its humanization—how else does the child learn how to keep and attract the attention of others (Brüggen 2009)? Yet these seductions are always asymmetrical and dangerous because adult sexual obsessions that are not sufficiently repressed or inhibited risk becoming untranslatable psychotic delusions for the child recipient.

Incestuous acts, within and outside Europe and over time, involve a fairly wide range of relations between people of the same age group or across generations; as a desire for a category of people excluded for sex or marriage, incestuous desire is not exclusively oriented to children or youth. Moreover, to the extent violations of the incest taboo are penalized cross-culturally, a wide range of means are employed to discourage these acts in different cultures and times, from murder to exile to public shaming (Ember 1974; Frazer 1910; Malinowski 1926, 1927; Spiro 1993; White 1948). Criminalization is a particularly modern and recent solution to problems of such transgressions of intimacy. And increasingly today, only incestuous acts by male transgressors with children and youths are criminalized.

Although cases of brother-sister or cousin incest was reported in therapy at KiZ, over the course of my fieldwork, not a single case appeared in the archives of the Berlin Ministry of Justice from the period 2001 to 2008. Cases of mother-son incest were also reported in therapy, though none were legally prosecuted. For women, more problematic in their relations to children than transgressions of intimacy, and more subject to the scrutiny of the criminal justice system, are abuses in the process of separation, prosecuted as crimes of neglect, infanticide, and murder (cf. Schepe-Hughes 1993). In any event, the child cannot do without attachment to a mother (or mother substitute), and most of these primary caregivers are women. Therefore, the risk of adult female transgression of the child's intimacy must be socially tolerated. That is not so with attachments to a father (or father substitute), where the risk of male transgression is less ambiguous and more likely to be perceived by the child as an immediate aggression.

But also, on another plane, I am suggesting here that male sexual desire and its criminalization are sites for the contemporary expression of the long struggle regarding sexual prohibitions and civilization, and indicative of a new symbolic order that we have not yet conceptualized as such, one that no longer rests, as the psychoanalyst Achim Perner (2006) has written, on "the despotic father of a paternal order." Perner asked, in the absence of the despotic father, who will be the guarantor of this new order, so that we need not give up the prohibitions on which it is based? In other words, which figure or institution will serve as the modality of law to regulate questions of physical intimacy that constitute the relations between generations and genders? Medical, pharmaceutical, and psychotherapeutic markets are already active in introducing new reproductive technologies, invasive surgical procedures to create transgendered beings, and forms of self-fashioning that erode the incest taboo as the guarantor of "the heterosexual-generative constitution of the social order and culture" (Berkel 2009, 88). The new markets effectively relocate the agency of order not only from the "despotic father" but also from the social to the individual, and increasingly from elderly to younger subjects—to subjects with the authority to decide but uncertain about the assumption of responsibility for these decisions (cf. Carsten 2000; Franklin and McKinnon 2002; Ginsburg and Rapp 1995).[28]

An examination of alternative modalities of responsibility awaits another kind of study, but here we can suggest a few more limited hypotheses: that in the West the incest taboo has been increasingly narrowed and the sex act criminalized to regulate lineal rather than lateral relations between kin; that the father is no longer the guarantor of this order but increasingly seen as a potential transgressor; that increases in the mother's authority have not thereby enabled her to assume the role of the guarantor of the incest taboo; and that this taboo is being eroded and redefined in a new postpaternal symbolic order, in which the legal field has become one site for a ritual neutering of men who violate the rule of rules.

THREE

Rehabilitation of Pedophiles

Rehabilitation is the official goal of the German penal system. As stated in the Penal Code, amended on March 16, 1976, rehabilitation aims "to enable prisoners to live in the future a life of social responsibility without illegalities; it should also serve to protect the general public from further criminal acts." In pursuit of these ends, a 2002 federal law (which went into effect on January 1, 2003) mandates that individuals sentenced for sexual abuse to more than two years of imprisonment have not only a duty but also a right to *Behandlung*, therapy/treatment.[1] Consequently, key to the rehabilitation of such offenders has become therapy, which is seen as the primary means for *die Aufarbeitung der Tat*, reckoning with the act or deed.

Among those categorized as sexual criminals, child sex offenders encounter an additional demand in their rehabilitation. To reckon with the act means also to find a mode of relating to, and modifying, the assumption that "pedophiles" have a fixed psychological predisposition and fixed sexual identifications. In Foucauldian terms, the act risks making offenders into a distinct "sexual species" (Foucault [1976] 1978, 43). Since the species-label "pedophile" assumes irreversibility in sexual orientation and being, men must challenge it even to be considered capable of rehabilitation. Following an accusation or arrest, most men do in fact vehemently dispute the ascription. Definitions of pedophiles vary considerably, of course, by time and place, as well as by the speech community to which any person belongs. It is a category that includes a wide variety of intentions and behaviors, but, as a working definition, I will follow popular usage and ignore the behavioral range, and construe a pedophile to be an individual with any sexual interest in children or youths under the age of consent.

In this chapter, I attend only to the division of child sex offenders into incest abusers (as men who have sex with relatives or children in their in-

timate groups) and pedophiles (as men who have sex with children outside their intimate groups), with the focus on "pedophiles." There are, of
course, many other distinctions that matter, such as, for example, age of
offender, emotional maturity of the child or youth victim, cognitive and
emotional capacities, and erotic-cultural dispositions toward children. Each
of these factors specifies a different relation of an offender to a child or
youth. Yet psychologists have identified a number of characteristics, which
seem to exist to a greater or lesser degree, for all or most child sex offenders,
incest abusers and pedophiles alike: emotional loneliness, high levels of
social inadequacy, low self-esteem (a partial explanation for the desire to
interact with children rather than adults), lack of empathy for their victims,
and "cognitive distortion" (defined as thinking errors about the sexual desire and will of children) (e.g., Beech 1998; Beech and Fisher 2002; Fisher,
Beech, and Browne 1999; Ward and Keenan 1999). Beech and Mann (2002)
have argued that rehabilitation is unsuccessful if all of these problems are
not addressed in treatment. Wößner (2010), in turn, has developed a typology of treatment-relevant characteristics to differentiate in diagnosis and
treatment between specific clusters of sex offenders (cf. Nedopil 2000). In
the two case studies below and in the conclusion, I return to how therapy
addresses these specific characteristics.

Here I address not *whether* therapy successfully rehabilitates pedophiles
but *how* it can be and often is efficacious. That therapy can be successful has
already been established by many scientifically controlled and comparative
studies in English- and German-speaking countries, a point I elaborated in
chapter 1. The question of how therapy is ritually efficacious is most readily
addressed by ethnographic means: on-site participant observation of the
process of transformation and rehabilitation that therapy intends to effect.

For society as a whole, successful treatment of child sex offenders tends
to be equated solely with reduction of the risk of relapse. For the offender, a
fully successful reckoning means that his risk of repetition will be assessed
as negligible or null and that he will be released from prison after serving
two-thirds of his sentence; a less than successful reckoning means that he
will not only serve his full sentence, but perhaps be confined to a psychiatric clinic or indefinitely detained, or, if and when released, placed by the
judge in charge of his case under *Führungsaufsicht*—extended, and perhaps
indefinite probation.

Increasingly today in the West generally the sex abuse of children is considered less a cultural transgression than a human rights violation, the most
stigmatic and shameful of acts, the worst of all possible crimes. A fairly
recent acknowledgment of the dignity of children, along with a decrease in

the number of children in upwardly mobile families worldwide, has accompanied an increase in their value, which in turn contributes to the stigma attached to the abuser. For the public at large, however, there is a phantasmatic quality—captured in the phrase "soul murder" popularized by Leonard Shengold (1991)—to the two most prominent categories of child abuse: incest and pedophilia (Godelier 2004; Laplanche 1989, 126). Discovery of the act often becomes an immediate national or global event, as interlinked media chains obsessively report such acts, exaggerating their *social* significance in front-page articles of newspapers and magazines or in lead stories for television news (Berkel 2006). Especially since the late 1970s, child sexual abuse has become a central security issue in northern Europe and North America, rivaled as a phantasm only by the threat of "Islamic terrorism."

Both as phantasm and in practice, to rehabilitate sex offenders of this type poses a supreme challenge: how to reconcile the hope of transformation with the widespread assumption that in their abuse pedophiles are expressing a relatively fixed sexual orientation or preference—a *pädosexueller* core.[2] If their desires are immutable, the therapeutic goal cannot be a transformation of desire or motivation but must be delimited to cognitive behavioral change alone. Public pressure for longer sentences and for preventive detention or restrictions on the movement of pedophiles, then, is buttressed by this general skepticism about the possibility of fundamental change in the nature of the self.[3]

In this climate of lay and expert opinion, the demands on therapists and legal professionals are much greater and paradoxical in the treatment of pedophiles than for all other criminal types. Any positive assessment of therapy or imprisonment that claims possible success through rehabilitation must be balanced against the risk of recidivism. One incorrect assessment can severely damage the reputation, if not end the career, of a therapist or judge or prison warden, as well as potentially retraumatize the victim. The demands of therapy on the pedophile are also great. The stigma attached to this act leads to cultivated concealment, lying, and self-deception, which in turn encourage perverse forms of internalization of the stigma. In therapy, offenders must work through the shame often attached to these perverse forms to transform that shame into guilt. Such a transformation would enable an assumption of responsibility for the act—considered an integral step toward successful rehabilitation. But to be effective in the eyes of the law, treatment must go further and also assure the public of nonrepetition of the crime after release from prison and after therapy has terminated. To speak to the insecurity and fear produced by pedophiles, one must go beyond cognitive behavioral assessments and attest to a "psychic change" in the self. To work toward a changed self in a new relation to the child as object of desire, therapists must gain access to the unconscious of the adult offender, where much of the knowledge necessary for a transformation is stored.

Incarceration and Therapy

Incarceration, or the threat of incarceration, is in the register of law, and in some sense antithetical to therapy. In prison pedophiles become *Sexualstraftätern* (sex offenders), *Verurteilte* (the sentenced), and *Gefangene* (prisoners), who are serving their sentences (*verbüßen*). In therapy they are called *Klienten*; no longer registered as "patients" of therapists, they receive a service for which they have responsibilities. The clients in group therapy include not only those who come from prison, either released for the purposes of the therapy session alone or attending therapy on the way back from a day job before returning to prison. They also include men who either have already served their prison sentences or attend therapy before their scheduled trial as a way to build a case to avoid imprisonment altogether. Although legal and therapeutic experts prefer not to use the term "forced therapy," group treatment contains both strong incentives and a strong element of coercion. Many men in fact do refuse therapy and prefer instead to sit out their sentences. The major justification I heard for refusing therapy is that the therapist available to them was unqualified. Of course, the profession contains both excellent and poor therapists. And some men have indeed been mistreated by psychiatrists or psychologists (who clients, to the extent they make distinctions, tend to equate with therapists). However, this opinion is usually based on experience with "treatments" that seem to encourage deception or playing along rather than experience with types of therapy that rely primarily on deep introspection and that reward clients for honesty.

Important to note here is that the experience or anticipation of incarceration itself factors into the efficacy of therapy, and it arises as an issue in nearly every therapy session. Men learn from each other what to expect in prison life and how to be proactive in negotiating penalization with both the Ministry of Justice (e.g., lawyers, public prosecutors, judges), which deals with sentencing and the conditions of parole, and the Ministry of the Interior (Bundesministerium des Innern, responsible for security, e.g., prison officials, security personnel), which deals with imprisonment and the mechanics of detention and parole. These two ministries generally work together, but they also frequently conflict as to the balance between the "civil rights" (specifically the right of "self-determination") of the accused and the "protection of society" (specifically an ambiguous preventive detention).

With respect to pedophiles and sexual criminals generally, this conflict plays itself out around the assessment of risk.

When judges are asked to revisit a case for the purposes of early release or parole, or receive a request from a state prosecutor for preventive detention (*Sicherungsverwahrung*),[4] they often ask for a letter from the therapists about the success of treatment; they may even telephone the therapist. The same interactions occur, though less frequently, with prison officials. All therapists are very careful to assure their clients of confidentiality and hence are reticent to reveal much about the content of the therapy in letters or phone conversations. Most of the letters that I read are short and merely factual (e.g., X completed so many hours of therapy, between these dates, attendance was ir/regular, prognosis good/noncommittal).

Judges, in turn, complain about the brevity and lack of detail in the letters or tend to dismiss them altogether. Most rely solely on outside psychological *Gutachten* (evaluations) to inform or justify their decisions. These outside evaluations, for which the court pays well, run up to seventy-five double-spaced pages. They are usually based on two or three interviews, rather than, on average, eighteen months to three years interaction and observation in therapy. The evaluators are not obligated to any notion of confidentiality and therefore are often quite willing to make dire predictions about the future behavior and sexual interests of the offenders. There is a noticeable trend in the decisions of judges toward mandating the serving of a full sentence, or minimally two-thirds. In decisions from 2002 to 2003, I noticed that some judges released men after half of the sentence had been served, what I am told had been a fairly common practice when social workers and psychologists wrote positive evaluations. I did not find a single case of release after serving a half sentence after 2003.

In discussions of the effects of incarceration, most men in therapy who have already completed their prison sentences do not report the prison experience as merely wasted time. In fact, they say that it often afforded them the opportunity to think through their pasts—having very little else to do—and to assess perhaps for the first time their own persons, including who they have become for others. This introspection is quite different from Erving Goffman's dramaturgical model of "impression management" (1959). Instrumental goals of trying to curry the favor of or ingratiate themselves to prison officials, or to intimidate or impress fellow prisoners, are of course never totally absent. Indeed, because some legal and prison professionals are concerned only with good behavior while in prison and a prognosis for abstinence on release, the incentive for prisoners to present themselves as "good" is strong. From what some of the clients said in therapy, they also encountered prison psychiatrists who shared these reduced goals. The narrowing of relevant "data" to impression management is also supported by a trend in prisons to hire professionals who employ models of cognitive behavioral therapy, including pharmacological interventions, rather than psychotherapists committed to asking about nontransparent and unconscious factors motivating the offense.

Irrespective of the kind of treatment offered, after the accusation of child abuse, child sex offenders—compared, for example, with men accused of murder, rape, or theft—must struggle with a reductive psychological classification of themselves. Their own usually very limited understanding of their own motivations and behavior is suddenly radically at odds with the understanding of others, whose alternative representation begins to circulate not only among prison intimates but also in families, the media, and the public at large. Nonetheless, at least initially, managing of the impression they make on others is not of the highest priority, for the simple reason that the accusation alone functions as a kind of branding impossible to resist. With the arrest most minds are already made up both in- and outside the prison. Rather than being primarily concerned with how to express themselves to others in prison and manage their appearance, offenders are largely engaged in an intrasubjective or intrapsychic discussion to confront their own dissociation between self-images and the behaviors and desires they associate with their newly ascribed label of pedophile. Under the intense coercive pressure of psychiatrists and psychologists within the prison and of other officials, they are most often, as I shall elaborate below, laboring both to deny the label's applicability and to arrive at an image of themselves that is somewhat coherent or consistent in its self-understandings and rationalizations.

Although I worked in an open, minimum-security prison, many men there did pass back and forth between this type and a closed, maximum-security prison. Only in the case of the latter—in Berlin, there is only one, called simply "Tegel" after its geographic location—would it be accurate to compare the German prison experience to Goffman's description of the "total institution: . . . cut off from the wider society for an appreciable period of time, [leading to] an enclosed, formally administered round of life" (1961, xiii). Even the borders between the outside and inside of the German maximum-security prison tend to be more permeable than in Goffman's US-based or Foucault's ([1975] 1977) historical model.[5] From a sociological perspective, Loïc Wacquant (2001, 407) was correct in arguing that the goal in the growing use of incarceration in Europe, versus the United States, is "more panoptic than retributive or segregative . . . to exercise a close surveillance of 'problem populations.'" If, however, there is one European response to these "problem populations" that resembles the US retributive and segregative response to social insecurity, it is in the response to male pedophilia. That said, elided in this panoptic perspective are the intended psychic transformations of the clients themselves—the work of therapy within a plan of rehabilitation—as offenders engage in mental work that exceeds what one might expect from the experience of incarceration or surveillance alone.

The Making of a Sex Criminal

A sex criminal (*Sexualstraftäter*) is made, not born. It starts with his arrest and continues through release from prison and the termination of therapy. Needless to say, experiences after arrest are as diverse as the histories of the individual men before the accusations of child sex abuse. Nonetheless, here I want to sketch this general process while, where possible, pointing to the variability of experience.

An arrest is usually made immediately, sometime within hours, after a plausible complaint of abuse to the police. But as the knowledge of abuse only occasionally surfaces within families at the time it initially occurs, these accusations are rarely made without a delay of years after the violation. Under German law at the time of this research, the case for such abuse must be criminally prosecuted within ten years of the alleged victim's eighteenth birthday. For pursuing civil damages, the German parliament in 2011 extended the statute of limitation to take legal action from three to thirty years after a victim's twenty-first birthday. Following the arrest, suspects are detained, usually in a maximum-security prison (*Untersuchungshaft*) before being brought to trial. The time served in custody awaiting trial counts toward the fulfillment of the sentence.

Prosecutors delay the trial until they are able to obtain from the accused an agreement to the charges, an adequate admission of guilt. This delay can be lengthy, with the accused in custody more than a year before being formally charged. If the accused has been released from custody but charges are pending, the trial delay can be several years. In this period of delay between arrest and sentencing, psychologists interview the child and the accused to gather evidence. Prosecutors encourage suspects to plead guilty, as judges nearly always impose a less severe sentence if an admission (and plea) of guilt is made.

In cases of sex abuse not involving incest, child victims or their families do not meet the accused between the arrest and the trial. At the trial, the victim usually does not testify because in the interim the accused has admitted to the crime or because the evidence submitted is itself sufficient for the judge to arrive at a decision. In the event victims do testify, they can be unpredictable: They might merely repeat testimony, but also they may give confused testimony or, in rare cases, plead for the judge to be lenient if not to forget the charges altogether. In the latter case, the judge must decide to enforce the law as interpreted by the state prosecutor or go against the prosecutor and convince at least one of their civil assistants to agree. At least one assistant must also agree to the content of the sentence (e.g., monetary or imprisonment, amount of money or length of imprisonment).

For the period I examined, the median sentence for child sex abuse is two and one-half years in prison, for aggravated child sex abuse three years. Few sentences are shorter than one year, and few are longer than three years, although they can run up to fifteen years. Monetary penalties are also imposed for lesser offenses. The justification for lesser sentences include such factors as, for example, the admission of guilt spared the victim (*Opfer*) from having to appear in court and testify, there was no prior history of crime (of any type), no force was used in commission of the crime, or the victim was postpubescent. Very few offenders are released from prison without being placed on extended probation, usually from three to five years. Probation requires regularly reporting to a probation officer and continued therapy.

Following sentencing, a psychological assessment is made in prison to determine where the convicted man serves out his sentence. If the sentence is longer than two years, he might be assigned to the open, minimum-security prison where he would be released to work outside the prison, having to report daily only for minimally eight hours of sleep. In maximum-security prisons, child sex offenders are treated by other prisoners as the lowest rank in the prison hierarchy and subject to discrimination, threats, and humiliating treatment. Therefore in Tegel they are segregated in a separate cellblock. In the minimum-security prison, offenders do not always share much time with one another and often do not know other inmates' crimes.

Hence, the psychologist's advisory opinion (*Stellungname*) is the first major assessment that influences the experience of incarceration. These opinions, based on a reading of all court documents and a personal interview, run from three to five pages. They assess, for example, history of illnesses, drug or alcohol consumption; interaction with children and single mothers with children; sex; work; prior criminal activity; relation to parents and partners (past and present); explanation of the crimes or crimes committed; and, most important, whether the convicted man has latent or overt "pedophile tendencies."

This opinion, then, contains a diagnosis of the offender and of his "treatability" and a prognosis of the recidivism risk. The major question addressed is whether the crime is part of a behavioral pattern or a single occurrence. The different histories listed above are analyzed together to predict whether the offender can benefit from treatment and what kind of therapy is appropriate—"psychotherapeutic," which enters into "personality development, or "social-therapeutic," which restricts itself to immediate cognitive and behavioral changes, such as, for example, avoidance of drinking, drug-taking, or contact with children.

If the advisory opinion recommends incarceration in the minimum-security prison, then the convicted man is immediately charged with finding a therapist. He may also request therapy while in the maximum-security prison, usually from a therapist employed there. Prison officials recommend therapists, but in the open, minimum-security prison it is the offender who must find one who has an immediate opening and will accept him as a client. Among the various professional therapists, psychiatrists were, in this study, most likely to conclude that offenders are "not treatable." Such a conclusion is most frequently based on assessments such as a "refusal to confess to the deeds (*Tathandlung*)" or "unwillingness to engage in therapy," but such assessments betray a general skepticism about the potential for change among pedophiles generally. After a negative diagnosis, the offender is under pressure to sign a statement waiving his right to keep this opinion private. The statement is then sent to prison officials and sets in motion new negotiations on therapy.

Treatment (*Behandlung*) in the open prison, as well as in other types of minimum security prisons, is primarily focused on meeting administrative expectations. Accordingly, the psychologists there procure for the offender, when legally entitled and qualified as treatable, a therapist outside the prison. In maximum-security prisons, a separate wing houses sex offenders, with its own specialists who focus on the nature of the delict and treatment aimed at avoidance. Nonetheless, prisoners even there do at times successfully petition for therapy outside the prison, and it is granted in cases where there is an unavailability of hours for therapy within the prison or when the patient makes a convincing argument about the utility of a specific outside therapist. The state, in any case, pays for this therapy only during the period of incarceration and only if approved by prison officials themselves. Prisons must operate within limited budgets and hence do not automatically approve all requests for treatment, even when it appears the law requires them to. Prisoners, of course, can challenge these decisions. If mandated as a condition of parole, the patient pays. The therapists at the center where I worked often informally reduced fees to a pittance when the clients were unable to pay.

At this center therapists conduct their own exploratory interview to assess the ability for and type of group therapy, in which they review the court's verdict with the client, asking him with which statements he agrees. Rarely do clients admit to all charges against them, so the question for this interview turns on whether the client admits to the core charge, or to sufficient details, to enable him to engage in therapy.

Based on the psychological assessment of the exploratory interview (whose results are written up) and the advice of the prison psychologist, usually after several individual therapy sessions, therapists assign offenders to one of the five groups mentioned earlier (incest abusers, *Pädosexueller*, learning disadvantaged, youth, or young adults). Some of these classifications overlap (e.g., a learning disadvantaged man may also be a youth or an incest abuser also a *Pädosexueller*); hence, some of the assignment is opportunistic, as therapists select clients from waiting lists, and at times assign someone to an approximate group rather than wait too long for a place to open. It is not unusual for clients to wait six months or longer to enter treatment.

Once assigned to a group, optimally of seven, clients report to therapy on their own (except in rare cases of individual therapy for men from a maximum-security prison, in which case the convict will be accompanied by a security official from the prison). If clients are not able to attend sessions, they are admonished to call ahead of time with a justifiable excuse, which they tend to do. Therapy sessions meet once weekly for two hours in four modules of ten weeks each. Three such series comprise a single year of therapy. The four modules focus on the sequence of events leading to the act (often called crime cycle), personal biography, relapse prevention, and empathy for the victim and apology. Two therapists, one man and one woman, conduct all groups.

In treatment, it is never clear to offenders what a full reckoning with the act (*Aufarbeitung der Tat*) means. Even if they have had prior encounters with the criminal justice system, they most likely have not encountered someone who demanded of them a deeply introspective account of their most intimate behavior. Initially, they all admit to a general crime but deny the specifics of the deed, offer a very sketchy or no explanation for why the abuse happened, and tend to be unreflective about their family histories and their own biographies. Each weekly therapy group begins with actual problems (*die aktuelle Runde*), where clients spend up to an hour sharing: seemingly endless problems with colleagues at work; tense family encounters where the crime is the elephant in the room; how someone in prison threatened them; why the social worker did not tell them something or is postponing their appointment because she will soon be away on vacation; how to deal with the court's judgment, a negative psychiatric evaluation, the conditions of parole, or a refusal to grant parole; and how and when to tell neighbors or friends or family about the crime. Much of this discussion is clearly circumlocution, an attempt to avoid bringing the deed itself into speech. On the other hand, prisoners are understandably anxious about how they will reintegrate themselves and their criminal histories into the world outside prison when such an eventuality comes.

Depending on the stage in their reckoning with the crime, clients are asked to address their own acts of abuse: recalling, analyzing, and resummarizing events; answering questions of the other members of the group; diagnosing themselves; examining empathy (or its lack) for their victims; relating the abuse to their own histories; discussing strategies to prevent recidivism. Therapists actively listen to their stories, offer sympathy and advice, or, alternatively, confront the clients in contradictions or evasions. Much of the therapists' work intends to uncover or create an internal monitoring voice from under layers of shame.

The fourth module involves developing empathy for the victim. This is approached by composing a letter of apology to the victim or parent, which is read to the group and discussed. It goes through many drafts until the therapists are satisfied that the abusers have gone some way toward understanding for what they are apologizing. Clients are asked not only to assume responsibility for the abuse but also to address the specificity of the harm to their particular victim(s). Usually the letter remains a formal exercise, important for the abuser's therapeutic progress but not for the victims or their parents, who are assumed not to want to receive such a letter.

Many of the men in treatment have themselves histories of neglect (*Verwahrlosung* and *Vernachlässigung*), where the adults in their lives seemed not to have made firm distinctions between their own needs and those of their children, and where they arbitrarily punished them or withdrew care. One of the most important factors in a successful therapy is to access the clients' own histories of loss or neglect in order to develop self-empathy that may in turn enable empathy for one's victims. To the extent clients experienced psychic change in their rehabilitation, they came to appreciate—symbolize, one might say—the separate emotional world of children. In short, therapy entails a movement back and forth between discovery and disclosure, a process that facilitates psychic change.

The Case of Konrad

Konrad is a man in his late thirties, a recovering alcoholic recently released from the special section for sexual abusers of a maximum-security prison in Berlin. After serving a six-year sentence for two counts of aggravated sexual abuse of a fourteen-year-old boy, he was released on probation, under police supervision (*Führungsaufsicht*), with the stipulation that he remain in therapy and take medicine to suppress his sex drive. He was referred to KiZ and, after three hours of individual therapy, assigned to a group for men classified as having a *pädosexuelle* orientation.

For the first nine months, Konrad behaved as if this group was his first encounter with therapy, even though he had years of experience at the maximum-security prison. He seemed unprepared, even irritated, by the questions. He suffered from depression and appeared distracted and uninterested, which I attribute both to the drugs—selective serotonin reuptake inhibitors (SSRIs)—to suppress his sex drive and the Zoloft for depression, and to his resistance to the "talking cure" and to what he might have gained by self-reflection.

In his first attempt to explain his delict to other members of the group, he claimed to remember nothing about the crime. He did not even remember having read the decision of the judge. When asked what he knows for sure about the delict, his response was "that I did something twenty-four hours ago and not now. Years have passed."

In fact, through the first ten weeks, Konrad conditioned his responses so as to give the "right" answer, but he did not invest anything of himself in them. He responded to all questions with simple adages: What is your explanation? "That I was neglected." Why did you drink so heavily? "Because I needed it." What are you going to use therapy for? "That this doesn't happen again." (*Das sowas nicht mehr vorkommt.*) How are you going to deal with your romantic desire for children? "Who knows what life will bring?" (*Wer weiß was das Leben bringt?*) Do you approach others for sex? "No." Why? "Because I fear I will relapse." (*Ich habe Angst daß ich rückständig werde.*) His resistance to becoming conscious of what he had done and who he had become was enormous. He had painfully learned not to know certain things about himself, and, while his story is tragic, he never appeared particularly sympathetic to others in the group. He seemed virtually incapable of introspection of any depth and therefore unable to empathize, what Heinz Kohut (1975, 352) called "vicarious introspection," with either his victims or the other clients in the group. The therapists appeared unable to find a language to enable him to become more conscious of his past and of those around him.

Through about six months of therapy, I had no basis from which to assess the truth of Konrad's story of what he had done. My focus, instead, was in accounting for his inability or refusal to remember his delicts. If it were due to inability, then he was containing somewhere in his unconscious the material that he had deeply repressed and made unavailable to himself; if it were due to stubborn refusal, then he was repressing nothing but merely unwilling to incriminate himself in front of the group.

At the fourth session, after a quite confusing recapitulation of his recent history, the therapists appeared perplexed when he began confusing the crime for which he had served his rather lengthy sentence with a previous delict. The first delict was for the seduction of a twelve-year-old boy in a summer camping place. It was the early 1990s. The Wall separating East and West had come down, and Konrad used the summers to do what had been denied to him as a GDR (German Democratic Republic) citizen: to travel in West Germany. The boy, Konrad said, visited him in his tent to drink and smoke because his parents did not allow him to, and they also left him sitting alone while they went from tent to tent drinking the whole night. One morning the boy told his mother that Konrad forced him into sex. She called the police and brought charges. For this, Konrad received three years' probation. The therapists asked him about his feelings on the morning after this first offense. He said that because he was so drunk and stoned, "On the next day I remembered nothing about what happened."

Konrad also claimed to not know that he had abused the fourteen-year-old boy in the second offense, the crime for which he served his lengthy prison sentence. After that arrest, he was so depressed that he twice attempted suicide. That boy had been a neighbor in Konrad's home village whom he ran into at a Dunkin' Donuts in Berlin where young male prostitutes hang out. After a few weeks, the boy showed up at Konrad's apartment in the village, moved in, and came and went as he pleased.

Two years later, he moved out, unprecipitated by a fight or incident, with no explanation. He simply disappeared and never came back. Two years after that, the boy, at the age of eighteen, brought charges against Konrad of sexual abuse with a minor. Konrad said he had been in love with him, but that he did not know until the trial that the boy had worked as a prostitute while living with him, nor, apparently, was he aware that the boy did not feel any love. At the trial, the boy insisted he had had sex with Konrad only because he needed a place to stay. Konrad countered that he had understood the boy's cohabitation, continuous visits, mutual affection, and willingness to put up with his drinking as a sign of love.

Given Konrad's low self-esteem, one goal of the therapists was to enable him to identify with himself as someone other than the worthless person he had come to be identified as. Perhaps if he empathized with himself, rather than wallow in self-pity, he could begin to feel empathy for his victims also. To do this, however, he had to work through his own history of abuse and self-abuse, what in therapy is called "biographical work." He did this in a singsong, whiny voice: He explained his drinking and depression as a result of his personal history. His parents both drank heavily and beat him frequently. In his early twenties, he had two loves in his life, which he says were mutual. Both men were in their late twenties at the time, and both died of AIDS. Konrad cared for them as they were dying. It was in this period of care and grief that he became addicted to alcohol, he said, although he had drunk before also, though not the entire day.

As for why he was now interested sexually in underage boys, Konrad adamantly refused to elaborate what it was about a boy that he found attractive. In response to questions about "type"—innocent, hairless, lively, stocky, pretty face—Konrad had a standard response—"I don't know."

The interaction between the two therapists, who had been working together over a decade, simulated a set of parents who could disagree and cooperate. Their conflictual yet open and facilitative relationship allowed the clients to switch identification from one therapist to the other, and for the therapists to switch roles depending on how they assessed client needs.

Konrad seemed extremely closed to both therapists for the first nine months. When he consistently refused to elaborate anything, the male therapist became more confrontative and challenging. When that elicited no response, he appeared to give up on Konrad and devote more time to the other clients. Meanwhile, the female therapist continued to show some sympathy, despite Konrad's apparent withdrawal, but this also for a long time brought about no further engagement—until a session about ten months into the therapy. Konrad was elaborating the story of the death of one of his adult male lovers, when he explained that his motivation after the death was to find a partner who, he said, "will not die before me."

This utterance, positing a link between his sexual desire for adolescent boys and his anxiety about death and separation, marked a turning point in Konrad's therapy. It is not that these words took away his pain of loss and fears of abandonment, but they offered the group empirical and conceptual access to an integral part of Konrad's experience and assisted the transference between him and others in the group that had been heretofore truncated. For the first time, others began to express empathy for Konrad that was believable to him, which, in turn, made him more confident in reflecting on his past relationships, as he felt others were actually interested in his fate.

The goal of the therapists was not to locate the origin of his fear of being left behind with the death of his two lovers. Most likely his anxiety of aloneness emerged from his relations with negligent parents, or out of belonging to a social underclass in the former GDR, or from a feeling of social exclusion based on an early discovery of his homosexual desire. Rather, for the therapists the point was that the loss of two intimate partners overwhelmed his ego, and he found himself in a space of deadness. They had only to access some particular emotional experience of loneliness to enable Konrad to enter the chain of associations and contexts to which his anxiety was linked.

It is highly questionable whether Konrad's fear of abandonment could have ever been alleviated through the anxiety-relieving, psychotropic drugs he was taking without also dealing with the history of this affect of deadness. What is even more doubtful is whether he might ever re-cathect to a different love object, an adult man, and displace his sexual attraction from those "who will not die before me," without first dealing with his fears of abandonment.

After this utterance, Konrad began to tell the group about distinctions he had deeply hidden from himself. Lacking language or words or friends to contain or take the place of his pain, he had turned to intoxication to anesthetize himself from feeling. His own indulgence in extremely self-destructive behavior might be understood as an attempt to kill something within himself. It showed a disregard for his own life. His attachment to underage boys was both an attempt to anesthetize himself against having to lose or separate from someone he loved and an experience of aliveness. To enable him to bear the thought of loss, he had to feel empathically understood before he could develop an ability to empathically understand and invest in the world of others. The therapists had to grasp the suffering behind Konrad's offense and demonstrably empathize with his pain before they could work on the conditions that might prevent a repetition of the offense.

Even into the eleventh month of therapy at the center, Konrad insisted on the correctness of his interpretation of events leading to his imprisonment. He doubted the boy's perception of abuse, and he doubted that the relationship existed only because he "bought the sex." He contended that the boy, along with two of his friends who testified as material witnesses, made the charges up. Hence, when it came time to submit to the group a letter of apology to the victim, Konrad was reluctant to show any true empathy for the boy. Some of the clients in the group, who otherwise remained emotionally distant from Konrad and critical of his general unwillingness to talk, sympathized with his version of the story, as it remained consistent and entirely plausible. Although Konrad was clearly using his age and permanent residence to seduce the apparently destitute boy, the boy already had some sexual experience with men, working as a prostitute. He also came and went as he pleased. His decision to live with Konrad and have sex with him was most likely not the result of Konrad's coercion but of accidental social circumstances outside the control of either of them.

Driven by questions from the therapists, the group also discussed the plausibility of the boy's account, since the recognition of abuse frequently occurs years after the event, especially among children, and the charges were filed only two years after the sex had ended. Konrad had indeed taken advantage of the boy's lack of other options at the time. Yet, it was difficult for other members of the group to assume that a fourteen-year-old boy was not yet *mündig*, mature enough to consent, although they acknowledged Konrad had violated the legal age of consent. Konrad's lack of empathy for the victim of his particular act of abuse did not, however, prevent him from seeing the wrongness of child sex abuse and neglect. After this session, he began in therapy to show a capacity for empathy that before had seemed entirely nonexistent.

In the last two months of Konrad's therapy, he underwent a transformation that surprised other members of the group, including a client who had before shared several years with him in group therapy in the maximum-security prison. Encouraged to comment on how Konrad reacted to therapy back then, this client said Konrad had always been *bockig* (stubborn) in his relations with the therapists; he had changed very little until the last month. The therapist in the prison had been extremely impatient with him. She had focused solely on the delict and countenanced no evasion, he said, techniques that were quite effective with him but that did not lead to any introspection by Konrad.

The sudden changes in Konrad coincided with success in obtaining an apartment for himself (he had been living in a group home) and then securing employment in a social service agency offering advice to underclass men like himself. He began to cut and wash his hair before coming to therapy and suddenly shaved regularly. He no longer complained about fights with his sister or father, or bureaucratic obstacles he encountered as an ex-prisoner, or the difficulties of subsistence by support through Harz IV, the 2004 governmental welfare reform that severely curtailed social benefits for the poor. He no longer always avoided eye contact with the other men or therapists, and often cracked jokes, showing a cynical and irreverent Berlin humor. He reported joy at having and decorating his own apartment and at serving coffee, cake, and cola to his father and sister. When others asked him to talk about himself now, the therapists had to stop him from going on. He was proud of being free of his alcohol addiction and expressed pleasure at his work, even though it was menial labor with menial pay and barely kept him subsisting. He even began talking concretely about what specifically might interest him in young men over eighteen.

Therapeutic Intervention

Despite the diversity among child sex offenders, efficacious interventions include some of the same key features enumerated in the case of Konrad. Efficacy entails changing the way the offender thinks about himself, changing the way he thinks about and with others, as well as a reassessment of what he has done (the wrongful sexual acts) as part of a reorientation to acceptable intimacy within the confines of legality. It also entails understanding how affect influences thinking. Psychic change is impossible by simply correcting what psychologists call "cognitive distortion." Therapy must also address the inexplicable affect offenders attach to their relations to children or youth.[6] For Konrad, the affect aroused by boys was disturbing precisely because he deluded himself as to what he was doing, and therefore had no critical perspective from which to understand his own motivations much less those of the youths he abused. He initially resisted therapy, fearing not cognition per se but that thinking the deed would empty his unconscious, outside of which, ultimately, might stand little more than that symbolic albatross "pedophile," or what was called in prison: *Kinderficker.*

In talking of affect, I rely on a strict and narrow definition offered in a 1909 essay by Sandor Ferenczi ([1909] 1952, 277–78), that "only such things (or ideas) are symbols in the sense of psychoanalysis as are invested in consciousness with a logically inexplicable and unfounded affect, and of which it may be analytically established that they owe this affective over-emphasis to unconscious identification with another thing (or idea), to which the surplus of affect really belongs. . . . [Symbols are] only those [substitutions] in which one member of the equation is repressed into the unconscious." Simply put, the unconscious might be conceived as the response to a surplus of affect, which by means of a repressive mechanism stores things or ideas. Problems with affect regulation have been shown to be greater in individuals who have not experienced secure attachments, a phenomenon commonly reported about sex offenders generally. One goal of therapy is to develop the ability to regulate this affect, which depends on gaining a capacity to engage in imaginative mental activity that allows for the interpretation of one's own and others' behavior as intentional (Fonagy et al. 2002; Fonagy and Target 1996). That is, abusers must come to recognize both their own interiority, about which many know little and over which most have little control, and they must come to recognize the separate—and what will necessarily remain to them enigmatic—interiority of the child.

Therapy at KiZ in the idiom of a "talking cure" offers, I would argue, the possibility of a self-transformation through access to the unconscious and therefore some degree of affect regulation. To be sure, my analysis here breaks from how most KiZ therapists might understand themselves. Most do not think of themselves as primarily concerned with unconscious activity. Nonetheless, the therapy for child offenders that I observed always tried to go beyond a narrow idea of reckoning with the deed to the affect attached to it. To "treat" the offenders, therapists at KiZ did not rest at the goals of behavioral, drug, or delict-focused treatments: an admission of the deed, an installing of impulse control, or an agreement to renounce drives. When therapy was most successful, clients arrived at an understanding of what their offensive acts stood for within their own very personal histories. Not merely a product of a specific kind of sex drive or orientation, the deeds are revealed to be symbolic substitutes in an infinite regress of prior, frequently ambiguous and fragmentary experiences (Obeyesekere 1984). Awareness of these substitutes enabled some offenders to develop a sense of self more open to imagining and assessing alternatives for a life of "responsibility without illegalities."

In this, the treatment orientation of KiZ therapists advances the more recent proposals by forensic psychologists to replace the dominant Risk-Need-Responsibility model (RNR) with what they call the Good Lives Model (GLM), to provide "individuals with the necessary internal and external conditions to pursue pro-social personal projects *that replace* previously offensive criminal behaviors" (italics added; Ward, Gannon, and Birgden 2007, 206; cf. Andrews and Bonta 2003; Ward and Gannon 2006). In pursuit of the goal of rehabilitation, then, treatment aims not only to avoid risk but also to enhance the readiness to change and to increase the responsiveness of the offender to a potential psychic change. The particular open prison where I worked in fact placed as much responsibility on the offender as possible in a system of incarceration, calling itself a *Selbsterstellmodel* (self-administered model), which is congruent with the further refined self-regulation model (SRM) advocated by Ward, Gannon, and Yates (2008).

This kind of treatment and incarceration must be modified for different individuals; it is unlikely to work for all child sex offenders. For some offenders, there may indeed be a singular drive behind the deed, in which case the task of the therapist would be to encourage the offender-client to externalize and make alienable a certain pedophilic desire, or pedophilic drive. For some, this drive may be internal to the self, and not only internal but submerged and unrecognizable as such, repressed and stored in the unconscious. For other men who are highly conscious of their desires and the means necessary to satisfy them while evading the law, there may be little repression. But in the case studies presented here, which are by no means exceptional or outlier cases, it is difficult to infer that the person speaking is externalizing pedophilic desire. This interpretation is in line with much contemporary psychoanalytic clinical practice, where, Peter Fonagy writes, "psychosexuality is . . . more frequently considered as disguising other, non-sexual self- and object-related conflicts than the other way around" (2006, 1).

When Konrad speaks he is not giving voice to a simple desire or motivational force that can be transformed according to Freud's initial formulation: "Where id was, there ego shall be." The "drive" that most motivated Konrad—as he and the therapists came to understand his speaking self after more than four years of intermittent therapy in prison and another ten months at KiZ—was not a "sexual interest in children," not even a sexual interest in youths, although his passions seemed to lead him, much like a drive, to seek out adolescent boys in need of attention and help. Rather, in response to repeated questions about sexual type, Konrad frustratingly reiterated, "I don't know." At the time, the therapists and I inferred from Konrad's "I," which insistently disavowed knowing itself, a resistance to introspection about his motivations. Instead, perhaps, we should have taken seriously his disavowal, for, as he himself later concludes, his behavior was not primarily about finding an appropriate object for his sexual desire, but about the repetition of a pattern, following the deaths of two lovers, to find a partner who "will not die before me."

The "Konrad" who was speaking to the therapists toward the end of his sessions—less wary, more optimistic, joyful in small daily acts, ironic, eager to share experience—is one who had remained for years, it seems, at least partially hidden to himself if not nonexistent. During the time of his abuses, he had neglected his appearance and drank huge amounts, as if the fog of intoxication might camouflage the phenomenal emptiness of his everyday. This neglect had much to do, I suspect, with his same-sex desire and the stigma attached to it as he grew up in East Germany. Later, his stubborn refusal to remember his offenses expressed that side of his dissociated self necessary to protect an inner self, less from accusations of child abuse than from the affect attached to memories of neglect from childhood and fear of abandonment by his lovers and acquaintances. That is also why, perhaps, when he spoke to the group in therapy, he adopted an unusual singsong voice of fake optimism, as if his fear of disclosure could be allayed only by putting the words to music. It seems likely that the deadness of his own demeanor and lack of attachments to others—he claims to have had no real friends, not even fleeting friendships since the time of his first offense— mimicked his relatively recent experiences of death and loss. The therapists at KiZ listened closely, empathized, pried, attacked, argued, and threatened, but for a very long time they seemed at wit's end to get behind the voice he inhabited in the group that comically flattened all differences within his experience into silly adages and homilies, ostensibly for them.

When the self emerged that he had sought to hide, Konrad twice attempted suicide. That step would have been an annihilation of both his manifest self that appeared unkempt, stubborn, pedophilic, and his latent, secret one. More disturbing for him, I suspect, was not the pedophile self, who was fairly recent in origin, appearing in full gestalt only as an adult in his late twenties, but the self reeling from loss and death. In any case, Konrad did not appear particularly shameful about his sexual relationships with the underage youths he had picked up; he had lived with them publicly in his village and in therapy addressed them openly, if consistently incoherent about what went on. His experience growing up in an entirely dysfunctional family had led to defenses—a surly, sullen, uncommunicative facade—to protect himself from revealing his vulnerabilities as well as from external demands. Konrad's hidden self was, compared to the person he presented in public, the more fragile, more interpersonally sensitive, more fearful of abandonment, similar to what D. W. Winnicott ([1960] 1965, 148) characterized as the True Self, which "does nothing more than collect together the details of the experience of aliveness." With the accusation of child sexual abuse, Konrad's search for aliveness in a relation to boys was betrayed, relationships that he had regarded as loving and caring turned persecutory.

Law was an essential instrument in transforming Konrad's experience of love into persecution. Raised in the former East Germany in a poor and "asocial" family, he had learned a strategy of survival that meant evading the law, in particular criminal law. GDR law, although authoritarian, also assured the advantages of a wide-net social welfare state (e.g., free health care, cheap subsistence goods and housing, easy if under-employment) without requiring much in return. Konrad internalized both versions of law: the paranoid-authoritarian and the minimally caring. Following his arrests and (after the second violation) imprisonment, he initially experienced the democratic federal law in the united Germany in the register of persecution alone.

Confronted with a state and social order that labeled him a pedophile—a label not widely bandied about in the former East but which became a major specter evoked by the newly freed and sensationalist press after unification—he was imprisoned with other sexual criminals, among whom he had the most abject status. These circumstances led him to drive his longing for the "experience of aliveness" deeper into his unconscious; his external shell, or what we might call the False Self (Winnicott 1965), was the only side he made available for others to see. Konrad then transferred this persecutory and nonreciprocal yet caretaking relationship with the law to the one he had with his therapists. As the demands for psychic change were great, Konrad initially resisted treatment more than most of the other clients in his group, and his transference relation with the group therapists at KiZ changed only several months before the end of therapy.

Law and Therapy

The label "pedophile" glosses over distinctions among the various types of offenders and the diversity of their behaviors. However, to the extent that every man accused of the offense is legally classified as pedophile, and most frequently treated in therapy as a *Pädosexueller* with a fixed sexual preference, each offender must address the same set of projections from the outside world. But the experience of offenders differs by the kinds of relations they have had with their victims, leading to widely varied degrees of internalization of these ascriptions. Although all clinical evidence suggests that adult relations are clearly more abusive when with five-year-old children than with eighteen-year-old youths, for example, offenders do not always experience it this way, and the law tends to treat all sex offenses as similar in kind.

Law tries to resolve the problem of asymmetrical experience by fixing an age of consent, generally fourteen in Europe, in some countries up to eighteen. Trying to specify an age alone as the marker for "sexual self-determination," or sexual maturity and agency, may establish legal clarity, but it also creates therapeutic problems by representing all victims below a certain age as "children." The uniformity of this category is contradicted by the varied experiences of offender and victim alike. While law in its interest in uniform application excludes this experience by relying on chronological age to define consent, therapy must take into account the experience of the offense, *die Tat,* to access the client's self. But because therapy is the key to a legally and socially consequential rehabilitation, therapists are always under pressure to prioritize legal assumptions and categories that assume a homogeneity in victims and in the experience of the offense. Such assumptions often run counter to the lived experience of the men they treat and therefore are counterproductive for therapeutic efficacy.

The case of Konrad presented here falls into an intermediate category; his victims count chronologically as children but are clearly pubescent, or adolescent, or the objects of "ephebophilia," the psychological classification most often used to delineate a sexual interest in mid- to late adolescents, girls fourteen to sixteen or boys fourteen to nineteen. His victims clearly had varied sexual interests, too, but, in their immaturity, those interests appeared highly ambivalent, confused, and embedded in other needs of which they were unaware. Therefore, relations with adults were highly susceptible to manipulation and abuse. Social and legal norms now dictate that those interests, however defined and determined, be categorically protected from adult sexual desires. Therapists charged with rehabilitation must minimally bring the attitudes and interests of offenders in line with these norms.

Men who repeatedly seek out prepubertal children for sex are certainly more difficult to rehabilitate than someone like Konrad, and they may in fact be less treatable through therapy generally. The choice given them is either complete sexual renunciation or chemical castration, since at the moment we are at a loss on how to imagine and create a socially acceptable sexuality for them. There appears to be more ambiguity and variance in the abuse of postpubertal children, however, and therefore more room for therapeutic efficacy.

In demonstrating through the case of Konrad not only that therapy can be successful but *how* it is, I drew attention to the importance of psychic change for men under the stigma of social abjection and the threat of permanent incarceration. The self tied to the act of child sexual abuse may actually be a False Self, which hides or protects the self that must be made to appear in therapy. For therapy to be successful, I have specifically identified the potentiality for authenticity inside interpersonal relations and affect regulation as integral to treatment. Treatment models limited to controlling impulses, cognitive behavioral correction of thinking errors about child sexuality, changing sexual object choice, or committing to sexual abstinence are inadequate for such a task. The regulation of affects is hardly a developed science, but we do know that access to affects is a uniquely individual process, not group- or type-specific, and crucial to begin the internal conversation the offender must have to reckon with the act. The offender after successful therapy should not only assume responsibility for the act but also find, as Christopher Bollas (1987, 62) wrote, "a more generative way of "holding . . . the self as an object of one's nurture." Able to nurture his self, the rehabilitated offender might open himself up to empathy for and life with others.

FOUR

Knowledgeability and the Materiality of Child Sex Abuse

Knowledgeability

Child molesters present acute challenges to knowledgeability. In therapy they are asked to come to know themselves through introspection and empathic understanding in a process that will never actually end. Yet if the therapists are competent and the treatment is at all successful in working through the offenders' defenses, the offenders come to know themselves differently and better than they had before. To use this knowledge not merely to control impulses and alter behavior, or to change one's relation to children, but also to transform the self, is a demand of a much higher order—and it takes time. The alternative to this transformation is to act on habit or its avoidance alone and risk mindless repetition of scenarios based on past experience. Hence, offenders are subject to strong incentives to change, but, given the public skepticism about this possibility, they also are subject to equally strong incentives to deny the accusations and avoid the full weight of the social stigma attached to molestation. Without some degree of transformation, and the ability to show signs of rehabilitation, however, reintegration into everyday social life will usually be made impossible.

To know exactly what happened in sex abuse is elusive, in part because it is based on memories of an act. One must reconstruct the act, or the event of which it was a part, to claim an experience of abuse after, often long after, something happened. This retroactive reconstruction through memory would seem to give force to the argument that most sex abuse lacks a materiality independent of the diffusion of meanings and discourses drawn from and promulgated by the various actors involved. From this perspective, the act materializes only after the event in its subsequent performance in which speech is central. Yet, as I hope to demonstrate in what follows, the actual act of abuse, aspects of which usually remain opaque, can serve as a material referent for the memory work entailed in understanding the crime of abuse.

Following arrest for child sex abuse, few men ever admit fully to the accusations at this early stage of the ritual process. When child sex offenders in Germany enter therapy, which most of them do—as a legal right, a duty, and a condition of sentencing—they usually have several individual sessions before joining a group. Therapists insist that they admit to their offense before entering the group, that is, that they admit to knowing something. All offenders withhold some things, however, both as a strategy to protect themselves from the accusation—a motivated ignorance of the facts, so to speak—and because to assimilate their experience into the crime of sexual abuse is a psychically difficult, self-incriminating process.

When I write of ignorance, I am referring only to not-knowing that is motivated—that is, to "motivated ignorance." To leave the state of ignorance is to become informed, but information alone will not suffice to make one knowledgeable. Therapy is supposed to enable the accused to recover both what he does not know and what he does know but is withholding. In both cases, to become knowledgeable is never merely a matter of elaborating that about which he is ignorant, nor is it a matter of making explicit what is implicit. To become knowledgeable is also a process of recovering bits of information—images, sensations, feelings, thoughts, speech—that have been made unavailable to memory or repressed. And after the suspect recovers these disconnected experiential bits, they must be combined into interconnected wholes, what Wilfried Bion (1984, 1962) called transforming "beta elements" into "alpha elements." That is, the accused must recover information that he has made difficult to retrieve, certain memories that he has made unavailable to himself, and think through the connections between these different bits of information. For the man accused of child molestation the process of discovery and recombination requires both introspection and establishing a relation of empathic understanding in his thoughts with the child he has molested.

To summarize: confronted with an accusation of sex abuse, suspected child molesters are first asked to recall and then to organize the details of an experience or experiences in a way that responds to the accusation. But that accusation is of "sex abuse"—an alpha element, an already coherent, organizing concept. If the accusation is true, the suspect knows he will be placed in the category of the modern untouchable, outside the moral bounds of the human. Hence, the first reaction to be expected, when accused of child molestation, is to protect oneself from this charge. To deny it. And that is what men accused of child molestation tend to do. In any institutional setting in German society, however, whether the home, the school, or the workplace, such denial is rarely accepted. The accusation alone is grounds for an inquiry; in fact it often mandates an investigation, usually by some agent of the state, someone acting for or authorized by the state. Such an investigation, even before it has reached the criminal justice system, initiates a ritual process in which the suspect repeatedly answers questions that entertain the possibility, or more likely presume, that he is hiding something. There is no presumption, however, that he is ignorant, only that he is motivated to ignorance.

Accusations are based on the experience of a child or youth. Nowadays, children are given the benefit of the doubt as to the veracity, or at least partial veracity, of their accusations. In northern Europe, at least, the long history of dismissing children's complaints as fantasies of adult abuse is over. Even in those cases of children's complaints based largely on fantasy, today they are usually assumed to warrant an investigation to determine their truth. And since some very public scandals in German schools and churches in 2010, public educators are increasingly active in encouraging children to come forth immediately when they suspect adult misbehavior, in a policy publicized as "No Room for Abuse" or "Zero Tolerance." Hence, it is no longer always the case that most statements of abused children are gathered long, even years, after the transgressive act. In the period of my research, however, most accusations were still made years after the violations, in which case they are not statements of children but statements of youths or even adults who remember an event.

In any event, it would be very unusual for that happening to have been immediately experienced as what we call "sex abuse," although it may have been experienced as transgressive, harmful, or injurious. To classify the act as abuse the child must do precisely what Bion describes as thinking under the pressure of thought: transform beta elements into alpha elements. This transformation of the act into the language of abuse is often a cumbersome and slow process. Certainly in the past, though somewhat less today, adults have been outright dismissive of the child's claim of abuse. But also, the child's language itself tends to be inadequate and children's testimony of sex abuse, being central to the recovery of the event, is usually based on an experience of ambivalence. The experience is, first of all, confusing, often with an adult with whom they identify, and then also painful, perhaps even simultaneously pleasurable. Only in retrospect, after children or inexperienced youths attain a certain maturity, do they have the linguistic categories, the emotional capacity, and the confidence in their own integrity to turn what happened, the lived event, into an experience that makes sense as criminal abuse.

If the victims are still children when the accusations are transformed into testimony for the court, an adult—for example, mother, high school counselor, psychologist, or therapist—usually becomes the primary inter-locutor in reconstructing the memory of a transgressive experience into one of sexual abuse and in producing evidence for the court. Fathers or close father substitutes are the most frequent child molesters. In those cases, if the abuse is revealed during the child's latency stage, it is the mother who frequently serves as adult interlocutor. Once puberty is reached, however, mothers usually become complicitous in the abuse. In those cases, third par-ties outside the family instead intervene to help the youths or adults form a coherent picture of what went on.

For the purposes of understanding the rehab ritual, this process of recov-ery of memory means that the suspected child molester must first respond to an accusation about a violent transgression that he is charged with ini-tiating, based either on the accusation of someone who is not capable of making the charge without the mediation and support of other adults, or on the accusation of someone who has reached a maturity that enables her to remember and now construe the experience as a connected whole. It is important to emphasize the temporal, adult mediation of the experience of abuse because adults today are very motivated to protect children from an unmediated experience of sex in the first place. Moreover, this motivation to mediate the child's experience is one that many adults will insist they are ignorant of. Rather, most adults, at least in Germany, will insist that they are interested only that the child discover sex freely, without coercion.

These conditions of recovery of what happened might create the im-pression that a true representation of the experience of abuse, in word and image, is impossibly elusive. Elusive, yes; impossible, no. However difficult it is to create a true representation, this seemingly elusive experience con-tains within it a truth that is capable of being grasped. That truth is necessary for the victim, in particular, because without knowing *what experience* exactly is behind the by now well-documented symptoms of sex abuse, one cannot address the consequences and effects of abuse. By the time that experience enters the ritual process of rehabilitation of the offender, it invariably in-cludes the social mediation of what happened.[1]

This is all to say that the experience of the transgression, for the abused child and the offender, is fully intersubjective, redefined through relations and interactions with various adults subsequent to the initial act. Children are ambivalent about this mediation, for it in many ways takes away an ini-tial experience by fixing its referents in adult terms. By seeking to make this experience fully discursive in adult language, it robs the child's unconscious. But to rob the child's unconscious is part of the process necessary to achieve the coherence of the category of "abuse" on which the court relies.

My focus in this chapter will be more narrow, not on what the victims of sex abuse experience or know but on how the offenders come to know, and what they then in fact do know in light of what we know about the intersubjective experience of the child. Consider this problematic through one offender's attempt to arrive at knowledgeability of his act of incest.

The Case of Uwe

Uwe, a thirty-seven-year-old man accused of incest with his four-and-one-half-year-old daughter, is atypical of German sex offenders in therapy in that he never disputed the descriptions of his daughter or ex-wife, and he was not arrested but only threatened with legal proceedings. What he shares with other men in therapy is the struggle with coming to know what went on, and it is this aspect of the case, the relation of knowing to the materiality of the act of abuse, that will be my focus in what follows.

Many of the men in group therapy do not talk much; some do not seem to like to talk. Uwe was most extreme in both respects. Although he was always alert and appeared to listen well, he went through entire two-hour sessions saying things like, "*Nichts neues.*" (Nothing new). Or, "*Ich weiss nicht, was ich erzählen soll.*" (I don't know what I should tell.) Or, in response to a therapist question, Anything new? "*Eigentlich nichts.*" (Actually nothing.) Or "*Bei mir gibt's nichts.*" (Nothing much, for me.) And at work? asks the therapist. "*Eigentlich auch nicht viel, nichts passiert.*" (Actually not much, nothing happened.). Or, when therapist #1 asks, Have you seen your children this last week? "*Gar nicht.*" (Not at all.)

This consistent recourse to the negative may seem like the result of defenses against self-revelation such as repression or denial. Repression would mean he is making his experience unavailable to conscious thought, denial a refusal to admit what occurred. But, after a year of observing Uwe, I concluded that he was neither repressing his experience nor denying the events. What he did, as he comes to understand it, alarmed him like a natural disaster would. He understood that he had committed an act considered so heinous that even murderers are treated with more sympathy. He sincerely wanted to know what he had done and how he had come to do something considered so despicable. Something that, if he had committed the abuse he was accused of, was absolutely repulsive to him.

Uwe usually came to therapy directly from work, odd jobs repairing or building things. Despite his reticence to say anything, he brought a tense, anxious presence to the group simply by how he looked: typically, tattered jeans with holes at the knees, a hooded zip-top sweatshirt, fashionable frameless eyeglasses sitting above an unkempt, straggly beard. All of this adorned a thin, reedy body with a long elegant neck, dimples, a wan, pleading smile directed at whomever addressed him, and quirky hair, which stood straight up, gravity defying, as if it were electrified.

I often strained to understand the speech in these groups. Many of the men mumbled or swallowed their words, talking in fragments comprehensible only within the larger contexts of their lives. Uwe muttered softly, often mouthing words that do not come out in distinctive sounds. The other men repeatedly asked, "What?" And they admonished him to speak up. Therapist #2 suggested that Uwe practice talking loudly to himself in front of a mirror. At his workplace, fellow workers nicknamed him *Der Stumme* (the Mute One). Here we have to speak, said therapist #1. Can we do something to help you?

Uwe shook his head and raised his eyebrows helplessly.

After about four weeks into therapy, Uwe had still not spoken about the deed, what he had done. The other men in the group were curious, but also a bit angry at his reticence, and they began to needle him. Uwe reluctantly explains: "My daughter, who was four and one-half, discovered that she could gratify herself (*Selbstbefriedigung*). I helped her, *muschispielen* (play with the pussy)." His ex-wife noticed that their daughter had discovered this. He talked to the girl's mother about it, and she said, "We all do that. But let's see if she does it at school also. You should have forbid this." The daughter apparently then played with herself at the school also. "*Muschispielen* was not my intention," says Uwe. "I wanted to distract her [*ablenken*], to play with her to divert her attention. It didn't work out. Then, I thought, stroke her behind, her legs, her feet, to take her mind off the vagina. This concept '*muschispielen*' was hers, she discovered the formulation herself. Shortly before Christmas, my ex-wife said our daughter could stay overnight, but I wasn't there. Then it came out. She turned to the juvenile authorities for advice, and she and I agreed I would come here to KiZ."

The initial goal of therapy is to bring into words the deed, thereby externalizing it as an object about which the offenders then can think critically and create the possibility for changing their relation to that deed. Over time the therapists tried several approaches with Uwe.

In a series of sessions, they reconstructed Uwe's biography and looked for some event in his life that might have prefigured the abuse. They asked about his relations with his parents, his early sexual experience, his time in school, job training, and work history. His parents divorced when he was six, and he was raised subsequently by his father, now deceased, whom he regarded as "somehow a friend." His childhood was unremarkable, he says, but he does not want to speak much about that period. He instead jumps over it to talk about his military service. He served as an orderly with the Red Cross in preparation for catastrophes, but he had done this kind of work before. It was nothing exceptional for him, he said. He felt prepared for the experience; it did not shock him.

When asked about his sexuality, he becomes visibly uncomfortable: He leans forward, then back, rubs his hair, looks up, exhales. He describes playing doctor as an eight-year-old with his stepsister, who is three years older, as "nothing bad." Sex was spoken about at home, he says, nothing unusual there, either.

Therapist #2 asks who was more active in playing doctor, his stepsister or Uwe, and he doesn't seem to understand the question, before finally conceding, "As far as I remember, she was more active. She examined me." Therapist #2 asks whether his sister already had breasts and pubic hair. "Yes," he says. One usually plays doctor much younger than that, explains therapist #2; twelve is particularly old for such a game. "We didn't know each other before that," Uwe says, as if they would have played doctor earlier had they met.

Were you discovered? asks therapist #1.

"Yes, I think so."

What was the reaction? "More amused than anything."

Did they forbid it? "We didn't do it often," he says, and explains that he had an interest in sex, but it wasn't exciting for him. For his sister, however, he grants that the play was about sex. Yet the family, he says, talked and even joked about this later, always with amusement.

Searching for other sexual experiences, he describes discovering a few years after this doctor play that he could masturbate. He says he discussed it with his father, with whom he lived at the time, even though his mother remained closer as a confidant. After the sixth grade he spent more time alone and no longer sought out close friends. He had no childhood crushes, he says, because he did not seek out a girl.

How did he experience his first love? asks therapist #1. Uwe explains that in his early twenties he was asked by a woman who worked in the state office in charge of drivers' licenses whether he had a girlfriend. When he said no, she advised him to search for one and offered to help him write a personal ad for the newspaper. The woman who responded became his wife. They were engaged three months before marrying and remained together for another three years. Asked to describe his ex-wife, he says she is open, social, and approaches people easily.

Asked to describe what he put in the ad, he says, "Loyal, somewhat odd, shy, in treatment." He laughs. The woman, his future wife, was a nurse, and she said she was seduced by his description of being "in treatment." "When I met her," he says, "I could talk a lot, not like now." They soon had a daughter, and then a son.

But his wife was always dissatisfied, he says. She insisted on moving frequently, to different parts of Germany. They first moved to Kassel, where they could buy a house cheaply. He moved there first and prepared the house. Within weeks after his wife arrived, she wanted to move again. At that time, pregnant with a second child, she revealed to Uwe that she was attracted to women. They moved back to Berlin and found a house there, which he painted and renovated. Then came the divorce, he says, and she insisted that he leave the house. She wanted, says Uwe, the son for herself.

When asked to account for his own transgression, Uwe explains, "It was because I was fixated on my daughter, without establishing that I was her father." He distinguishes between his initial feelings for her, how they developed, and how he sees them now. After the separation from his wife, he enjoyed joint custody, but the children largely lived with their mother. When he arrived to pick them up, his daughter initially avoided him, hiding and not wanting to go with him. He realized he had to do something to change this, he explains, and offered his ex-wife to take care of the children more often. That proved convenient for her, as she had begun to take classes in night school. Over time the daughter then developed a deep intimacy with him and started in fact to resist returning home to her mother. She began to say things like, "I want to remain with you forever." On retrospection, he notes that back then he had devoted all his time to taking care of the children and to creating closeness with his daughter, instead of taking care of himself. He also ignored his friends.

And your son? asks therapist #2. "Our relationship has been more constant," he explains. "It was different. He knew that I was his father. And there was a time when he was with me more than with his mother." Shortly after the birth of the second child Uwe's ex-wife sought a new relationship and found a woman friend. When asked by another man in the group whether it bothered Uwe that his wife "turned lesbian," he says, "yes," adding, "at some point she would have noticed that she wasn't interested in men."

In a session that followed the attempt to create a biographical sketch, the therapists concentrated on some details of his sexual experience. An entire session was devoted to his relations with his sister. Therapist #1 asked what the age difference meant, that the sister was twelve and he nine. "This is hard for me," Uwe prefaces his remarks, "generally hard [to talk about my experience with my sister]. I never had problems with her. We understood each other before we had sex play and after it also. She left then, started her own family."

Therapist #2 interjected, It's not about a problem. You were the small brother. What was your feeling for her, and what did you feel in this close sexual contact with your sister? Children experience this in different ways. A nine-year-old-boy is still a young child; a twelve-year-old girl can already be quite grownup. Uwe replies, "We slept together in the same bed, and I never noticed her physical proximity. It was a game for me."

The therapists sense that he is being evasive, and therefore are suspicious on his insistence that his experience with his sister was neither sexual nor ultimately traumatic. Not a sexual game? asks therapist #2. Uwe answers, "There was no sexual sensibility back then." And for your sister? Uwe concludes, "The sexual experience was very pleasant for her, for me it was a game. She was my stepsister, we were not related. And we didn't grow up together. She lived with us in our family for only three years."

Did you not feel exploited? asks therapist #2. Uwe shakes his head no.

In another session, the therapists ask the men to fill out a questionnaire. One question read: "Your sexuality, it did not play any role, but instead . . ."

Uwe first says, "I have no idea. I wanted to distract her."

From what? asks therapist #1.

"From masturbating," says Uwe. He adds, "I'm guilty in that I continued to stroke her while she masturbated. I thought it was something private, but she was with me. She wanted attention."

You encouraged her in this, says therapist #2. Would she have masturbated if your ex-wife were there?

Tears began to roll down Uwe's cheeks, and he wipes them away. "I stroked her because I thought it would get her thinking about something nice (*etwas Nettes*), something else, and then she would stop."

But stroking her did not set any boundaries, says therapist #2.

"That's my problem," says Uwe. "I have to learn how to have authority. Or I have to pay attention to what I am feeling also."

You sound helpless, say therapist #1. You have to learn to say no. And what about your son, do you discipline him?

"No, I also don't set boundaries with him," says Uwe, and he begins to cry again.

Do you make any decisions? asks therapist #1, visibly frustrated. He reminds Uwe of an event he had mentioned in another session, about how Uwe responded to a physical assault by a coworker by smiling at him. You never resist, he tells him.

"Yes I do," Uwe defends himself.

When? "I changed my residence a number of times."

Therapist #1 returns to probing Uwe's sexual fantasies: What do you think about when you have sexual feelings?

"I do it alone."

What do you think about? the therapist repeats.

"A woman."

In perhaps a third of the sessions, the therapists keep returning to the question why Uwe encouraged his daughter to fondle herself. Most of the time, he gives the same answer: I wanted to distract her.

Once therapist #2 asks, Did her wish shock you?

"Yes," he says, "looking at it that way. In that moment, when it happened, [however], my expectation was that it was something nice. A situation comparable to play."

Another time, the therapists distinguish between setting boundaries and distracting, and ask, If the goal was to stop your daughter from pulling down her pants and playing between her legs, then why would *stroking her* help achieve this? Uwe is silent.

Therapist #1 says, for six months your attempt to distract didn't work. Did you try something else?

"I wanted her closeness," replies Uwe.

Why didn't you share this problem with your ex-wife?

Uwe remains silent.

Increasingly Uwe's ex-wife refused to talk with him and prevented him from having any contact with the children. No letters, no answering his telephone calls. For a while, she let him see his son but not his daughter. The social worker who is to mediate his relationship with his family informs him that his daughter does not want to see him anymore. But then he learns from his son that his daughter began complaining: If her brother can visit him so should she be able to. The therapists counsel patience.

After I quit observing the group, Uwe continued therapy for another year. His ex-wife, the therapists told me, was happy in her new relationship. They described the daughter, whom they had observed in a separate therapy, as a lively, delightful child, not affected as far as they could tell by the early history of masturbation in front of her father. The children now have two mothers, and they cut off all contact of Uwe with his daughter. He seldom sees his son anymore either. Uwe continued in therapy with other incest abusers for another year. Near the end, he reports that his ex-wife informed him that she planned on leaving Berlin with her new partner and the children.

I asked the therapists to give me a final sketch of Uwe's development. They were ambivalent in their final diagnosis. On the one hand, they agreed that Uwe had a minimal sexuality, if any, and that his drives appeared consistently weak. On the other hand, one therapist suspected he might have an orientation toward children, in which case he should have been treated in a group with men who had abused unrelated children or youth rather than in a group of men who had committed incest. Following a new trend in German psychology to classify pedophiles as a third sexual orientation alongside hetero- and homosexuals, one therapist considered that he might be a *Pädosexueller*, a third orientation alongside hetero- and homosexual, but she had no further evidence for this ascription. The other therapist was more skeptical of this claim.

The Limits of Empathy

Uwe never did go to trial. But if he had, and if a judge had arrived at a verdict, she would have had to first assess the truth of various utterances, a process of making objective and explicit the various motives and perspectives of the experiences of the child and the adult. Such a legal process of producing and evaluating evidence is similar to that of the humanist or social scientist engaged in reaching an understanding of the truth, except that the judge, oriented only to a determination of guilt or innocence, to whether the deed fits the legal definition of crime, is restricted in the kinds of permissible evidence. We, by comparison, are oriented to producing a fuller version of the truth, and therefore in the interests of knowledgeability are wise to consider a wider range of evidence than is a court.

Whatever conclusions we arrive at in our understanding of Uwe and his daughter, they will not be the result of the uncovering of the "truth of sex" in the sense of Michel Foucault, which he hyperbolically described as the "existence of a discourse in which sex, the revelation of truth, the overturning of global laws, the proclamations of a new day to come, and the promise of a new felicity are linked together" ([1976] 1978, 7). The "truth of sex" about which Foucault wrote was, arguably, the dominant ordering discourse about "sex" and the body in certain institutional settings from the late-nineteenth to the mid-twentieth century. It still exists, and speculation about Uwe as *Pädosexueller*—an ontological category, an attempt, in Foucauldian language, at "subjectivation"—is part of this discourse. Indeed, on the surface Uwe's experience interpreted through this discourse, and through the entire ritual rehab process, appears as if oriented to producing a certain kind of sexual subject. Yet the therapists who treated Uwe struggled with experiences of his that were not included within the discourse on sex, and ultimately they were inconclusive about how to define him as a sexual subject.

There are nonetheless obvious similarities in Uwe's case with the processes examined by Foucault, such as the "pedagogization of children's behavior," in the attempt to find the causes of the young girl's masturbation and of a sexuality in Uwe through what appears to be a confessional setting ([1976] 1978, 103–10). But the formal similarities between confessional and therapeutic settings are not borne out in Uwe's experience. The therapists are most intent on finding out what actually happened and what Uwe's motives were in his relations with his daughter that might have led him to encourage her to masturbate. They go through a lengthy set of questions that might lead Uwe to define himself as a sexual subject, but they do not end there. Their intent is ultimately to elicit from him an explanation in his own words rather than a particular "confession." To follow Foucault's analytic lead here, as does Judith Butler in her influential *Bodies That Matter*, would lead one to a question about how "regulatory power produces the subjects it controls" (Butler 1993, 23), or, in another formulation, to understand "the matter of bodies as the effect of a dynamic of power, such that the matter of bodies will be indissociable from the regulatory norms that govern their materialization and the signification of those material effects" (Butler 1993, 2). In other words, bodies are "indissociable" from regulatory norms, based on knowledge that is an effect of power.

Yet "the process of materialization" (Butler 1993, 9) of Uwe's body and that of his daughter cannot be ascertained by reading the effects of regulatory norms in discourse. Even after their bodies are marked by the act of transgression, noticed in the school, and talked about with Uwe's wife and later by Uwe himself in therapy, the materiality of the interaction between Uwe and his daughter is separable from the regulatory norms expressed in language. In fact, for the therapists the deed must remain separable from the language they use or they are not doing their jobs, which are not ones of labeling or interpellating but of open discovery. The norms, which certainly exist, are not cited like law, as Butler defines the performative workings of regulatory power, but merely one interpretive reference to appeal to in everybody's attempt to interpret the meaning of the exchange between Uwe and his daughter.[2]

The verb *muschispielen*, for example, which comes to be used by the girl to describe a form of precocious sensual play, is the effect of a dynamic of power only if one reduces all of the young girl's interactions with adults to dynamics of power. *Muschispielen* does not appear to be the reiteration of anything, but instead is a novel act that confounds its participants. Uwe's encouragement of this play and later difficulty of bringing the deed into speech is due precisely in part to the absence or ambiguity of regulatory norms, and to the difficulty of interpreting them. Likewise, the process of uncovering what happened is not brought under a single rule or under language as such. The attempts of therapists in this case to understand Uwe's deed as an expression of sexuality ultimately went nowhere.

That is because the therapists held onto a conception of the event's materiality—that something did happen, even though it may be difficult to get at—as that which Uwe must reference and work through. By asking questions only of the discourse of sex and its production through a matrix of knowledge/power, Foucault's analytical focus elides the materiality of the intersubjective. There is a truth in Uwe's case, but it is not an effect of the discourse. The truth has an integrity not as an *effect* of the efforts of Uwe and the therapists to bring the act into speech, but one that can be approached *through* and resists these efforts. If the theoretical goal of the therapists is to bring Uwe closer to the truth of his experience, Uwe's goal is ultimately knowledgeability: to understand his act through introspection and empathic understanding. If that is our goal, we readers replicate Uwe's efforts.

What did go on for those six months in Uwe's relation with his daughter? What is the truth in the materiality of the events? Uwe's explanation is consistent for what he agrees, in retrospect, is a transgression: that he wanted to distract his daughter from what she called *muschispielen*. Why, then, as the therapists repeatedly ask, did he stroke her other body parts when she engaged in this sex play? It remains a mystery where she learned the word *muschispielen*, though it is highly improbable that she learned it from her father or her three-year-old brother, the only males she had contact with. It is likely that she heard it in interactions with girls or women, including her mother, or put the two words *Muschi* and *spielen* together into a compound noun, as is allowed in German syntax. At any rate, *muschispielen* is merely a label for an activity, a symbol for the child's attempt to please herself, initially only in her father's presence.

Uwe has no answer for why his daughter discovered this behavior in interaction with him or why he seemed to encourage what most adults today would call masturbation. When asked, he repeats his initial motive: He stroked her to distract her (*um abzulenken*). That motive is indeed plausible, but my first reaction is that it is too transparent and partial an explanation. Too transparent because it is not consistent with Uwe's motives in other domains where they remain generally hidden to him, and though he may not have a large ego, he nonetheless has feelings and interests and drives that are not merely reactive to those of others.

It would also be a mistake to assume that Uwe is pursuing certain interests out of a rational calculation or carrying out a desire based on either a rational understanding of his passions or an innate drive that he cannot properly control. As we have seen, Uwe has no particular passions and little "inner passion," and he is hardly a rational-choice type. Throughout therapy it proves difficult for him to retrieve a sense of his own self-interest. He makes few decisions but mostly follows the initiatives of others. When therapist #2 challenged Uwe about not making decisions and failing to defend himself, Uwe became agitated and insisted, "Yes I do." When? asked the therapist. "I changed my residence a number of times," replied Uwe. Yet earlier Uwe had complained about his wife's wish to constantly change residence, suggesting that even this decision was not based on his initiative or interest, though, when cornered by the therapist to defend himself, he recalled it as such.

If we follow D. W. Winnicott ([1960]1965) here and ask whether Uwe is showing us in therapy a False Self protecting something from disclosure, that something could in fact be an interest in sex with children. But we have evidence of only one such example in his life, that of his relations with his daughter, and one experience is hardly enough evidence to infer a primary interest in children or a sexuality based on such interest. The therapists' discussion of whether he had a *pädosexuelle* orientation was ultimately inconclusive, as they had insufficient evidence to infer a particular sexuality of any kind.

A more promising approach might be to ask not about his formation as a sexual subject but about how his experience is relational and leads to a strongly intersubjective sense of self. In therapy Uwe is always smiling at the other men in the group, even when they are saying things critical of him. He smiled the same way, apparently, at work when a coworker struck him. This smile might be a way of protecting himself from disapproval by others, but it is also a sign of empathy. Rather than assert his own interests and indulge in his own feelings, he consistently tries to intuit and share the feelings of the other. His authentic self appears all too eager to feel the other's interests or perspective rather than his own. Even when another man asked him whether he was disappointed or angry that his wife had left him for a woman, to "become lesbian," as he puts it, Uwe does not react angrily. He merely admits his disappointment—in a single word, "Ja." And then he goes on to account for his ex-wife's motives: Eventually she would have discovered her sexual interest in women anyway. In other words, rather than dwelling on his own disappointment or accusing his ex-wife of trying to punish him, he offers the other members of the group a statement of empathy for her reason for leaving him.

Could it be that Uwe was reacting to his four-and-one-half-year-old daughter out of the same sense of relation: both protecting himself from disapproval and being empathic? That is, as his daughter begins playing with herself, Uwe enters a dilemma, knowing that society would think this is wrong, therefore trying to distract her, but also not risking her disapproval by affirming her interests in her own body by stroking her bottom, her arms, her legs. He admits to his pleasure in this tactility, but that does not imply he was motivated by self-interest or passion. That pleasure, so he reasoned, was limited and solely a result of his daughter's initiative.

His explanation—intending to distract her in her initiative—was of course self-serving, assuming that his child had a will clearly demarcated from his. Was the daughter, however, not taking her cues from her father and performing for him? To what extent is the *Muschispiel* an attempt by the daughter to relate to her father in the absence of her mother? The most likely explanation is that Uwe, in his sorrow and abandonment, elicited an emotional reaction in his daughter, and that she therefore was reacting to his suffering.

The daughter's motives are more difficult to interpret, as we have no record of what she thought or felt, of how she was experiencing Uwe's co-participation or, in his words, his "attempt to distract" her sex play. To be sure, the daughter may have discovered masturbation on her own; it may be a product of her own fantasy and discovery of her own body. The fact is, however, she made this discovery initially only in front of her father. His presence appears crucial and causative of her behavior. His wife had left him, he was lonely, quiet, needy, but unwilling or incapable of expressing himself in words. His only joy seemed to be the visit of his children. He suspended all other activities and friendships. Therefore it is most plausible to assume that Uwe did in fact elicit his daughter's reaction, but that both his message and his daughter's reaction were unconscious.

In sum, to become knowledgeable in way that approaches the truth of what really happened, to know the materiality behind the story, we must foreground what is communicated unconsciously, taking into account that which could not become material information for a court of law. This is true especially in cases of the sex abuse of children where the unspoken and sometimes unspeakable is crucial to accurate description. Such diverse psychoanalytic approaches as those of Melanie Klein and Jacques Lacan have maintained that most adult communication with children is unconscious, even more so when the children are very young. A great deal is learnt before children acquire language, and in that early phase of life children initially take over from adults their unconscious. Jean Laplanche (1999) developed this line of thought most fully, arguing that the adult's excitation is subject to "intromission" or "implantation" by the child, resulting in a "message" that in translation creates the child's unconscious—communication that does not depend on words.

Uwe claims that he became more nonverbal after his divorce. It follows that after his separation from his wife, his communication with his daughter and son also had come to be primarily nonverbal, meaning that he communicated largely by mood and look—his wan smile, his searching, pleading eyebrows. Lacking speech, he probably thought that his smile and his eyes were telling his daughter little about his inner state, which in any event was not transparent to him either. But rather than project into Uwe her own feelings, which, as a child, were highly susceptible to adult influence, she was more likely engaged in interpreting and translating his messages, however subdued and subtle in expression. She, the prescient child, in other words, understood his desire better than he himself did. She inferred from his nonverbal communication that the message was a desire for what he described to the therapists later as "something nice" (*etwas Nettes*). In short, neither Uwe nor his daughter was acting out of any conscious self-interest or stable drive or desire, nor were they, in those six months of transgression, the subjects of any authoritative discourse. They were acting out of understandings reached through an intersubjective process of largely unconscious communication.

What makes Uwe's case so unusual is that his offense seems to be due in part to an excess of empathy. Since the 1980s, most programs of treatment for sex offenders have included a component on empathy, based on the assumption that sex offenders lack empathic skills. They lack the capacity to know emotionally what the child is experiencing within the child's frame of reference. Therefore they are not easily convinced of having harmed a child when told that they use children for their own sexual pleasure, imposing on them an adult sexuality for which children are by nature unprepared. More recently, scholars have amended this assumption, arguing that sex offenders are not marked by the lack of empathy generally but by the lack of empathy for their particular victim only (Brown, Harkins, and Beech 2011, 15). Uwe's relation with his daughter does not appear to fit this model, yet because he seemed to encourage his daughter's sex play, his transgression was considered abuse.

From the daughter's point of view, was it the "sex" that was damaging or the social elaboration and interpretation of this sex as abuse? Uwe had in fact not engaged in physical abuse, which would have likely overwhelmed the senses of his daughter. Nor did he engage in deprivation or neglect, which would have starved those senses. The fact is, the daughter never seemed bothered by the evidence of her sex play, at least according to what the therapists who treated her told me, even after the scandal around the accusation of her father's abuse. Why the sex abuse did not result in symptoms may be in part a result of her father's empathy, which in turn led him to not overreact to her precocious sexuality. The same might be said for the early intervention in the child's behavior by the mother, the kindergarten teachers, and the therapists, whose empathic responses to what happened foreclosed the possibility that play might become abuse in her memory.

Nonetheless, the expert professionals—child psychologists, therapists, judge—all agreed that Uwe was motivated to ignore the potential harm he was inflicting on his daughter. Almost from the start of therapy, Uwe concurred about the question of harm, though he persisted in doubting that his motivations were sexual. The unknowability about whether Uwe was actually harming his daughter while he himself was sure of his nonsexual motives is probably what, I suspect, often drove Uwe to tears. Acting out of what he thought was empathy, he could not bear the thought that he had harmed his daughter. Even after therapy, he was left with a fundamental uncertainty about the consequences for his daughter of the sex play during her childhood. An explanation incorporating his unconscious motivations, as I attempt here, might have provided him a perspective from which to understand better his motive of distraction. But the therapists did not probe his action as part of an unconscious exchange with his daughter. Rather, they insisted that his explanation of "distraction" was merely a rationalization of a sexual motive that they ultimately were never able to clearly define.

Yet we should not lose sight of the goal in Uwe's therapy: to overcome his resistances and arrive at a transparency of self that would not tolerate his silences or possible self-deceptions. Therapy and the law approach Uwe's ignorance through a critical discourse of the self that is not merely confessional, not satisfied with a particular historical "truth of sex," but intent on finding out "what really happened." This critical discourse is also not primarily oriented to classification of sexual types but instead calls for Uwe to engage in a relentless revelation of what is most authentic in himself through an examination of his history and actions in their finest details.

As we have seen, empathy with his child was necessary for Uwe to arrive at an understanding of events. But empathic understanding finds its limits when he is asked to say no, to authorize an action that entails not a mimetic relation to the other but a negative judgment. Initially his inability to be sufficiently introspective, to more fully understand his function as parent, limited his ability to go beyond his self-understanding as a supportive, empathic, facilitating person. To become informed and knowledgeable required of him a reflexive interpretation of himself and his actions that worked through his own unconscious transference with his daughter. His interpretation should have broken with his own self-understanding of what being supportive and facilitating means. In this process he would have, to paraphrase his own words, become a father who says no, both to himself and his daughter.

Given the outcome of events, it is obviously too late for him to rectify his inaction now. Most important, however, is that from today's vantage point, what happened appears to have caused his daughter no harm. Yet the fact that his ex-wife moved to another city and, with the support of the social worker in charge of his case, removed his daughter and son totally from his care introduces another context into his daughter's memory of what happened. That removal may lead the daughter to assume she is the cause for the separation and thus guilty of betraying her father. In that case, the materiality of what happened will be transformed through memory into a different kind of abuse.

For contemporary critics of the family, the Oedipal dynamic assumes an illegitimate authority along with the father's guilt, making it difficult for them to understand the frequently compromised position of the mother and the agency of the child (cf. Bell 1993). For contemporary critics of the state and law, Uwe's case can serve as an important reminder that the threat of imprisonment through law does shadow the treatment, but the state in this case neither overreacts nor is entirely absent. Rather, the state seems to allow various social actors and institutions to work their way toward an understanding of the event and to reckon with the transgression without making the deed into an illegality. This enables the mother, the father, and the daughter to resist identification with an overdetermined event that might create the trauma they seek to contain.

FIVE

Seduction and Empathy

Seduction and Empathy

The thought of adult male seduction in child molestation brings into play the two contrary meanings of the word "seduction." Seduction can be the charm of making oneself attractive to others, or it can be the attempt to lead someone astray, intending to make someone act against his or her own will. The former values seduction as a skill, the latter condemns it as a threat. The two meanings are not fully separable yet rest in an uneasy and unresolvable tension. At present in the West, the ubiquity of the fear of child molestation leads to an emphasis on the second meaning—of luring, tempting, unfairly enticing. And this stands in opposition to the valorization of sexual self-determination, which since 1973 is also a European legal right, invoked and enforced to various degrees by different courts. Even early in life, the child is now assumed to have a self and therefore, as much as possible, should have a general right to determine what he or she does and what can be done to him or her without feeling threatened. In Germany and most of Europe, the right to positively assert sexual self-determination begins after fourteen.

Yet the condemnation of seduction is never without ambivalence, because, as I've argued in other chapters, following Jean Laplanche (1989), adult seduction of the child is enigmatic and necessary—how else does the adult keep the child's attention despite its growing autonomy needs? And child seduction of the adult is a necessary part of its humanization—how else does the child learn how to keep and attract the attention of others? Seduction is, moreover, closely connected to empathy, for successful seduction often relies on the ability to feel what the other feels. Empathic understanding, then, though generally considered a skill, may serve both ends of seduction: It may lead to the ability to charm, or it may lead to an exploitative enticement. It all depends on what use one makes of this understanding.

The asymmetry between child and adult places the child in a precarious and vulnerable relation, structurally in the position of not initiating or willingly participating in anything but of always being taken advantage of. Perhaps not "defenseless," but rarely able to defend him- or herself adequately against adult aggression, whatever its form, and at risk of being denied the ability to determine an emergent self. An adult already has physical and psychic defenses; elaborate ones at that, to defend itself from unwanted attentions and attachments. These defenses may be inadequate also, but they are not always so. Structural vulnerability is perhaps the major reason why the prototypical abuse is that of the child. Still today, in one place or another, one can hear attempts to defend sordid forms of horrendous abuse—racial discrimination, torture, rape, murder. Increasingly, though, no one defends child molestation. Even after the child has acquired the necessary skills to seduce the adult, it remains difficult for it to engage in abuse of adults. Structurally, it is assumed, a child cannot victimize. This perspective becomes less coherent, however, when it comes to adult relations with youths, or with those on the cusp of adolescence.

To be sure, adult seduction of youths, like that of children, can be oriented to sexual abusive. And empathy can be used to manipulate and to lead the child or youth "astray," to get the child to act against its interests if not against its will, as well as to understand and to sympathize. Youth empathy has not been much studied, but my own work with a group of youth offenders at KiZ suggests that empathy is a skill precisely *not* cultivated during adolescence. It is likely that children generally have more empathy than youths. Many studies confirm that especially children readily and unconsciously assume they are responsible for the misfortunes that befall their parents or siblings, even when these misfortunes are unspoken. Building on the foundational work of Melanie Klein ([1937] 1975), there is a huge literature dealing with children's guilt. Youths, by contrast, are not always troubled by guilt. They are entering into another kind of relation to others, one where mastery of the craft of seduction becomes most important not for the relation to parents but to join and develop peer groups. The awkwardness of their status and location in the social, the sudden changes in their bodies, the growing needs for approval and recognition, are all accentuated by the emergence of genital sexuality.

Consider this dynamic of seduction, empathy, and abuse today, in light of the increased agency given to or assumed by the child and the expansion of the category child into and often through adolescence. One way to make this shift in the agency of the child clear is to interpret the experience of abuse through the myth of Hansel and Gretel, perhaps the most widely read children's story that deals explicitly with seduction and the threat of abuse.

The following case of Reinhard's molestation of Olga begins an explication of this dynamic.

The Ritual Process

In 2007 Reinhard was sentenced to two years and three months on probation for the sexual abuse of a twelve-year-old girl. The judge then asked for a psychiatric evaluation, which is quite common following sentencing for the crime of sex abuse. In this case, the evaluation should help the judge to set the conditions of parole. The psychiatrist, after an interview of several hours, concluded that Reinhard was severely depressed, "dangerous, with a chronic *pädosexuelle Neigung* (orientation)," and that he suffered from a "personality disorder." He recommended commitment to the psychiatric ward of Berlin's maximum-security prison. The judge then asked a therapist from Kind im Zentrum, whom he had asked the advice of in a prior case, to conduct another evaluation. That therapist concluded that Reinhard was not dangerous and was also capable of therapy, and therefore should need neither be sent to a psychiatric ward nor incarcerated in a maximum-security prison. The judge followed the therapist's recommendation. Four weeks later I met Reinhard in therapy.

A lengthy ritual process that began with an accusation was now supposedly nearing its end: to assess the conditions necessary to determine the optimal conditions of psychic change. What might the justice system, acting in the name of a democratic state and in the interests of German society, compel Reinhard to do to effect a self-transformation? The expert knowledge of psychiatry, which, as we will see below, had in the past been used to abuse Reinhard, was again called on to aid in a legal decision. To be sure, psychiatry is a large field, with many different orientations. Another psychiatrist may have followed an alternative school of thought and reached conclusions more similar to the therapist, educated in an eclectic mix of psychological techniques. In fact, in the cases examined in this study, an almost equal number of psychologists—again, a diverse crowd—were asked to do psychological evaluations following sentencing.

In the case of Reinhard, however, this psychiatrist followed a categorical logic and language most characteristic of contemporary work in "forensic psychiatry": Reinhard was a category of person—"*der Pädosexuelle*"—who has a type of "personality disorder" that makes him "dangerous." The potential consequences of this disorder makes him a security risk for society and mandate a withdrawal of most of his freedoms along with compulsory psychiatric treatment in the psych ward of a maximum-security prison. In the end, the judge rejected this diagnosis and stipulated conditions for parole that allowed for maximum freedom and a treatment that would facilitate a less coercive self-transformation. The judge's decision here, to reject the advice of the highly qualified psychiatrist, should not be understood as either typical or usual. I did not encounter another case where a judge so directly rejected the recommendation of a psychiatrist, although I am told it has happened, if infrequently. What is typical is the framing of the problem and the kinds of ritual expertise judges have come to rely on to make decisions about sentencing, terms of incarceration, and parole.

From the start of therapy at KiZ to its end, Reinhard told a consistent story about what he had done to the girl, whom he called Olga, and about why he thought it was abuse. It happened only once, one night on a weekend, three years before the court sentenced him. His world was in order at the time; no specific problem or cause precipitated the abuse. But he knew immediately that it was wrong, he said, and on the way home that night, in a masochistic impulse, he took pills to numb himself, after which he was committed to psychiatric care. The psychiatrists at the time did not know of the events that led him to take the pills, and he did not tell them. They diagnosed and treated him for depression only. Only several years later did Olga make an accusation, bringing Reinhard's abuse to light, leading to his arrest and, in 2007, to a trial and conviction.

Reinhard's Past

Reinhard spent most of his childhood in an orphanage for boys, from the ages of seven to twenty. His parents had separated when he was six months old and sent him to a home for infants. After six years there, he returned to his father, who had remarried. His stepmother, he said, beat him regularly and forced him to work for her in the house. After a year, his father sent him to another orphanage. "The boy's home was the best time for me," he explains, "everything was structured, everything secure. But I didn't learn anything there, I didn't learn how you live outside the home."

He is now fifty-one years old and works as a specialist in care for the handicapped and elderly. He is tall with wide shoulders; his hair is tied up in a ponytail. In one of the first therapy sessions I attended, the therapists asked him what he wants from the group. "I see myself as a ghost, a pedophile, unlike others, unlike you," Reinhard says. "I want to take out of my experience here what I can do to help others. For two years I have prepared for this. I want to talk now. After 1989 [the opening of the Wall and collapse of the East German state], everything was all of a sudden speakable. I want to leave the [therapy] group more stable [than I am now], and I want to say, 'I am not the person that the psychiatrist said I am.' That is false. The evaluator had some personal problem with me, about what I did to him. Now I am ready to bring the time before 1990 into therapy, the eight years I sat in Bautzen."

Bautzen is the East German prison where most political prisoners were sent. By the time he entered group therapy at KiZ, Reinhard had become wary of all forms of psychological treatment because of his experience in that prison. About nine years before the Wall came down, he had attempted *Republikflucht* (the crime of flight from the republic) in the German Democratic Republic and was sentenced to serve his time in Bautzen. When the therapists at KiZ initially asked him how he relates his situation today to the time he spent in Bautzen, he became suddenly totally despondent, dropping his head and retreating into himself as if he needed every last ounce of energy to survive that particular moment of thought. The psychiatrists in prison had mistreated him, as is well known about psychiatric treatment of political prisoners in the former East Germany. For the first ten months of group therapy at KiZ, however, Reinhard would mention this mistreatment but then refuse to talk in any detail of his experience. In individual therapy, however, he had already revealed to a therapist that he had been raped many times while the guards looked on, after which they sent him to the psychiatric division of the prison. That therapist kept this information to himself until Reinhard indicated he wanted to discuss it with the group. "I began to live only in 1989," Reinhard says; 1989, the year the Wall came down, roughly coincided with his release from prison.

Seduction and Abuse

The night of the molestation, nearly three years before his sentencing, he was doing well, working twelve hours a day, "more than I wanted to," he says, "taking care of seventeen- to eighty-year-old handicapped people. I enjoyed it. I am the type who must always be working. I can't just lay on the beach." He was in a relationship with a woman he had met through a personal ad in the newspaper. Reliance on such public mating services greatly expanded during the 1990s, which was especially important in areas of the former East Germany. Friendship circles that had been an important part of the social fabric while living under an authoritarian regime with a large surveillance apparatus, and might have formerly opened some new networks, often fell apart. And many people took advantage of newfound freedoms following the dissolution of the authoritarian state, especially freedom of information and increased mobility to travel. His new partner seemed to complement him. But after three months together, she began having problems with her ex. And Reinhard felt as if he were shrinking as a person. His self-esteem plummeted, and he began to drink and to take antidepressants, which he obtained easily enough at work, to quiet him down—"to take away my consciousness," he explains. Nobody noticed, he said, as at that time the GDR was in a state of disintegration. This political chaos was accompanied by the dissolution of social controls, which facilitated a break up of friendship circles and, for him, a new anonymity in public life.

His partner assumed responsibility for everything at home and expected only that he be thankful. When she said, be home at eight o'clock, he was home at eight o'clock. They enjoyed being together, he says, and the sex was okay for the first two to three years, but she clamored for more love than he felt capable of giving. "I am very careful in such things," he says, "not so fast with love."

He stumbled on the child Olga through a friend whom he had met on a retreat to recover from his drug addiction. This friend, who is very shy, is attracted to obese women, and his neighbor, Olga's mother, is obese. He asked Reinhard, who is friendly and outgoing, to seduce her for him. Reinhard agreed without taking the time to think through the potential consequences, although he was not attracted to her.

"She is not my type," protests Reinhard, "but my friend convinced me to put the move on her, since he wasn't good at such things. Then I noticed she wanted something from me, not from him." Nonetheless, Reinhard's friend did manage to have sex with her a few times, but the relationship never went anywhere. He did not want to commit to her anyway, explains Reinhard. Suddenly, Reinhard found himself visiting a single mother and her two kids, little Olga and her older brother. He couldn't figure out how to extricate himself from the situation.

Reinhard noticed immediately that the family was very weak and needed his help, and this he found appealing. The mother was born in Westberlin but moved to the East shortly after the Wall came down because the social welfare payments were better there. On his visits, Reinhard played mostly with Olga, who was ten at the time. Although her brother was only fourteen, he chain-smoked in the apartment and seldom went to school. His mother did not seem to notice his truancy. And she did not object to his smoking since she smoked too. Even Olga smoked. The father lived in Westberlin and had no contact with them—and also paid no alimony.

Because of the mother's obesity, she had difficulty moving, so she rarely went out and did very little even in the apartment either, which Reinhard noted was filthy. The kids took advantage of her immobility and ignored her.

Reinhard told his partner, who had training in pedagogy, about the family. She offered to help out. The two of them spent an entire weekend together cleaning the family's apartment. After that, his partner said, never again. Undaunted, Reinhard continued his visits alone, and later even renovated the apartment.

After a year, his partner warned him that Olga also wanted something from him, that he should be careful. She always waited for him at the door, she called him often at his home, and when he went some place, she insisted on going along. She even got angry when he went anywhere without her. Yet he remained oblivious to how their relationship was developing, even though, he revealed in therapy, he had once before had a similar experience, assuming the care of a needy single mother with children in another city where he had lived. Only leaving that city fully extricated him from that particular family, although he still maintains contact with them.

"At first the mother slept on the sofa, and I in her bedroom," he says. "She wanted me to stay over every night, so I could make breakfast in the morning and she didn't have to do anything. Sometimes, if she had a guest, or wanted to stay up and watch television, which was nearly every night, she would say, you can sleep with Olga. So it became habitual, when I came, I'd sleep with Olga." Soon Olga became attached to him and increasingly jealous of any attention he gave to her brother or mother. She sent Reinhard love letters, saying she wanted to be with him all the time. He began to dream of some-how raising her that she would be with him permanently.

"What did Olga offer me?" asks Reinhard of himself. "She paid attention to me. She paid more attention to me than my partner did at the time. I suf-fered from an emotional deficit, and Olga was always there."

"It went on a long time without any sensual contact," he explains. "For about a year we only cuddled. I thought she was really neat. When she did something wrong, I wanted only to look away. For example, when she stole from me, cigarettes or money. I didn't scold her; I kept quiet, consciously. Olga is not my type, really. I have always dated women. But at another level I was thinking that the reciprocity will come. . . . Something began in my unconscious. . . . The weaknesses of the other meshed with my own weak-nesses. I would lay on my back, and she on my belly. I was not aroused, I felt good. It was nice, it was tenderness. After about nine months it developed into affectionate contact. She tried to feel under my T-shirt, I said no. [Yet] I enjoyed this. There was no longer any tenderness with my friend at the time."

"Nothing happened for about two years. Then I noticed I could stroke her in other places, on her genitals also. How was she? She was very still. I thought that it pleased her. Now I know that this wasn't true."

"Right after [the molestation], I fell asleep. But I knew that it was a punishable crime *immediately* after I did it. On the way home I took pills to numb myself. And then six months later, in psychiatric treatment, they heavily sedated me."

After Reinhard was released from the psychiatric institution two years later, his partner moved out. While in treatment there, he had told her about his relation with Olga. At that time, only she knew of his abuse and the story behind his attempt to sedate himself out of existence. Being abandoned and having no job led him to return briefly to the psychiatric hospital.

"When I came out again, I went to Olga," he said. He waited outside the apartment building and called her on the intercom. She came down to talk to him. "She stood there, and she was afraid! I knew what was up, that she had probably told her brother. I thought, what should I do now? I stayed. Then her brother came out with a friend to talk to me. We smoked together. Olga had told him that this man and that man had fondled her. I don't know what is true. He asked me [about what she had said]. We had been a team, and he would have believed me. I knew, as I stood there, that she was calling the police. They came after an hour, arrested me, put me in handcuffs." He was sent, again, to the psychiatric ward, this time in a prison. After his trial he was freed on probation, with the stipulation he enter and remain in therapy.

He met Olga once more while on probation, after the sentencing. "She told me that everything [about the relationship] pleased her up to that point. She had written love letters to me. I was also in need of love. I had photos, letters, all kinds of things I wanted to take with me into the trial, letters that we sent to each other, where I wrote I didn't want to be more intimate with her. But I didn't take them with me, I couldn't. So they sent me to the psychiatric ward. As a mature adult man, my thoughts were distorted. I thought I always wanted only the best for such families, but I wormed my way in. I chose socially weak families, and today I avoid my old group of friends and have built a new circle [of friends]."

Introspection

Therapists at KiZ periodically throughout and at the end of therapy ask the clients in their group to summarize their progress for others in the group. Where are they now in understanding themselves in their relation to the act of abuse? Reinhard now thinks it is no accident that he committed this crime. He need not have done it, he says, it was a calculated choice about which he was not fully conscious. "For me," he explains, "there was no resistance in the family. I gave Olga money. She had a poor family background, I had a poor family background. I wanted to make it better for her. With the value of hindsight, I know now that this motivated me. I never satisfied myself physically with her, though I cannot say how that would have worked out after another year. She wanted to come and live with me, she needed love. I thought that I would raise the girl. There was nobody in her family for her to turn to. And I gave her love. She became dependent, and I believed she would stay with me forever. Ultimately, it was about power. Children get from us something they do not get from their parents. They insist on this, in fact. And I projected my own deficits onto this child."

Reinhard goes on to explain that he feels incapable of having relationships with adult women. He concludes, it is my "fear of women who are equal to me. When I see women who are superior to me, I run." Since the sentencing, he has had only Platonic relations with women. At the start of therapy he had two girlfriends, one twenty-four, the other thirty-four, and within a month had developed a relation with a third. Unable to choose between the three, he ended all of them to avoid hurting someone. "I seek helpless women," he explains, "and when they aren't helpless any more, I run away. I have to be with someone who is needy. I always look for someone who has it worse off than me. Then I feel strong. But then the relationship inverts. In my last relationship she was really very needy, and for two years it went well, then it turned around. As someone from an orphanage, I don't know how to construct a relationship. I studied psychology to find out. I learned that it wasn't about others but about my own needs. I didn't want to show my flaws anymore."

"[Now] I have a new friendship circle. I broke with the last one. I sought families with deficits, because I feel good among them. I buy things, I cook. I once had a friend, whose parents were alcoholics, and I took a bottle of liquor with me whenever I visited them. I don't even drink! I hadn't learned how to distinguish between helping someone and my own interests. My new friends are not needy."

Do you have fantasies for children? asked the therapist.

"No, not for children. I fear fantasies of children," he replies tartly. When they run in front of you, what do you think? asks the therapist. "They have no meaning for me," replies Reinhard. He admits he is attracted to unblemished beauty, which he explains as compensation for his own imperfections and feelings of inferiority. Unlike some other men in the group who desire children because they are hairless, Reinhard likes hair. He points out that in the boy's home where he was raised, they were proud if they had hair on their bodies. Others were jealous of those who were the first to grow body hair. So he does not associate beauty with lack of body hair or with other signs of puberty.

Today, he says, he fears all relationships, he fears taking responsibility for them, for their gestalt. "I am addicted to harmony," he explains, "I run away, fast, when I am fed up. I close the door. I strategically avoid confrontations." While in his last year of therapy, Reinhard completed an advanced course in caring for physically handicapped individuals. The state paid for the first half of his training. He likes such work, and the patients, he says, like him, also, because he is patient and has the strength to deal with them physically. Given the very few men who do such work, he has highly valued skills. Employers seek him out.

In his final summary of his progress in therapy, Reinhard responded to the therapist's request to, once more, explain why he abused Olga, "It satisfied my lust, which I now have under control. I allowed my lust to drive me, I turned off my interior laws in a wave of lust. Perhaps in thirty years sex with a fourteen-year-old will be normal, as homosexuality is today. But the nature of affection and the boundary between affection and abuse is difficult to draw. [Olga and I] shared this, and at that moment you don't think about the act as criminal."

What does Reinhard mean, then, in declaring himself a pedophile? It does not surprise him that when he found himself in the presence of a pubescent, neglected, admiring young girl growing into womanhood, he would find her attractive and imagine the possibility of making this presence permanent, turning his bond with her into a family of his own making. His explanation of motives—driven by a "wave of lust," failure of "interior laws"—places the responsibility for the act fully on himself, while also placing the act in its contexts. He understands that he has to avoid a dynamic of repetition. In acquiescing to the pedophile label, he complies with legal and therapeutic demands to acknowledge that he overstepped a "boundary." Yet the expression of lust and the failure of interior laws is in tension with a self that is responsive and caring but also, as he says, "addicted to harmony." In all of this, the native's points-of-view that he offers largely replicates the regnant normative point of view of German society or the West. That normative point of view is replicated not only in Reinhard's accounting, but also in the views of the therapists and legal professionals who are to help and punish him, and in the lay majority viewpoint, which tends to judge and condemn him.

Reinhard has made this normative point of view internal to his own ethics, and he acknowledged having transgressed the norm almost immediately after the act. He in fact began punishing himself for this transgression two years before Olga's accusation, two years before the police arrested him. Nonetheless, to judge the wrongness of Reinhard's act of abuse, to make an ethical pronouncement, the normative framework of prohibitions or legal codes is insufficient. It is necessary to make an epistemological break from those norms and arrive at an analytically defensible interpretation of his transgression that does not replicate but nonetheless incorporates the various native's points-of-view. While Reinhard's introspection enables him to address fully the security concerns of society, his own violation was also about something else. That something else is his erotic interests, which are being awakened and redefined in a newly reconstrued Oedipal dynamic. We might understand this reconstrual through a retelling of the tale of Hansel and Gretel, which returns us to the question of seduction with which this chapter began: From where does the threat to the child come?

Hansel and Gretel Retold

The folktale *Hansel and Gretel* is the telling of an Oedipal drama: There is a father, a (step)mother, two children, and a witch who seduces the children, with cannibalistic intent, after they are abandoned by their parents. Hunger formally drives the story: Because the parents fear starvation, and the children eat too much, one night the mother proposes to send them deep into the forest with a loaf of bread, a plan the father opposes but relents to. The next day the parents take the children into the forest, but they find their way back. The following day they repeat the trip to the forest, and the children do indeed get lost this time, but eventually find a witch's house comprised of gingerbread and cakes. The witch offers them the house to eat, but then locks Hansel in an iron cage to fatten him up to eat and makes Gretel into her slave. When she tries to coax Gretel into the oven, the girl instead shoves the witch in. The witch burns; Gretel frees Hansel; the children discover a vase of treasure and precious stones and return home to live happily with their father (the mother has since died).

This story has been used as an archetype for a wide variety of child and familial dramas, from Henry James and Edgar Allan Poe in the United States to Nathalie Sarraute, Gottfried Keller, and Günter Grass in Europe, to name but a few authors, and it has been subject to consistent psychoanalytic readings. A cursory search of literature in the last quarter century alone finds that the tale is rich for many other perspectives: It has been used to interpret problems of Canadian adolescents, to train drama students in role playing, to dramatize the life of a woman with an alcoholic father, to name the dynamics of a cannibalistic fish population, to represent pictorially the "woman in the woods," to name an evolutionary adaptation syndrome, to frame survivor fantasies, to explain the relationship between economy and culture, and many more.

My question has to do with the framing of the Oedipal dynamic in the folktale, premised as it always is on a set of structural positions, or functions, and how Reinhard's case changes this framing. Freud interpreted the dynamic of Oedipus as a myth about the necessary functions surrounding the investment of libidinal energy. The "mother" and "father" in this account are functions, in the sense of different positions necessary to occupy in a structure. There is nothing natural about who specifically occupies these positions, but the psychic structure of human development demands that they be occupied. This occupation or relationship to objects Freud calls *Besetzung*. We grow up with a psychic representation of a central, motivated triangular constellation of child-parent relations that is necessary for development but by nature conflictual. In translating into English the German word *Besetzung*, James Strachey reverted to a Latin word, *cathexis*, to capture the wider range of meanings that *besetzen* has in German. One definition of *cathexis* in English is the emotional and mental aspects of investment of libidinal energy in the occupation of functions in these relationships.

According to classic psychoanalytic theory, the initial mother-child dyad—a unity in which the child sees him- or herself as part of or joined with the mother—is disturbed by the entrance of a father, who brings language and law to the child and creates the Oedipal dynamic. Without this disturbance, separation from the mother is more difficult, as there is no psychic demand of the child to work through his or her initial unity, or desire for unity, except perhaps in the imagination.[1]

Our theoretical focus must take into account a wider range of Oedipal-like dynamics but should remain on the triangular constellation of positions, meaning on how a third mediates every dyad, including the relations of mother-child, husband-wife, and child-parent. Functionally speaking, wherever there is an Oedipal dynamic, the father mediates the mother-child relation, the child mediates the husband-wife relation, and something outside the family mediates the child-parent relation. In the tale of Hansel and Gretel, the children's separation is from the parental unit, not only from the mother. They are already alienated from the mother and have only a strong emotional relation with the woodcutter, identified in the story as their father.

Separation is thus initially dramatized through the figure of the witch, who functions as a third in relation to the father-child bond of the Oedipal complex, or, one might say, the witch presents the possibility for a new triangulation. She does not fulfill her function, however, as the siblings form a pair to thwart her designs. Her attempt to mediate the relation of the children to their parents (or, more precisely, the father)—to enable a separation—fails, as she wants them for herself rather than merely wanting to redirect their libidinal investments. Moreover, she wants to ingest the children, to cannibalize them through an oral seduction (the trick of offering them to eat the gingerbread house she provides for their lodging). In other words, if separation for the children means annihilation, then they must return home.

Traditionally, the development of autonomy is linked to this separation; its management is to bring about a kind of autonomous self—an individual with a degree of self-security, open to new attachments, able to connect with and love others, rather than remain in the position of the child vis-à-vis the mother. In other words, the development of autonomy is to make difficult a regression to the function of infant or infantile. In *Hansel and Gretel*, however, the threat of hunger and cannibalism leads the children not to regress to the infantile but to bond with each other and to their own discovery of wealth. In the event, they return neither to the mother nor to the parents but to the father alone, and with wealth taken from the witch. This means, I assume, they are returning after having effected a separation. No longer really children, they have achieved some level of autonomy and can now make their own contribution to a larger social unit.

Reinhard also goes through a series of triangular constellations: He comes from a nuclear family, which he does not experience consciously as an infant; his mother and father abandon him at the age of six months to an orphanage with multiple caregivers, in what might initially appear to him as a non-Oedipal setting; he grows up in this orphanage run by social workers employed by the state; he returns briefly as a conscious child at the age of seven to a classic Oedipal dynamic, where the father seems to neglect him and the stepmother abuses him; he returns to a group home; he lives in a dyad with a woman; he enters into a single-mother family as a substitute father; and ultimately he lives alone. His self in these constellations is defined with reference to different functions in which he is placed.

In a later or an alternative version of the Grimm's *Hansel and Gretel*, a stepmother replaces the mother, I suspect to save the figure of the mother from a charge of abandonment; only the stepmother could be evil enough to be cruel. Or, in structural terms, the child's emotional ambiguity is affirmed in the tale by complementing the good (biological) mother with a bad (step)mother. In response to criticism after their initial publication, the Brothers Grimm edited and sanitized many of the tales they gathered;

they made darker, sinister versions into less dark and less sinister ones. For Reinhard, however, his first mother has already abandoned him. The function of the mother and father are negatively occupied; the stepmother only adds the element of physical abuse to his ordeal of a relation with a mother.

After a year with his father and stepmother, Reinhard is abandoned again and sent to another orphanage, also run by the state, where he experiences security and care in a group setting. The state, that is, for Reinhard assumes the function of parents. Most of the writing about experiences of the modern orphanage paints a consistently negative picture of these institutions, as if they are run by bad mothers or witches. The origin of such institutions can be traced to the fifteenth century in Germany, when the state began to assume responsibility for care of children abandoned by their parents. Reinhard depicts his experience of the orphanage as positive. For him, the institution was one of care, structure, and security, one that prepared him to love and care for others, which he subsequently learned as a profession and at which he now excels. On the other hand, he says, he did not "learn how you live outside the home," by which he means how to negotiate the complex Oedipal dynamics of separations. He did not learn how to make distinctions and create emotional boundaries between kin and nonkin, insiders and outsiders. In the orphanage, he was always only inside.

Reinhard's subsequent attempts as an adult to enter into dyadic relations with female partners fails in part because he has experienced caring only in an egalitarian boys environment, with state employees—professionally trained social workers—mediating the relations between the boys. To be sure, the boys had their own hierarchies, especially age hierarchies, independent of their caregivers, but, at least in his orphanage, the experience within the home was of a bunch of formally equal boys without girls. The atmosphere, as he describes it, was of mutual attunement to the needs of others, which facilitated the development of an empathic capacity. Reinhard explains that when he is not the one caring for his (female) partners, he senses that they are "superior" to him, and he is inadequately prepared to negotiate this inequality. Thus, while he has some childhood experience negotiating relations with men and not only boys, all of whom he came to know only within the institution of the orphanage, he was denied any comparable experience with women due to the abandonment by his mother and stepmother.

Parental abandonment followed by the collective environment of care created in Reinhard a strong internal voice of responsibility. It was this voice, and not a pedophilic desire, that he developed, making him relatively defenseless to the demands of others, especially women and young girls. Growing up outside the family seemed to have made him particularly vulnerable to appeal from members of broken families; he wants to repair the perverse aspects of their functioning. Inexperienced at the usual modes of deception in such families, Reinhard could understand himself only as inhabiting the location of the pedophile, condemning himself as such even before his arrest and suicide attempt. "I see myself as a ghost, a pedophile, unlike others, unlike you," he says to other members of the group, but he adds a caveat, "I want to say, I am not the person that the psychiatrist said I am." He openly identifies with the ascription and reconstructs a story of his desire for Olga that assimilates his experience to this identification. Yet his own sexual history reveals an entirely different person, a "ghost," a more complex person ("not the person that the psychiatrist said I am"), one with no pattern of abuse of any sort but with a primary sexual interest in adult women, specifically in women who allow him to assume responsibility for them.

He enters into a relation with Olga's mother not out of his own erotic interests but as a favor to a friend—similar to the favor of a brother (in fact he uses the word *Kumpel* in therapy, meaning buddy)—who asks him to seduce her for him. The mother has two children; their father has abandoned them. Lacking a husband and a father for her children, she places Reinhard in these functions, for which he is ill prepared. She appears to use the children, specifically her daughter Olga, to seduce Reinhard into caring for them. He interprets this family through the lens of his experience in the orphanage, as needing his care, which, of course, they actually do. In both the seduction of Olga's mother for a friend, and in the assumption of responsibility for Olga's family, Reinhard again shows the empathic capacity he learned in his childhood. After two years of caring for them, one evening he sexually abuses the daughter.

What in *Hansel and Gretel* was the threat of hunger and cannibalism now becomes the threat of genital sexuality and sex. An adult male who seduces children for sexual needs replaces a witch who seduces children for oral needs. Hansel and Gretel return home to live with their father, the woodcutter; the mother who had sent them into the forest is now dead. Olga and her brother, by contrast, reject the (substitute) father to return to, as they now consider him a sexual threat. They have not yet separated from their mother, perhaps because their attachment does not appear to ever have been strong. In the rejection of Reinhard or another husband/father-substitute, and in the neglect they experience from their mother, Olga and her brother appear to be on their own, though there is some evidence that they have a bond with each other.

From the perspective of Olga and her brother, then, the Oedipal dynamic looks quite different than it has been represented in early modern European folktales. As folklorists and anthropologists began to reexamine these tales in the 1970s, they remained consistent in their interpretations to the spirit of early modern Europe (Mallet 1984; Schumann 1972). Despite quite radical changes in family and political structures since the origin of these tales, there has been little inquiry into how these might have affected the Oedipal dynamic or the psychic apparatus (cf. Loewald 1980). The psychoanalyst Bruno Bettelheim ([1976] 2010, 162), for example, had depicted *Hansel and Gretel* as a tale about "the destructive aspects of orality." Today, however, orality seems to be of little concern; one would instead talk of the destructive aspects of sexuality. Bettelheim argued that the father is merely a "shadowy figure," while the mother is "all-important," ignoring the significance of the children's ultimate return to live happily with the father, not the mother (160). Olga and her brother, by contrast, seem quite autonomous. They appear to make few demands of their mother, nor does she make any of them. The fact that they do not leave their mother has little to do with emotional dependence; more likely, it is a household arrangement supported by the state. Their actual father was not even a shadow—he was never present. Moreover, when a substitute father, Reinhard, appears, they cooperate to send him to prison. Thus, the story is no longer of the type, as the folklorist Alan Dundes (1992, 167) has it, where a "girl outwit[s] a 'bad mother' figure." In this contemporary translation, the girl outwits both her mother and a father substitute.

Finally, while Hansel and Gretel in the nineteenth-century version of the tale are rewarded with precious stones and a return to the father for inflicting on the witch (pushed into the oven and burned) the murder she had planned for them, Olga and her brother in the twenty-first century achieve justice by abnegating the authority over them of all father figures. This justice, achieved by the state on behalf of children, may not have actually been their conscious goal, and it comes at a cost: Olga and her brother return to a relation of mutual neglect with their mother. This is not to say that what Reinhard did to Olga was right or proper or ethical. He did wrong Olga, transgressing the social boundaries intended to regulate intimacy with children and protect them from adults. Nonetheless, Reinhard was perhaps the only person at the time to take an actual interest in caring for Olga and her brother.

The child Olga herself has ambiguous and changing interests: a premature sexuality, introjected from the messages of her mother and her substitute father, Reinhard, and no doubt from messages of her peers and of a very sexualized adolescent popular culture. Olga, the child, obviously fell for

Reinhard. She finds in him an adult man from whom she can learn the art of seduction, on whom she in turn can practice that art. This is necessary to obtain the love and adult care that her mother appears unable to give her. She indeed obtains some of this love and the care that she needs from Reinhard.

Ultimately, however, Olga becomes the love object of an adult male with a genital sexuality; she enters into a relationship that we today define as likely to result in child sex abuse. After two years he shows her this sexuality, practices it on her. It is abuse because we assume that she cannot understand what message he is conveying; her experience is categorically defined as overstimulation. Unprepared to leave the domain of fantasy, Olga's experience remains latent—not brought fully into discourse, only hinted at to the brother. Yet a year later, in an encounter with Reinhard, it overwhelms her with fear. She calls the police and brings in the law of the state. Olga's call illustrates a certain direction in European law, in which the "right of sexual self-determination," formulated in part to protect the privacy of the adult practice of sexuality from state or social interference, is increasingly invoked to protect the child or youth from a sexual experience with older youths or adults. Olga at twelve is on the cusp of adolescent, no longer the child of ten whom she was when she met Reinhard but not yet an adult legally capable of making her own decisions. Yet, even though she is incapable legally of consent, she no longer requires the mediation of an adult woman or man to become the agent of the law. She makes the call to the police all by herself, uncounseled by brother, mother, or friends. Lacking a parent to fill the classic function of the father, she herself becomes—belatedly, after the violation but perhaps before much psychic harm (of this we are uncertain)—the guarantor of the incest taboo and all the extensions of this taboo.

SIX

New Germans

Citizens with a Migration Background

In 2005, the Federal Office of Statistics in Germany replaced the category *Ausländer* (foreigner/without German citizenship) with a more inclusive one, *Staatsbürger mit Migrationshintergrund* (citizens with a migration background). Of the 80.4 million legal residents in Germany in 2011, 19.5 percent had such backgrounds. Germany, in fact, has the third-highest number of international migrants worldwide. Of those with migration backgrounds, 7.9 percent are foreigners, the rest largely children born in Germany to non-German citizens, children with one foreign-born parent, or children born outside Germany to Germans with foreign citizenship who then migrated to Germany.

One of the many criticisms of this more inclusive category is that it risks forever making migrants and their descendants a marked category; they can be depicted as bearing the stigma of migration over an infinite number of generations. Along these lines, in 2013, Alice Bota, Khuê Pham und Özlem Topçu—three young journalists who write for the important weekly *Die Zeit*, proposed that we simply call them "new Germans." I borrow their self-ascription for the title of this chapter. The assertion of the new Germans of a right to name oneself expresses the spirit of the times. But the advantage of the statistical category is that it does not mirror how people wish others to see them but instead emphasizes a historical perspective on German if not European reality: Irrespective of the land of origin, the descendants of migrants share in the histories of cultural displacement of their genitors, without always being able to identify what exactly they have inherited. This inheritance is what Jacques Lacan referred to as *le nom du père* (the name of the father), a concept I will query throughout this chapter.[1] By this he meant that a third party is necessary to break the exclusive relation between mother and child and enable entrance into the symbolic order of desire. In the case of migrants to Germany, the question is what the inheritance of the name of the father means for them, and to what extent they must distance themselves from the father to enter the symbolic order of desire of Germany.

The overwhelming majority of cases of child sex abuse that enter the ritual process—from accusation to therapy, punishment, rehabilitation, and social reintegration—involve native Germans. Few residents with migration backgrounds accused of molestation ever make it to group therapy, and thus never make it to rehabilitation. First-generation migrants often lack the German language competency necessary to reflect on their experiences in such a group. Also, families with migration backgrounds are under more social pressure to hold together, giving the taboo of child abuse greater force and leading to more underreporting of cases of abuse. Therapists, however, have told me of many isolated cases of such abuse, most of which have been handled in individual therapy. I was unable to observe individual therapy sessions, but I took notes whenever someone talked of cases of residents with migration backgrounds.

Because I have also conducted ethnographic work on relations between fathers and sons in Syria and Lebanon, I am particularly interested in what happens to men from these cultural backgrounds when accused of child abuse (Borneman 2007). Arab men do not represent all migrants, but they highlight certain aspects of paternal inheritance that characterizes migrant families generally. The following case of a Syrian man who is a legal resident of Germany and whose children are German citizens came to my attention during fieldwork, and I followed closely the therapist's perspective as he experienced the unfolding of the case. Unlike in the other chapters, I have only a description of the facts, which is not mine but a summary of different versions I was told over time, some transcribed from recordings. This case, therefore, is not reflexively written as are the others because I had no personal encounter with what is described; I observed nothing myself. To protect the anonymity of all involved, I did not make any direct contact with either the accused and his children or the other therapists, social workers, and judge involved in the case.

Suleyman's Abuse

A Syrian man in his mid-forties, whom I will call Suleyman, entered court-ordered therapy in October. He and his wife had moved from Damascus, Syria, to Berlin (actually when it was called West Berlin), in the mid-1980s. In Berlin his wife gave birth to six children, who all obtained German citizenship either subsequent to the amendment of the Nationality Act in 2000 that grants citizenship by place of birth or, for the older ones, through a separate petition to the Federal Foreign Office. The children grew up speaking Arabic at home, German in school and with friends. As is true of most migrant families, then, the children early on had better linguistic skills than their parents, who in fact learned much of their German from their children. That the father does not represent language for the child challenges one of Lacan's fundamental assumptions. He argued that the father brings to the mother-child dyad language and the law. Language for Lacan is always a form of castration, as it comes from outside, belongs to the social, and never really belongs to its speaker; and submission is essential because without language one lacks the primary means of self-articulation to enter society and become social. In Suleyman's case, the father's authority is not propped onto language and the law but severely challenged by both, which are foreign to him and to which he also must submit. His submission to German, unlike to Arabic, he experiences consciously as an adult, making him more aware of his lack. Over the years the parents kept in close contact with their kin in Syria, the entire family returning yearly for visits.

In August Suleyman's twenty-three-year-old daughter accused him of sex abuse. Together with her two siblings—a sister aged twelve and brother aged eighteen—she lodged a complaint with the Juvenile Authorities (JA). The children reported that they feared their father's abuse. He had, they said, molested his oldest daughter and he was abusive at home—striking the son, forbidding the younger daughter to play handball. Earlier in the year, the oldest daughter had broken her leg. The bandage on the leg made it itch, so she asked Suleyman to massage it. She claimed that her father was sexually aroused (*erregt*) by the massage, and his hand went too near (*zu hoch*) to her vagina. The JA contacted Suleyman, who denied the charges of molestation. Nonetheless, as required by German law, the agency immediately removed the children from his care and placed them in different group homes, cooperative apartments (*Wohngemeinschaften*) monitored by resident social workers for children and youths with problems.

After several meetings with Suleyman, the social worker in charge of the case, who had migrated to Berlin from the Czech Republic about the same time as Suleyman and his wife had done so from Syria, called a therapist, who I will call Martin, to ask whether he would accept Suleyman in therapy. She sent Martin a report summarizing the charges, signed by her and her superior, both of whom have known and worked with him on other cases over the years. And she informed him in a telephone conversation that Suleyman was very concerned about his children and wanted them back. He had appeared on time to each appointment the JA scheduled. He was very unhappy now, she said, as he considered himself a good father who was no longer able to take care of his children. For Suleyman, the ability to care for his children was of utmost significance, at the very core of his definition of being a man.

Suleyman undoubtedly experienced all of this as strange and new. In Syria children would never even think of going to some state authority to accuse a parent of abuse. Children are taught to respect and honor their parents, irrespective of how they are actually treated by them. Matters such as abuse are addressed informally within families or kin networks, if at all. Occasionally advice may be sought from religious authorities (e.g., Christian, Druze, Alewite, or Muslim). Fathers still have tremendous authority over their young children. Attachment to mothers is very strong and lifelong. In the event of divorce, women obtain custody over their children rarely, and only when the husband agrees to yield it (Borneman 2007).

Martin called Suleyman to set up an appointment for September, but Suleyman did not show up. Martin then called him again, and Suleyman explained that he had been sick. (Later, however, he revealed to Martin that he was absent because he did not know where to go to meet him.) They agreed to another appointment for October, and that meeting went as planned. Martin had four subsequent individual therapy sessions with him.

In the first session, Martin did not question the veracity of the accusation but merely tried to clarify the charges against Suleyman and determine whether he could work with him as a therapist. The written document from the JA that Martin received did not state that Suleyman had been accused of child abuse. He was accused of "molestation of his oldest daughter," a charge that he denied. The word "incest" appears nowhere. Because the oldest daughter is no longer a minor, I was surprised that the case did not fall under the jurisdiction of a regular adult court. That was because the younger daughter, who was underage and therefore still lived with her father in his apartment, was also pressing charges. The JA was charged to intervene on her behalf and in the interests of the family unit. The report by the three children of their father's abusive behavior seemed to imply that the younger girl was also at risk for sex abuse, like her older sister.

Martin asked Suleyman about the massage and the charge of abuse. He granted that he had hit his son but vehemently denied the charge of molestation. He did massage her daughter's leg, yes, he admitted, but correctly. Martin then explained to him that the charge of sex abuse means, minimally, that the adult man is sexually aroused in the interaction. Suleyman appeared pleased by this definition, which he had not heard before. He insisted that he was definitely not aroused as he massaged his daughter's leg.

He then added, *"Sie ist aber ganz schön dick!"* (But she is really quite fat!), as if being overweight made her unattractive for sex, additional evidence that he would not want to molest her.

For Suleyman the idea of arousal (*erregt*) is open to an interpretation that differs from what a German therapist might think. When sitting in public drinking tea or coffee, men from lower middle classes in Syria often keep themselves in a state of arousal by holding or even massaging their penis. There is no embarrassment in this, no sense of exhibitionism as there would be in Europe. Through crude jokes referring to the penis men will often bring this arousal into language, with an explicit agreement among them that one is not talking about a real event but just joking. To insist on reference to reality would risk insult and anger among the men. On the other hand, the arousal of "sex" is usually restricted to an excitement referencing what adult men and women do in bed, sexual intercourse. Pious Muslims also associate sex with reproduction.

When Martin asked Suleyman what he did for "sex," Suleyman said that he had none since his wife left him. She had betrayed him with his best friend and announced this in front of their six children. In Syria the wife's claim that her husband is not sleeping with her can be used to effect a divorce. Claims of being unsatisfied in sex are of another order, and although the wife has a claim on satisfaction also, it is often assumed that her satisfaction is contingent on being able to satisfy her husband. A revelation of betrayal such as Suleyman's wife made might lead a husband in Syria to murder his wife, and the community in which the couple lives might well think this is justified. In Germany, however, there is a very public and disapproving discourse on "honor killings." In public discussions and in the media they are often used to assert an essential difference between Muslims and Christians, and to claim the impossibility of integration of Muslims into "Christian Europe." In post-unification Germany, there have been a number of widely publicized trials of fathers and brothers for honor killings. Suleyman and his wife surely were not ignorant of this publicity, which likely emboldened the wife to make her announcement of a sexual affair openly, before the children, without fearing her husband's wrath. In addition, after several decades living in Berlin, she might have been influenced by the post-1970s European discourse that asserts women have a right to satisfaction in sex.

Suleyman did not react to his wife's announcement with wrath, however, but instead agreed to a separation. That must have humiliated (*demütigt*) you, sympathized Martin. Suleyman found that the concept *demütigen* (to humiliate) described precisely his experience, and he immediately incorporated the word in his own reflections on the affair his wife had with his best friend. Sometime in the spring of 2011 she returned to Damascus with the three youngest children to live with her parents. The three older ones did not want to return with her and thus remained with their father. The uprising in Syria against the authoritarian regime of Hafez al-Assad, which began in mid-March 2011, had not yet spread to Damascus at the time of her return. However, by December of that year the fighting had spread there also, eventually turning the peaceful uprising into a full-scale civil war, killing more than 190,000 and creating more than a million refugees. Having severed ties with her husband, the wife had little choice but to suffer through the war with her three youngest children in Damascus.

"You are still young," Martin addressed Suleyman, "aren't you still sexually active?" "No," responded Suleyman as he squirmed in his chair. "I have had sex only with my wife." The word "sex" alone, Martin told me, made Suleyman uncomfortable. "I have had no sex since my wife left me," Suleyman repeated. "Did you try visiting a prostitute?" asked Martin. "No, no, no," repeated Suleyman, and then sat silently. Several other approaches to the same question resulted in simple responses of "no."

"Well then," said Martin, standing up as if preparing to leave, "if you refuse to talk with me about this, I have nothing more to say. I know it is difficult to open up about this. If you don't talk, however, then there is no way I can help you." For the therapist, Suleyman's unwillingness to discuss the nature of his desire, associations, and fantasies would make treatment impossible.

With this threat and promise, Suleyman relented some and began very slowly to talk about his circumstances. Sexually, he thought only about his wife, he repeated. No other women came into the picture. But when she told you of her betrayal, before your children, after she dishonored you, asked Martin, didn't that have an effect on your erotic feelings for her? Suleyman began to sweat heavily, "No," he said. "I am a good Muslim. I go to the Mosque every Friday."

In the next two sessions, Martin tried further to coax Suleyman into talking of his fantasies. How do you live your sexuality? he asked, repeatedly. "In every fifth sentence," explained Martin to me, Suleyman would reiterate a religious conviction. Such convictions seemed, for Suleyman, to take the place of a description of his sexual desire. Most frequently, he answered Martin by saying "no," or "I go the Mosque." When Martin twice suggested appointments for therapy on a Friday, when he had an opening, for example, Suleyman replied, "On Friday, I go to the Mosque."

Toward the end of the third session, Martin exclaimed, "I don't believe you. You are a man, you are alone. You must have some kind of fantasy. When you see a beautiful woman on the street, do you have no fantasies about her? "No, no, no," was Suleyman's response. Have you ever looked at pornography? "No," said Suleyman. Not even on television? asked Martin. "No," he replied again.

In the fourth session, Martin asked, How about when you sleep, do you wake up aroused? Yes, Suleyman confessed to this. Do you masturbate? Suleyman also hesitantly admitted to this, without using the word. But when Martin asked, again, about the specific images he had in his head, Suleyman returned to a fantasy of his wife. Perhaps you are interested in men, said Martin, assuring Suleyman that their conversation was private and that no possible response could offend him. Martin actually meant the question ironically, hoping to provoke Suleyman into some lightness or humor. But here, too, Suleyman held firm in his defense of whatever images constituted his interior self and responded with an adamant, "no, no, no."

Despite what seemed to be a reticence to reveal anything intimate about himself or to reflect on the nature of his desire, Martin felt the sessions were going well. Suleyman's trust in him seemed to be growing. He was making an effort to be introspective, even if the results as yet seemed meager. Martin began to feel he had interacted enough to assess the situation and Suleyman's range of motives. He also began to have serious doubts about the veracity of the daughter's accusation of sex abuse.

In December the JA scheduled a meeting, to be attended by Suleyman, Martin, and the social worker and her superior, to assess the results of the therapy and the status of the complaint. Martin showed up and found only the social worker in attendance. Her superior had called in sick, and she then called Suleyman to tell him not to come, but she could not reach Martin because she did not have his cellphone number. Martin used the time to confer with the social worker about developments in the case. She told him that the children were not happy in their different group homes. The oldest daughter was living in her own apartment. The younger daughter was lonely and missed home. The son, in particular, was not doing well. He neither attended school nor worked, so he had nothing to do. The social workers responsible for him in the home characterized him as "very undisciplined" and "leading an asocial life." He did not listen to them, and they reported that it was impossible for them to monitor him. They called Suleyman, who attributed his son's behavior both to not wanting to work, generally, but also to hanging out with the wrong crowd (*schlechte Kumpels*). After this exchange, both Martin and the social worker expressed grave doubts about the charge of molestation itself.

This suspicion was confirmed the end of January, when the children appeared again before the JA and asked to withdraw their complaint. The social worker there called Martin to inform him of this request. Based on the separate statements of the therapist (Martin), the son, the father, the oldest daughter, and the social worker, the JA could now submit a petition to the judge in charge to cancel the proceedings. However, the judge nonetheless had first to order a psychological evaluation of the daughter's credibility. Now, said the judge, it became important to check also whether the withdrawal of the complaint was not a result of pressure on the children by the father. If the psychological evaluation determined that the children were not coerced into changing their story, all that remained of the complaint was to reinstate the custody of the father, which the children now indicated they wanted. However, the JA could not automatically restore his *Erziehungsrecht* (custody/education rights) until the judge in charge of the case made a determination that the father was "capable of raising the children" (*erziehungsfähig*). In short, the charge of molestation could not be automatically dismissed without first carrying through on the process to determine its veracity. The children, therefore, were to remain in their group homes until these issues were settled.

The son then informed the social worker that he had already, without their approval, moved back into his father's apartment. He said that he no longer feared his physical abuse. Now that he again lived with his father, he was even assisting him at his work, an auto repair garage run by Turks. Since the father was accused of molestation of a female and not a male, the JA relented to the son's decision to return to his father without court approval, as there were no grounds for suspicion that the father might sexually abuse him.

Martin had another appointment with Suleyman scheduled for the end of February, and, given the course of events, Martin thought it would be the penultimate appointment. To Martin's surprise, Suleyman arrived with his son. They entered the therapy room and sat down. The son sat with his legs crossed and turned away from Martin. Martin asked what he could do for him. He wanted Martin to put in writing that his father had never molested his sister. That evidence, he thought, was necessary to reinstate the father's custody, which the children wanted. He and his sisters agreed that the group homes were far worse for them than living with the father.

Martin explained that he unfortunately could not provide this written statement, but it was perhaps ultimately unnecessary. A final meeting with the JA, he explained, was what they needed. Up to this time, Martin and Suleyman had always communicated in German. Suleyman is competent enough to converse fluently, as long as Martin does not resort to technical terms. But here some of the issues were legal and technical, so Martin frequently asked the son to translate some of his remarks into Arabic for his father's sake, which he did.

Were the charges fabricated? Martin asked the son. He said yes. What were his motives for agreeing to this accusation against his father? Martin asked. The son explained that after his mother left for Damascus, his father became stricter at home, hitting him when he would return in the evening from meeting his friends an hour or more after the time he had agreed to return. And the motives of your siblings? asked Martin. The son explained that his younger sister was forbidden to wear certain clothes, in addition to not being allowed to play handball. The oldest sister had a German boyfriend, and she was forbidden to see him. They all resented these controls and wanted to escape what they considered unnecessary discipline.

Martin then turned to the father. He explained that since the children had grown up in Germany, they behaved as other children in Germany behave. If every father hit his son for returning home an hour later than planned, there would be loud (*Knallen*) explosions overall in Berlin. The son found this statement amusing, and his attitude toward Martin began to change. From the start of the session he had watched Martin closely and suspiciously. Now he began to identify with Martin, and with his authority. Being more than twenty years older than his father, Martin was positioned as a grandfather to the son. Grandfathers in Syria exert authority over their sons, often to the benefit of the grandson. Aware now that Martin was no longer on the side of his father, specifically of his father's disciplinary function, he opened up some about the actual relations he had had with his father at home. He made no further mention of his mother or her absence. He played down his father's physical abuse, dismissing it as not that severe. Even though Martin encouraged him to express what kind of restrictions he thought would be fair for his father to place on him and his siblings, the son refrained from repeating his complaint. And he began to translate Martin's statements to his father without being asked to.

As for the father's treatment of his daughters, Martin was also clear. He admonished Suleyman: They should be free, as are German girls, to date the boys they know from school or work. He asked, What would you rather have for your daughter, a German boyfriend who works or an Arab boyfriend who does not? Of course, Suleyman responded, a German boyfriend who works.

Martin then asked the two men how they evaluated the actions of the JA in their case. Did the JA act against the interests of the family? Suleyman did not respond, but his son said yes and questioned the agency's authority over him and his family. Martin explained that the JA in Germany acts as the law compels it to. They, the three children, had made an accusation of molestation against their father, which the JA was required by law to act on. It acted in the interests of the son and his sisters throughout, Martin asserted, and ultimately the father had suffered needlessly not because of the JA but because of the false accusations of his children. The father nodded agreement; the son listened without expression.

The admonishments of the therapist here appear to overstep the mandate of therapy. Narrowly conceived, the therapist is asked only to elicit the self-understandings of his clients and help them reckon with the self thus revealed. Yet, in working with the JA, the therapist must modify his mandate. To uncover the self-understandings was insufficient; he must also ascertain whether they are true. And then he must also mediate those understandings so as to enable the youths involved to live within the law in Germany. In this mediation, the therapist approximates the goal of rehabilitation, working to reintegrate someone set aside from the social back into society. But rehabilitation of whom? In this case, the JA was not dealing with a crime committed by youths but one against them. When confronted with a charge of child sex abuse, the JA's primary responsibility is to protect the child from this abuse. If any rehabilitation is asked for, then, it is not of the children but of the father who is suspected of abuse. But here the son and his siblings were also in need, or so thought the therapist, of a different understanding of their relation to the social. Any transformation of the self, which might be a later goal, has as its prerequisite a better understanding of the relation to the social environment.

Once the therapist uncovered the truth in this relationship between father and son, he took up his second task, which was to clarify to the son and father that the JA was not acting against their interests and that they were being treated the same as any German citizen. This clarification is especially important given the complexity of German rules and regulations and the lack of transparency of German society and bureaucracy to citizens with migration backgrounds. Very often families of citizens with migration backgrounds are not privy to the implicit knowledge one learns by being an insider to this society over time.

By contrast, not knowing why something occurs at the level of the state and its institutions is part and parcel of life in Syria. The authoritarian state in which Suleyman and his wife grew up used the arbitrariness of rules to establish authority. People expected little transparency of rules and laws. The state established its authority over its citizens in part by withholding and giving arbitrarily, a condition conducive to paranoia and thinking in terms of conspiracies. The therapist in this case took note of the son's skepticism that the JA acted in his interests and those of his siblings. In fact, the JA and those it employed, not only the therapist, went out of its way to determine what those interests were and to reconcile them with German law.

As this session with the father and son drew to a close, at 13:55, Suleyman asked whether they could return around 16:00 to get a paper signed. Martin said yes, but warned them to be punctual; he had another appointment that began at 16:00 promptly. The current session, he added, would have been fifteen minutes longer if they had arrived on time. The son then asked Martin for his telephone number, so he might call him and return if he has some personal problems. Martin gave him the number of the office.

Suleyman returned alone that afternoon, but fifteen minutes late. Martin had to leave a therapy session in progress to sign the form. Suleyman immediately apologized, however, noting that he was late.

The appointment before the judge of the family court to determine whether Suleyman is *erziehungsfähig* (capable of raising his children) was delayed for two weeks. Martin called Suleyman at his work to inform him of this and to remind him that there had to be a final discussion between Suleyman, the therapist, and the social worker before this court date. Suleyman's son answered the call—his cellphone was now also in the hands of his son—and agreed to tell his father.

On March 21 Martin arranged a meeting with the three children, their father, and two representatives from the JA. Shortly before the meeting, they had heard from another therapist that the younger daughter was not feeling well because she sensed that her two older siblings were making her carry the major responsibility for their family dilemma. The two women from the JA arrived for the meeting and informed Martin that they had forgotten to invite the oldest daughter. Only the younger daughter showed up. Suleyman arrived and said that his son was taking a special course in a school and therefore could not come (a surprise for Martin, as the son had previously dropped out of school). Suleyman had not seen his daughter for nearly a year. She cried and hugged him.

Then the women from the JA began talking to the younger daughter about her sense of guilt. It was she, they said, who had lodged the initial complaint against her father for sex abuse—but at the insistence of her older sister. This was new to Martin, who had always assumed in his discussions with Suleyman that it was the accusation of sex abuse of the eldest daughter that resulted in the denial of custody of his children. In fact, from the start it was a double claim of abuse: that the eldest daughter had been molested while the father massaged her leg and that the younger daughter had been sexually abused (triple abuse if one accepted the son's charge of physical abuse). Suleyman apparently had felt so embarrassed about the sex abuse claim of the younger daughter that he never mentioned it in therapy sessions. The eldest daughter reinforced the gravity of the charges by stating, in her initial report to the JA, that if the two younger children remained with their father, her younger sister was in danger of being further sexually abused.

Unbeknownst to Suleyman or his therapist, the younger daughter had been in treatment with another therapist. In these sessions, she revealed how horribly guilty she felt, as if she bore the responsibility for her father's ordeal. The daughter's therapist reported this to the social worker at the JA. The representatives of the JA and the two therapists (one for the father, one for the younger daughter) then suggested another meeting, this time with the entire family, before they would ask the judge to reinstate Suleyman's legal custody over his children. Meanwhile Martin gave to Suleyman a bulletin, which an assistant had alerted him to, issued by a private association (*Verein*) in the district of Neuköln-Berlin, where Suleyman lived, which advises immigrants on problems of integration in German culture. One of the association's activities is to organize groups of immigrant parents of Turkish and Arabic backgrounds to come together to discuss problems they have raising their children in German culture. Martin suggested Suleyman attend such a group, and he readily agreed to do so.

The final appointment of Suleyman's therapist, his younger daughter's therapist, and the social workers was cancelled three times because the daughter's therapist forgot to schedule it; she was busy doing something else; and she was on vacation. Nine months after the charges were withdrawn, the family members met together with the therapists and social workers and recommended to the court that the family be reunited. At that time, the younger daughter was permitted to return and live with her father.

Le nom du père

Once the mother departed for Syria, the three oldest children were left in a relationship to a father formally in charge of their care but who had little authority. We do not have enough detail to understand the meaning of the mother's absence. We do know, however, that the father is asked to replace her caregiving function, but he appears to overcompensate for his inadequacies in her absence by increasing his disciplinary functions. And he attempts to enforce submission to the rules not of German society but of what he remembers as a Syrian symbolic order. It is highly unlikely that the children approved of their mother's affair with Suleyman's best friend, but her admission of this affair in front of her children made them complicitous in disempowering him. In their eyes and in his own, he had become less of a man, a cuckhold. They watched his humiliation. His ineffectuality in the face of such a serious admission no doubt resulted also in a loss of respect in the eyes of his children.

Migration had already changed the conditions of what the father stood for. The move to Germany imposed a new symbolic order on the family, a new language and new laws; the move set the stage for the first disempowerment of the father. In this new milieu, the parents had to renegotiate Syrian rules—of gender, sex, patriarchy, marriage—in light of the language and law of Germany. Neither parent was in a position to help much in this negotiation; that task was largely one for the schools and, ultimately, the JA— both institutions of the German state. In light of their experience in German schools with German children and German teachers, where the authority of the father had been severely undermined through the losses of two world wars and an occupation of a half century, the children found whatever disciplinary functions Suleyman had retained after the move irrelevant, if not oppressive (Borneman 2011, 2004, 1992). The younger daughter wanted to do sports, the son wanted to stay out late with friends, the oldest daughter wanted a German boyfriend of her choosing. Suleyman appeared relatively unprepared for these desires, awakened through the German context, though when the therapist suggested he had to adjust to them he was able to acknowledge the needs of his children.

Suleyman's children accused him of not exercising the "no" of the incest taboo that he is charged with enforcing, what Lacan calls the *non du père* (the no of the father). As in the case of Olga and her brother in chapter 5, the children themselves become the enforcers of the taboo and turn this "no" back onto the father or, in the case of Olga, onto the father substitute. In this accusation, they are both completing the mother's castration of their father and also becoming new Germans, for which separation from the father is also a demand (Borneman 1992). Suleyman's children appear to know that the accusation of physical abuse in German society is insufficient; molestation is the only charge that can guarantee their freedom. As Tarek El-Ariss (2007, 96) writes about what has become a very popular self-representation among Arab women seeking protection or recognition in the West, "by denouncing and exposing [the] father's abuse, she strategically lays the grounds for 'denouncing and bearing witness against' that which underlies and legitimizes her father's authority." Traditionally in Syria the son would ally with the father in enforcing piety on his sisters; the most extreme form of enforcement, what in Europe are called honor killings, often unfold according to this logic. But here, Suleyman's son shows no solidarity with his father in helping to enforce a patrilineal discipline. Instead, he joins his sisters in a collective demand for emancipation from the father.

After the JA and the judge complete their legal obligations to investigate the accusation, determine its plausibility and the credibility of those making it, the two younger children do return to live with their father. Vigilant therapists and social workers eventually arrived at the truth of events, and throughout the process created remedies that might inflict the least harm on the participants. Perhaps all is well that ends well. Perhaps not. By not expediting the reunification of the children with their father, the state, in the form of a judge and other employees, inflicted considerable unnecessary and perhaps permanent psychic damage on the father and his younger daughter. It is difficult to see how the father in his paternal function can reclaim a relationship with his children that is not constantly inflected by the wounds they have inflicted on him. It took an extra nine months after the accusation had been withdrawn to effect legal reunification of the children with their father. In this period, the younger daughter, whom her siblings had put into the decisive position of child sex victim to obtain their freedom, developed a guilt complex regarding her father that will surely result in considerable restitution needs. Bureaucratic due process here trumped the needs of the children pace children, a not uncommon event in the lives of families who in some way get caught in the caregiving apparatus of state institutions.

SEVEN

Loose End

This final chapter presents a series of odds and ends, each of which discusses issues that deserve separate accounts but whose elaboration would require lengthy descriptions and digress too much from the central theoretical arguments of this book. It is not to be read as a conclusion but as a series of openings to further research.

Chaos Reigns

Perhaps the most challenging mandate for the therapists at KiZ is to treat youth who molested children. In the group I attended, most of these boys could also be classified as children, most were in the throes of the *Sturm und Drang* time of adolescence, and most suffered from neglect and were themselves abused, though not always sexually. Most were simultaneously in group therapy and in individual therapy or psychiatric treatment. Most paid little attention to the others. Most did not listen well and had little interest in engaging in introspection, fearful that the other members of the group would disapprove of them. Most were ashamed of what they had done and were easily shamed. Most left the group sessions to return to family or group home settings that they experienced as uncaring or hostile environments, not highly supportive of critical self-reflection.

In light of these conditions, the question of the function of therapy for juvenile offenders generally could not be posed in the same way as it is for adults. The person who appeared in therapy was often not fully aware of social norms and hence had an undeveloped superego. The "I" or ego of the person who spoke in therapy groups, the first-person voice, was insecure, either unaware of its "self" or lacking in confidence. If unaware of its "self," it could not easily introspect and objectify that self, which is the primary goal of adult therapy. If lacking in confidence, it sought to speak not in its own voice but in a voice the others would approve of. The foremost question of the youth groups seemed to be how to create and sustain a group dynamic and a holding environment in which each individual could eventually speak about his problems. Yet most individual members were either indifferent toward or fearful of the others in the group. The therapists ultimately directed most discussions to clarification of transgressions, boundaries of the self, and respect for others.

Seven boys between the ages of thirteen and seventeen gathered weekly in the youth group of sex offenders I observed. About eight months into my research, a therapist I will call Nicole asked me whether I would sit in the full circle with her and the six boys. I usually sit behind them, so as to be out of their direct line of vision. The other, male therapist had fallen ill. The boys all knew me by name and had initially consented to my presence. Recently they had become particularly rowdy, so the therapist thought that my presence in the group, as a physical replacement for the male therapist, might help to quiet the boys and strengthen her authority.

In the very first session I had attended, I explained my role in this group as an observer interested in the problems of young sex offenders and the effectiveness of therapy. I told the boys that I intended on writing about it. The therapists thought that my intent to listen and my lack of judgment might serve to reinforce the boys' sense that their problems were being taken seriously. They needed recognition. All except one, the very youngest, came from broken homes and had suffered from various degrees of neglect or abuse. Sometimes the therapists called on me during sessions to confirm an opinion about America, which came up surprisingly often as a cultural reference (e.g., rock music, movie stars, the prevalence of guns or violence, the treatment of prisoners, the small size of the state welfare system), or the scientific status of an explanation they proposed. The boys often proposed explanations that the therapists sought to refute. But on the whole they and the boys seemed to totally ignore me.

The youngest, at thirteen, exhibited acute attention deficit disorder, swinging his feet and, when possible, swirling around in his chair, loudly slurping tea or coffee, eager to provide uninvited updates about his endless series of high school romances or to ask questions that had nothing to do with the topic at hand. (Example: "I have something to say, I have something to say." Ok. What? "Last week, I was in school and this girl looked at me twice, and I think she likes me.") The other boys disliked him and ignored his statements, while the therapists kept trying to affirm his sense of self-worth and convince him that he actually belonged in the group. His systematic attempt to get attention considerably infected a few of the others, who used it as an excuse also not to listen to the others or not to think. One exceptionally witty boy of seventeen who flirted with Goth style—always black—frequently expressed impatience with these antics (as occasionally did the therapists, who once made the thirteen-year-old sit still and face the wall). The others reacted openly only during the fifteen minute break in the middle of the session by completely ignoring him.

The group had become increasingly chaotic over the year, however, and this session began that way, with the boys unusually loud and, from the start, demanding coffee and tea, which was usually provided only on birthdays or when someone left the group. Nicole agreed to their demands this time and promptly disappeared to the kitchen for ten minutes to make it. On her return, the boys quickly emptied the contents of the sugar jar into their cups. The thirteen-year old was particularly enthusiastic about sugar and filled half his cup with sugar before filling the rest with coffee. The phrase "chaos reigns" played like a repetitive soundtrack in my head.

Nicole then followed the usual protocol and went from boy to boy to ask how his week was. Each gave the usual depressing reports: Nothing happened; I won a scholarship to a poetry contest but for mysterious reasons am not allowed to go; I had a conversation with a girl and she likes me; I have too much stress working and attending therapy; I had a meeting with my social worker, it went well; I hate my mentor in the group home who is so dense. The boys refused to listen to each other, as usual. But instead of focusing on one theme or on the problems of one boy for the day, Nicole tried to give attention to them all. They all seemed clever at sensing a weakness in a therapist or a tactical advantage over the others of getting the kind of attention they wanted. One slipped off his seat and sat down, cross-legged, on the floor (Nicole eventually told him to sit up, but he refused); others kept filling their cups with more coffee or tea, and when they emptied the pitchers, they asked for more.

To that request Nicole did not respond, whereas I wanted desperately to yell at them. The emptiness of the coffee and tea containers mirrored the emptiness of the speech I was hearing, and I was at a loss to see any therapeutic end to this session. Whatever stabilizing function I was supposed to have was not apparent. Earlier I had cautiously mentioned to Nicole that I thought the boys derived too much oral satisfaction from the drinks; they should be asked to talk instead. When Nicole did not respond for their request for more to drink, one boy asked whether she could prepare something for him to eat, as his attendance in the group would made him late for dinner back at the home where he was staying. She complied good-naturedly and left to prepare a sandwich. I sat silently with the boys, again, and they broke up into smaller groups to talk. When Nicole returned, the hungry boy munched on his sandwich angrily without saying a word while the others seemed to have made pacts with each other and thus were even better prepared to find ways to refuse seriously responding to any of her questions.

Finally, I could bear the tension no more—and kept hearing that soundtrack "chaos reigns." I blurted out, "You should show some respect for Frau X (Nicole, the therapist). This therapy group is for you. But you all behave as if she is the one who needs therapy. She is here for you. Use this time to discuss your problems." They all looked at me blankly. I had said so little in the past eight months that they were probably stunned to hear me speak. My words had no apparent effect. Their relation to adults and adult admonitions was in any case seriously disturbed. Nicole continued to ask questions which they ignored, or refused to answer, or answered by turning the question back to her, until time was up.

The next session was more orderly. Both therapists were present. I sat in back again. The boys ignored me. They again asked for (and received) coffee and tea. Periodically therapists asked the boys whether they wanted to remain in the group. Most decided to stay. Sometimes the therapists asked the boys to switch to groups more appropriate for them. But they always resisted switching.

Trust

One day two men in a group for "pedophiles" were particularly nervous and studiously avoided each other, whereas previously they had been supportive of each other. They seemed to identify with each other even though their crimes and circumstances were very different. One, whom I will call Helmut, was very articulate, able to make connections quickly for himself and for the others, and he asked astute questions. The other, who I will call Karl, spoke only when asked to, and then grudgingly, slowly, with little insight or interest in what was being asked of him. Helmut was on parole, convicted for viewing and circulating child pornography; he lapsed twice during the time I attended the group. Karl was also on parole, convicted of aggravated abuse for molesting several adolescent girls, in a series of repeat offenses; each repeat took him temporarily back to prison. Despite the convictions, both men managed to retain their jobs—and Helmut had a particularly good paying job requiring specialized computer knowledge—but both had problems with their coworkers, to whom they had not disclosed their crimes.

The therapists began the session by discussing the rule at KiZ that all clients were forbidden to have contact with each other outside the sessions. When someone is accepted for therapy, he must sign a contract with KiZ, committing himself to attend and pay for the sessions, and to not befriend the other members of the group until after all therapy has terminated. The therapists fear that in private meetings outside the sessions the men might unite against them, or begin to see themselves as victimized by society, or exchange child porn, or, at worst, strategize about how to establish sexual contact with a child or youth again. Not all therapy institutions hold to this rule. At some, such contact is considered unavoidable, or forbidding it is considered unenforceable, or it is allowed and even justified as an extension of therapy. Clients rarely have anyone they trust with whom they can discuss what they had done and talked about outside the sessions. Given the social isolation and secretiveness in which they live, clients have only acquaintances from the group in whom they can confide.

Karl, afraid that his parole would be revoked, had revealed to one of the therapists that he and Helmut had been meeting privately outside the group. Helmut felt seriously betrayed and abandoned by Karl, and he reacted aggressively to the therapists' attempt to shame him. He was indeed ashamed, turning deep red, but reacted as if the group had unfairly wounded him. He appealed to the difference in rules among different therapy institutions and insisted that he and Karl had actually been helping each other, therapeutically, by enabling further talk and reflection outside the group setting. He argued that he had no friends and had only his sister to talk to, but she was cold and distant since his initial arrest, so he could not talk to her either. Karl sat quietly with his head down, ashamed of violating the rules and ashamed of having betrayed the confidence of his only friend. Given his extreme social awkwardness, he appeared even more isolated than Helmut.

The therapists asked the other men in the group what they thought should be done about the violation. One argued that their behavior endangered the entire group, and the two men should be asked to leave the group as penalty for the violation. Their places should be given to other offenders who were on a waiting list for a place to open in the group session. The other clients were less forthcoming about advice, but nobody defended openly what the two men had done.

One therapist confided in me that he had seen clients together in cafes in the past, but never reported it to the other therapists. He personally disagreed with the policy but since it was group policy he went along. Another therapist explained to me the importance of setting boundaries, obeying

rules, and that this was just another test for the offenders as to their willingness to submit to social norms. It was evidence of whether the men could
be trusted to actually respect the boundaries they had violated in the past.

After the break in the middle of the session, Helmut did not return. And
he did not return for another two weeks. Then, he suddenly reappeared,
having privately confirmed to the therapists that he agreed to obey the rule.

Countertransference

About five months into the therapy sessions of one group, a client refused to
respond to particular questions posed by one of the therapists. He said that
my presence made him feel insecure and compromised; he did not trust I
would respect the confidentiality of the session. I had in the very first session
explained why I was there and what I would like to do—assess the work of
therapy, including that of the therapists. And I told the men in the group
that they could ask me to leave any time they wanted. In no group did they
ask questions of me at that point, though some did later. Several times men
approached me personally in the break they took halfway through the session to ask about my work. I always told them that it would be easy to look
me up on the Internet, should they want to see what my research in the past
has been about.

In this case the two therapists vigorously defended my presence, arguing
that it is important to have an outsider observe the interactions of the group;
that my attention to them suggested how important the work they did in the
group was; and that they should fear the US tendency to simply lock people
up and give convicted offenders long sentences. Inevitably Germany adopts
US models, and the excessive penalization of the US model is increasingly
appealing to many German jurists and the German public. German group
therapy presented an alternative model, and it is important to inform the
public about what goes on in these sessions. Perhaps it is especially important that an American inform himself of how Germans conduct therapy with
sex offenders. I explained to the group that I was evaluating the effectiveness
of the therapists in helping their clients, which should be in their interests.
The men took a vote and agreed unanimously to let me remain in the group.
The discussion then turned to the issue of paranoia and trust among members of the group.

With very few exceptions, I was quiet. Once and a while therapists would
bring me in as an expert on America, to confirm or contradict some statement about how things are done in the United States. Rarely did the therapists reveal how they suspected I influenced the group or what bothered

them, probably out of politeness, but also because of a high degree of professionalism in their relations with me. On a couple of occasions, I felt they projected onto me their own discomforts with a particular session or frustrations with the limitations of their own therapeutic skills.

One therapist told me he thought I was too empathetic with the offenders. Another said that it bothered her that I nodded off during a session. "Thank God I didn't snore," I joked. She smiled slightly and repeated, "It bothered me." On that occasion, I was returning from a transatlantic trip and had come directly from the airport for that session; I indeed struggled to stay awake. Her investment in my alertness suggests that she had entered into countertransference not only with her clients and the other therapist with whom she worked, but also with me, an informed observer. She wanted my alertness.

Failed Containment in the Field

The prisoner had been convicted for abusing the daughter of his girlfriend and was sentenced to three and a half years imprisonment. He had a prior conviction, eleven years before, for abuse of a stepdaughter in his second of three marriages. From a quick read of his profile, I ascertained he was in his mid-fifties, had dual Swedish-German citizenship, lived alternately in both countries, and had a regular work history of different relatively unskilled jobs. As he entered the room, the prison psychologist greeted him without expression and asked him to sit down. Based on an interview of less than one hour, she was to determine the kind of prison in which he would serve his time, either a closed, maximum-security kind or a minimum-security, self-administered one where he would be able to leave and work during the day (*offene Strafvollzug, Selbststelleranstalt*). She would then write an advisory opinion (*Stellungnahme*) also assessing the utility of therapy for the prisoner, along with his possible rehabilitation and risk factors.

He broke the ice, saying, "I think we know each other." Her expression remained blank, but she did pause, and then introduced me (who sat behind her) and explained I was observing her conduct the interview. She asked whether he had any objections to my presence. When he said no, she wrote up a statement, and they both signed it. The entire interview consisted of empirical questions: family history, work history, criminal history.

After he left the room, she asked me for my opinion before offering her own interpretation of what had been said. In most situations she asked me to express myself before she did. I took it to be a test of my competence as well as a bit of sadistic play. I first asked some questions to make sure

I had understood approximately what had been said, or not said. Then I cautiously described my impressions and what more I would like to know before making an assessment. I said that the man appeared to me to be forthcoming; he looked her in the eyes and did not hesitate in his answers, though I had no way to verify what he said. I would need to know more about his social situation outside the prison to assess his risk factor.

The psychologist was incredulous and visibly upset by my reaction, "He is a psychopath, can't you see? Everything he said was a lie."

"Even the stuff about his employment history?" I asked. "We don't know," she said. "We cannot trust anything he said, because he makes no clear distinction between reality and fantasy."

Either I missed something, or a lot of things, or she had information about him that I did not. She had already interviewed him once, shortly after his first conviction, which he had tried to acknowledge as he entered the room. She ignored that plea and chose to remain polite yet formal and distant, showing as little affect as possible. Yet her reaction now was about the affect she had repressed. She had felt disgust and nausea during the interview. I had not noticed that reaction, neither from her voice nor features. There was, she said, something slimy and irredeemable in this man's way of relating to himself, his past, his sex abuse.

I appealed to my incompetency and lack of experience. She interpreted my caution as an attempt to withhold judgment, perhaps an inability to feel the emotional disgust that she felt. On another plane, my lack of an emotion suggested I did not have access to the unconscious-to-unconscious transference that she relied on in arriving at a professional judgment in this case. What she understood to be all "lies" she inferred from both a certain deadness that this man had projected into her and from a prior meeting with her—a covering up, papering over, not taking seriously, of the crimes of sex abuse that she now, for the second time, had to evaluate.

In this situation generally, where she usually was alone and sought a pause, I provided her the opportunity to elaborate these projections so as to make her psychic distress—the disgust she felt—more tolerable to her. She had often complained of somatic disturbances—for example, discomfort, skin rashes, sleeplessness, which she attributed to the emotional burden of dealing with violent, psychically wounded, and frequently sexually perverse men. Yet this opportunity to elaborate was foiled by my inability to contain her emotion. My incapacity for empathy with her in her reaction to the offender, in parallel with my avoidance of acting out in any way, did not permit the elaboration of her painful feelings.

Plain and simple, I did not share that moment with her, and she felt abandoned by me. This would not have been the case if she had not made herself so vulnerable to me in the first place, which she did at my request, inviting the intrusive ethnographer into her workspace. First she helped me to obtain research approval as a "scientist" from the *Genderbeauftragte der Senatsverwaltung der Justiz* (person in charge of research on gender in the Berlin judiciary) and from the Berlin *Justizvollzugsanstalt* (penitentiary), and then she allowed me to observe her work. This required trust, and my lack of response suggested either an inability to contain her emotions or an ineffective containment. To be fair to myself, she brought with her into the interview a picture of the man's previous abuse, along with an accumulation of pictures of abuse of other prisoners. My impressions were limited to his rational statements and the looks and gestures that went on in the interview, whereas she was asking questions and more actively listening, creating a more dense world of voices and images from which to interpret the unconscious communication that was going on.

Peer Review

Reasons why a research proposal is supported or rejected for funding are varied and not usually predictable, even more so when the evaluators come from different academic disciplines. Having sat on review committees for approximately thirty government agencies and foundations in four countries, I know that it is often difficult even after funding decisions are made to conclude exactly why some proposals are funded and others not. I applied for only two grants to support this research. One agency, for which I had reviewed applicants for more than a decade, rejected it in the first round of discussion; I was told privately that it was in competition with three grants "on incest," all by accomplished senior scholars, and that my ethnographic study was considered more risky (because it was about child sex abuse) than one by a historian (about definitions and cases of incest in the past) and one by a literary critic (about representation).

The other agency to which I applied, the National Science Foundation (NSF), approved the proposal for funding after three rounds of reviews by both the Cultural Anthropology (CA) and Law and Social Sciences (LSS) divisions. It took nearly two years from the first application to approval of funding, and by then I had completed my first year of ethnographic research without external support (I was supported by a semester sabbatical pay from Princeton University stretched over a year). Because of the delay in this lengthy review process (eliminating the possibility of funding the nine months of on-site research), and in response to one reviewer's comments (which I interpreted as largely a rejection of my proposed budget), I reduced the initial budget from more than $249,000 over thirty months (of which the university's direct costs totaled 37 percent of the total) to $45,000 over nine months total—summer research for three consecutive years.

In the first review by the NSF, the CA division suggested resubmission but the LSS concluded there were no "socially scientific insights on law." In the second round of review, the two divisions reversed themselves, the LSS encouraged resubmission, the CA declined as "not competitive." In the third and final review, both approved, though there was still considerable skepticism among some individual reviewers. Altogether, approximately twenty scientists reviewed the proposal.

A summary of the reasons for rejecting the proposed research suggests a very broad array of interests at play, as well as much discomfort with the topic. I number the reviewers to keep them distinct. In the first submission, Reviewer 1 scoffed at the proposal and dismissed most of my questions as beside-the-point, concluding, "After all, child abuse is about little girls being abused by men." Reviewer 2 doubted that I would have the "linguistic data" necessary for analysis without tape recording conversations with therapists and their clients, and my own conversations with prisoners. Reviewer 3 insisted that I obtain "written informed consent" from each prisoner or individual in therapy with whom I spoke, to ensure noncoercion (that they were not coerced into talking with me); she was skeptical of my ability to determine when the offenders would lie to me or their therapists. Reviewers 4 and 5 doubted that I would be "able to gain access to sexual abusers" and so chose to ignore the necessary permits I had already obtained from the Ministry of Justice to work in the prisons, and from the therapeutic center Kind im Zentrum. Several reviewers also insisted the research could be done in the United States, that I had not made the case why it needed to be done in Germany. The assumption was that all research outside the United States would replicate the US situation; therefore only proposals that demonstrated before research began that a non-US place was different could be justified for funding.

For the second submission, I reorganized the proposal substantially and addressed all of the reviewer comments either in the proposal or, when I disagreed, directly in footnotes. Reviewer 6 began with a putative compliment, a "very well-written essay on an interesting topic"—which was actually a coded dismissal, and then suggested I send the proposal to Fulbright or Guggenheim. I interpret this as meaning that because the proposal had some narratives within it that were interesting to read, it did not strictly follow scientific style, which would have had a more clearly defined hypothesis and entailed more elaboration of specific scientific methodologies linked to specific data I would gather—for example, about the duration of "interviews," the number of prisoners to be interviewed, the standardization of questions, the way of obtaining informed consent, the small size and randomness of my "sample." These are all legitimate issues, but I could not have known about them in such detail until I already engaged in on-site research. (For example, initially I was unsure how much access and what kind I would have to the therapy groups, but once on-site, the woman who ran KiZ suggested I observe them directly, weekly, if the other therapists and their clients of the groups assented.) When all questions can be anticipated ahead of time, the research is no longer fieldwork but some other type—perhaps sociological/ survey, historical/archival—of formal data gathering.

Reviewer 7 said the need was to research victims of sexual abuse and not the offenders. Reviewer 8 wondered, since the study was in Berlin, whether I was aware that the "history [there is] quite different from other parts of Germany." She requested more of what she called "background" and asked the proposal to address how "sexual perversion [is] tied to German history, including the Holocaust." Reviewer 9 insisted such a study would be incomplete without research "on the importance of media in framing debates." I should include a study of "public discourses and debates around sexual abuse." Reviewer 10, noting the difficulty of linking this proposal to the incest taboo and debates on incest alone, suggested I link it to anthropological discourses on the state, power, and sexuality. Reviewer 11 insisted that before research began I include in the proposal a more extensive (I had only three paragraphs) legal history of "sexual self-determination." Reviewer 12 wanted to know why I did not do this study in the United States instead, which, the reviewer, wrote, would provide a "multicultural perspective," unlike Germany. This reviewer was skeptical that the German context, which ostensibly would be more expensive for the research, could yield any alternative data. Some of these same reviewers praised other aspects of the proposal, but the points of agreement tell us less about the reception than the criticisms.

I suspect some of these concerns were formulated to camouflage a reticence to support the research topic itself. Several reviewers, not only the ones cited above, stated explicitly that the research focus—sex offenders and their legal and therapeutic treatment—should instead have been on the victims (although such research is extensive, while research on offenders is meager).

Given this frequent prejudice against the topic itself, some of the demands for revisions were absurd. For example, there is no way one can tape-record a therapeutic session to obtain linguistic data. Confidentiality is a premise of both therapeutic work and ethnographic research. Taking notes itself may be risky, but, unlike journalists, not a single ethnographer, to my knowledge, has endangered her research subjects through notetaking. But tape-recorded sessions in this research setting are unduly risky. Both the therapist and client risk legal jeopardy if a court were to subpoena the tapes. Clients might also sue their therapists for violating their privacy by allowing me to tape. The same absurdity is revealed in the request that I do a history of sexual self-determination in a proposal. If I had written such a history at the proposal stage, one could easily have argued that there was no need for further research.

Several reviewers seemed to suggest that I hold naive notions of cultural relativism and of the native's point of view, which may in fact be a general assumption of nonanthropologists about ethnographers. Cultural relativism, most anthropologists would agree, is a necessary starting point for ethnographic work, as is eliciting the native's point of view, but these are preparatory positions and usually just steps toward a critical analysis.

A few reviewers also appeared to think that ethnographic method, requiring on-site negotiation in real time, evades the specific ethical and scientific-methodological problems that other disciplines (e.g., psychology, history) better control for during the research through methodology alone. The ethnographic approach differs crucially from isolated interviews and more controlled experimental research in that there is no controlled deception. For fields like experimental psychology, some deception is necessary to set up a control group. For fields that rely on surveys, posing the same question to every subject, and the same or very similar question over time, allows for comparison. But isolated "interviews" with therapists or their clients, or with officials involved in the legal processing of offenders, yield "opinions," data of how people represent what they know. Opinions are insufficient, however, to infer what sex offenders actually know or how they actually behaved or will behave, much less to ascertain what kind of self they are becoming through therapy.

The deep skepticism about approaching topics with ethnographic methods is often framed as a problem with the feasibility of pursuing such intense levels of personal engagement, wherein the ethnographer is continually arrested in the act of perception in unanticipated moments in real interactions in real time (Borneman and Hammoudi 2009). Feasibility concerns are indeed of extreme importance, as the difficulty of obtaining approval for projects and finding ways to access our subjects can doom extremely important projects. This holds especially today for research on or concerning prisoners or children. But I had already obtained these permits. Unable to be explicitly skeptical about "traditional" ethnographic methods (which would be unacceptable on an interdisciplinary panel, as it would be considered a disciplinary bias), some reviewers instead insisted that I could not do the things I had set out to do, or they demanded detailed methods that could be worked out only on-site.

Although many fields of study outside anthropology have taken over and modified the ethnographer's method of on-site "fieldwork," rarely do they engage in the kind of sustained research in contexts not constructed for or by the researcher. These contexts demand the skills of improvisation and trust building, and a willingness to be critically reflexive about what one is learning. The real time of anthropological fieldwork stands in sharp contrast to most other research paradigms, which usually operate outside real time. Those other paradigms—primarily census data, surveys, textual archives, or opinion polls obtained through random sampling—must make unreal assumptions about time to produce stable dependent and independent variables for particular research designs. Based on these unreal assumptions, they claim to be able to "bracket" the influence of researcher relationships with the subjects they study.

Anthropological Ethics and Disclosure

Anthropologists cannot in all honesty formulate ethical prescriptions for fieldwork behavior, as each encounter occurs with a different interlocutor in a different speech setting with different needs and wishes. Although deception as practiced in other disciplines may clearly produce useful information, anthropologists generally consider it unethical. Yet they also do not disclose everything to their interlocutors immediately, for good reason: to avoid overdetermining the research situation. Ethnographic research of any depth entails many gradations of disclosure depending on with whom one is communicating, from imagining and setting up a project through the fieldwork encounters and the writing up and publishing of results. In any event, it is illusory to think that it is possible to be fully aware and explicit about our motives at the beginning of a research project. Even after completion of research, one is still becoming conscious of what acute ethical questions were posed in the encounters and interactions. And only after a period of reflection is it possible to articulate these questions with any degree of clarity.

When the principle of indeterminacy is not central to research design (Moore 2009), when one appears to know exactly how to find out what one wants to know before commencing with research, interviews or linguistic protocols tend to substitute for intermittent and happenstance discussions or observations over time, questions are standardized and fieldwork entails little depth of interaction with few unpredictable face-to-face relationships. For Malinowskian-style modern fieldwork, however, to assume transparency through disclosure and to standardize encounters with our interlocutors effaces these encounters of the contingency central to a situational ethics.[1]

The call to disclose is always counterbalanced by the need to hide things, to resist the contemporary obsession to make everything transparent. Foregrounding disclosure as an ethical issue before any fieldwork encounters risks unduly restricting the principle of open-ended discovery central to fieldwork. Anthropologists hide sometimes not on principle but to protect themselves or to get better access to data and at other times to protect research subjects. Yet, taking away the capacity to hide, or to protect the unconscious from the law, is precisely what the Western legal system does when it comes to criminality. In this respect, both child sex offenders and abused children are forced to disclose memories that they have tried, for different reasons, to make unavailable to themselves. I, then, compared to those I am doing research about, am not subject to the same ethical demands. This asymmetry is built into the idea of research, and not merely ethnographic research, and it is integral to generating a special, scientific form of knowledge. It is very likely at the time of publication that I know my interlocutors and their social landscape better than they know themselves, perhaps even better than I know myself.

Because of their crime, sex offenders often lose the kind of basic freedoms that we assume belong to humans, including the right to a private life and the right to hide anything. In addition to imprisonment, they are asked to lay bare their inner lives, to reveal their deepest, unconscious motivations. For the criminal justice system, therapy initially assists in reconstructing the actual deed and how it was experienced so that judges can decide on sentences and conditions of treatment. Nothing can be legitimately withheld; everything is to be spoken. Release from prison results in other restrictions, as it is often contingent on the renunciation of freedom of movement (e.g., no walking past or living near children's playgrounds), monitoring of dating patterns (e.g., no dating single women with children) and Internet access (e.g., no viewing of pornography).

The demand on sex offenders of revelation, of bringing what happened into speech, is justified as ethical because society (specifically the law, democratically enacted, popularly supported) claims to need to know to provide collective security. Individual therapists (though not as many psychologists or psychiatrists as one might expect) have special obligations to their clients, and hence reservations about serving the law in this way. Many therapists still insist they can work effectively only when their clients trust them, which means that much of what goes on in therapy sessions remains confidential, not to be shared with the criminal justice system. It also means that therapists respect certain reserves or defenses of their clients, in other words, that they accept and allow clients to hide embarrassing details that might overwhelm them with shame or abuses that did not result in prosecution. Because most therapists are reluctant to tell all, judges most frequently turn to psychiatrists and psychologists who do not share this reticence to tell all to external authorities.

This all has a bearing on anthropological ethics, on the nature of my ethical obligations relative to those of my research subjects, and on my relations to them and to the situations or communities in which I do research. The concepts "individuals" and "community" provide a different set of referents for many anthropologists today than they did in the first decades of the twentieth century. At that time Franz Boas elaborated methodological and epistemological ideas around the principle of cultural relativism, which became the de facto ethics of anthropology. His initial goal was to avoid ethnocentrism—judging the morality of whole societies or cultures based on one's own assumptions—and instead to insist on an empathic relation with research subjects. It was crucial to assume cultural relativism to delegitimate claims that non-Western (e.g., primitive, savage, illiterate) societies were either in a prior stage to those in the West or inherently inferior. In other words, the principle sought, first of all, to regulate a fraught, asymmetrical relationship and to shackle the moralizing tendencies of Western researchers.

Boas's student Melville Herskovits (1955, 351) formulated the classic definition of cultural relativism: "Judgments are based on experience, and experience is interpreted by each individual in terms of his own enculturation." He turned to the contrast between polygamous and monogamous families to illustrate this principle, and he claimed that polygamy "performs essential tasks. Otherwise the societies wherein they exist would not survive" (349). While still important as a nonjudgmental point of departure in an inquiry, this principle no longer adequately frames the kind of ethical obligations most anthropologists confront in their relations. Above all, the focus on enculturation implies the necessary survival of societies or cultures by the enforcement of norms, that is, it assumes that social production depends on the production of a particular kind of person.

German society does not need rehab rituals to reproduce itself. There is no functional necessity to correct the wrong of child sex abuse through a ritual process of accusation, imprisonment, trial, therapy, and reincorporation. The justification of rehab rituals lies elsewhere. The ethical question for German society, as Germans themselves pose it, is not one of survival of a culture but rather how to balance the rights of the individuals involved (e.g., children, parents, sex offenders) with the need to provide collective security. Culture here is thoroughly permeated by relations with rights and the state, and it is more focused on the malleable self than reproduction of the cultural person. Perhaps I overstate my case. Public debates about who is German erupt all the time. But with each passing decade in the last half century, German residents have become more multicultural, binational, or of mixed origin. Debates about monoculture and its reproduction are increasingly displaced by those that focus on the boundaries of the self and the forms of legitimate intervention into this self.

This particular project draws out some of the complications of disclosure that accompanies changes in fieldwork situations and objects. These complications make it necessary to go beyond an ethics of cultural relativism to a situational or relational ethics. Such ethics is not universal but functions more like an intersubjective third, contingent on the ethnographer's relation to the concrete situation in which research takes place.[2] Ethnographers have obligations minimally both to their research subjects and communities, and to the scholarly community generally. My primary obligation is to do no harm: to my interlocutors and to their community (in this study, a country, Germany). Also, I am to anticipate the harm I might do through intervention as a researcher in pursuit of a particular set of questions and to respect the scholar's commitment to truth in research. Social scientists in other disciplines usually verify (to the university-run Human Subjects Review Boards) that the people they study have not been subject to harm by obtaining from them a statement of "informed consent."

Although in this project I did indeed obtain formal consent from my interlocutors, the process of verification of intent to do no harm actually tended to create suspicions and undermine the trust necessary for ethnographic research. When asked to orally agree to or to sign a statement of consent, offenders usually assumed that I am not an independent researcher but in the service of my government. They saw my attempts to inform them of the noncoercive nature of the discussions I would like to have (that they can stop talking or refuse to meet me at any time) as at best naive on my part, at worst a muddled disguise for an agent of a secret service.

Outside of reading prison documents, most of my activity was listening and observing. I of course engaged in many discussions, during which

I repeatedly posed open-ended, naive (from the native's point of view) questions; I tried to establish a working equality of status (although the power differential is by no means one-sided, as I was quite dependent on the generosity of my hosts and research subjects). Informed consent is a reaction to past abuse of research subjects, primarily in the area of medical research, and nowadays it is seen as an important condition for research in the Western academy. Also, universities monitor and increasingly restrict research in the attempt to protect themselves from potential legal liability. But a formal statement of informed consent is not, in my experience as an ethnographer, particularly important for my interlocutors. Their overriding motivation in granting me access was that they were curious and sought at some level to learn from my presence. This was also true of the therapists, the prison officials, and, I would say, eventually even most of the offenders. Without curiosity key acquaintances would not have facilitated my access to the observation of actual exchanges between therapists and their clients and between prison officials and their wards. It helps also that German law grants a special status to scientific inquiry, which enabled me to read documents generally protected under strict laws regulating the dissemination of data (*Datenschutz*). This curiosity did not foreclose instrumental interests on the part of my research subjects, which entailed many other kinds of claims on me (especially on my time, skills, and resources).

The challenge for me in this work has been to engage ethically with a ritual process that is a response to a widely considered social evil. Engagement with the transgression in itself makes me suspicious of sympathizing if not participating in the offense. Individuals accused of child molestation have all done something wrong, from today's moral perspective one of the worst possible deeds. Most members of German society (including legal professionals, the therapists, and some of the offenders themselves) presume that the accusation alone implies unethical, criminal behavior. Conviction is the justification for incarceration and, in some cases, for permanent surveillance after serving a sentence. Rehabilitation is, however, the ultimate goal in Germany, and the key to rehab is full disclosure: breaking down in therapy the resistances of offenders—about intimacy, sex, and violence—that hide or camouflage the offender's inner life. It is my impression that anthropologists today avoid much important research on the intersubjective self and its boundaries because they do not want to confront the quandaries and aporias of disclosure. To justify this avoidance is to compromise our accountability to truth (Borneman and Hammoudi 2009).

Psychic Change

Psychic change is a thick concept linked to a maximum expectation of re-habilitation, a transformation of the self through therapy (Joseph 1989). Behavioral modification is a thin concept linked to a minimal expectation of adjustment to social norms through rehabilitation of the person. Most therapists are satisfied with behavioral modification, but the criminal justice system often demands evidence of more substantive change. Therapists at KiZ worked with a much thicker concept of rehabilitation, but most would have reserved the claim of psychic change for only some clients. Nonetheless, built into their therapeutic techniques is the assumption that success in changing the psyche of the clients entailed some concentrated thinking through of their motivations and biographies, a kind of thinking that depends on an ability not just to adjust to norms but to symbolize the act of violation itself. Nearly all of the sex offenders I encountered in therapy groups found it acutely difficult to symbolize the motivations for their offenses.

Perhaps finding words to depict a sex offense against the child tests the limits of symbolization itself. And symbolization is the task of therapy. In bringing punishable actions and the unconscious motivations for them into language, child sex offenders are asked to symbolize what appears to have no reason, the unthinkable, the unnameable, a putative soul murder, the very essence of negativity and evil. Such acts of speaking, what Siegel (2006) simply calls "naming," tie the individual to the very meaning of the social; they demonstrate the essence of the relation of language to social order, and the highly coercive nature of speech on the subject. That is, during rehabilitation, the therapeutic subject, under the threat of incarceration or under surveillance after release from prison, must bring an act into words that construct him as someone outside humankind, incapable of the change that rehab rituals are supposed to bring about.

While they speak, offenders are asked to organize their disparate actions sequentially in terms of their own personal biographies. The purpose is to create a coherent plot that defines them in relation to their own actions and the effects these actions may have had on their victims, and, finally, to arrive at an understanding of the self that emerges from reflection and introspection in the presence and with the help of therapists. A primary goal of therapy is to create through objectification a self not identical to the "I," a self that can be viewed as external to the person who is speaking, as an object to contemplate, to criticize, to empathize with, and to understand. A self is what one has become but about whom there is the possibility of transformation that society generally acknowledges. Upon entering therapy, the core of the offender's self is associated with an evil act that, after rehabilitation, one would no longer commit. This primary goal is supplemented by the punishment of incarceration—the unfreedom and imposed discipline of the criminal justice system, which exploits the tension created between the person who wronged society (and is therefore imprisoned) and an externalized self produced through therapy, the self of introspection. The "I" that results would be able to speak, think, act, judge, and evaluate in a way that assumes responsibility for the act. This assumption is evidence of a psychic change.

Culture Shock

Ethnographers do not have the luxury of claiming to "bracket" their presence in the field and hence cannot easily retreat to an objectivity based on distance alone. Being there is a condition of research, and being there is the means to establish a relationship to our objects os study. That said, it is in no way clear what, if any, our own presence and experience among the people studied has on the accounts we gather and the stories we tell about the people we study. At least since the 1950s, one measure of the significance of ethnographic research has been how experience in the field changed the anthropologist. Anthropologists coined the term "culture shock" to capture the bewilderment or distress experienced when an ethnographer must adapt to a strange set of cultural referents and when, upon returning home, after immersion in this other cultural environment, she finds it difficult to readjust to her own environment.

For the last half century scientific journals have widely circulated the term "culture shock," making it into a popular and standard descriptive concept. At the same time, within anthropology the concept always provoked controversy. On the one hand, some anthropologists implied that they had "gone native," meaning fully assimilated to the norms and behaviors of the people they studied. For this claim, they were attacked by other scholars for being naive, at best, fraudulent, at worst. Was not the point to stress the differences between cultures? And could an adult in fact become such a radically different self?

About thirty years ago the term "culture shock" seemed on the verge of disappearing altogether from the anthropological lexicon, as did many of its associated concepts, such as "immersion" and "assimilation." Today even "culture" has become a problematic term—though nonetheless still widely used. The many criticisms of these terms were not without justification, and they opened the discipline to substantial change in fieldsites and objects of study. With new justifications at hand, over this same period an increasing number of anthropologists turned to study their own homes or cultures or countries. In addition, many "native anthropologists" from other parts of the world entered the Western academy with the expectation that they represent themselves and knowledge about the places from which they came, making terms such as "culture shock" and "assimilation" unnecessary if not irrelevant for their ethnographic research. Above all, if the site of study is a place with which one is familiar, the dialectic of nearness and distance appears no longer central to knowledge production. And it is unlikely that the researcher would experience anything resembling culture shock.

Yet the sense of unsettlement, of identity thrown into question, both upon entering the field for a distinct period and upon leaving it to return to the academy, remains an integral part of fieldwork experience for ethnographers, including many who study home or at home. To learn from experience in and of the field was always much more than a simple registering of facts, the testing of a preformulated hypothesis, accumulating "native points of view," or, in the case of those working "at home," reproducing without alienation what one had already learned about one's own culture. It was also a reckoning with the unusual transferences and countertransference of emotions, indeterminate but strong libidinal investments in others' lives, persistent projections on the ethnographer that resist correction or modification. Learning from the experience of fieldwork also demands of the ethnographer a high degree of reflexivity, which in many ways resembles a type of psychic change. Along these lines, Waud Kracke (1987, 59) has argued that culture shock is evidence of "a psychic transformation in the ethnographer" that is simultaneously "cognitive, ethical, and conative or emotional." This shock, he writes, is especially evident "in readapting oneself to one's own society."

That said, psychic change in the experience of culture shock is not usually of the same order as the wished-for psychic change in the ritual process of the rehabilitation of sex offenders. For one, except for the radical case of "going native," the change for the anthropologist is usually merely a relativization of the order of the person; for the sex offender it is a transformation in the order of the self. For another, the anthropologist voluntarily submits; the sex offender must submit to the coercive authority of the social. In ethnographic fieldwork, adjustments in the order of the person begin with entry into the field (if not preparation for this entry); continues through the learning of language, adjustment to forms of everyday life, and participation in ritual process; and culminates with a published monograph. In rehab rituals, the transformation of self begins with the accusation and arrest, continues through incarceration and therapy, and culminates with release from prison and reintegration into the social.

It is possible that in rehab a sex offender relativizes his person only by presenting a different face to therapists, judges, and prison officials. In that case his adjustments leave the self and its interior life unchanged, but in public he appears more normatively attuned, a normatively adjusted person. It is also possible that the anthropologist only simulates in fieldwork an adjustment to the norms of another society rather than undergo a self-transformation. If, by contrast, her experience leads to changes in her inner life, she is in some way "going native," assimilating herself into the culture of those with whom she interacts in research. In the case of a transformed self, changes in the unconscious or inner life are evidenced in dreaming in another language or register of images, in engagement with an order of phantasms that are no longer easily brought into consciousness and, because of that, difficult to consciously access but nonetheless important for unconscious communication with others in that particular culture. For child sex offenders, the challenge is to come to understand the radicality of what is demanded of them: To become a better or more normatively attuned person is not enough. Child sex abuse is, then, not simply an act to be avoided, a risk to minimize, or a motivation to be repressed, but a social transgression that demands of them a psychic change in the order of self.

Interiority

Among anthropologists, the notion of "interiority" presents two problems. One group questions whether interiority always exists in every culture and place over time; the other questions whether one can access this inner life of the person using techniques of participant observation. One response of those critical of exploring interiority has been instead to stress, as has Clifford Geertz (1973), the public nature of symbols and their performance. Recently Joel Robbins and Alan Rumsey (2008) reopened this question from a new angle, drawing from ethnography of the South Pacific, to focus on what they call the "opacity of the mind thesis." Unlike in the West, where it is assumed everyone has an inner life that can be accessed, the people in the South Pacific assume the inner life is largely unknowable and place little or no value on transparency of motives. Across the South Pacific region, concealment, the capacity to hide inner thoughts, is highly valued. There appears to be a fear of the loss of autonomy entailed in the revelation of secrets, of which there are many, personal or communal.

Accordingly, individuals in the South Pacific claim that the mind of the other is opaque, that his or her intentions cannot be understood, and even speaking in the first person "I" is no index of true intentions. As Webb Keane (2008, 474) has rightly concluded, this is not an argument of comparative psychology (whether interiority exists), although usually framed that way, but "a metalinguistic claim about the relations between public evidence and private states" that is part of a "moral psychology." Revelation and concealment are political claims, "less about intensions than the talk about intentions," not about whether one can know inner thoughts but about the "capacity to hide them" (475, 477).

Indeed there is, to my knowledge, no ethnographic evidence in any culture region of individuals lacking interiority or lacking a moral psychology about its valuation. The question is instead about the variability of access, the complexity of the life of the mind, and the willingness to explore the mind. Within anthropology, questions that focused on interiority were of central concern to a number of research programs: for example, the relation of culture to personality (M. Mead 1928; Wallace 1970), the historical development of individualism (Durkheim 1969; Dumont [1983] 1986), the cultural construction of the self (Hallowell [1955] 1967), the social construction of the self (G. H. Mead [1934] 1964), and the cultural diversity of concepts of self (Geertz 1973; Schweder and Bourne 1984). For the most part, these programs made weak if any analytic distinction between person and self, as they were primarily interested in explaining relative moral psychologies, differences between the West and non-Western cultures. To the extent they claimed something distinctive about the self, it was often attributed to modernity, as in Arthur Kleinman's (1988, 51) statement, based on the analysis of illness narratives, that "the self as we come to know and experience it is a 'construction' of modern culture."

What makes the self an important object for modern culture concerns not its constructedness per se, but its focus on a specific quality: how it makes explicit an interiority that is accessible through talk and cultivated introspection and capable of transformation. The (cultural) person and his public representations have been essential to the construction of modern nationalism and "orientalism," as ways to differentiate collectives and, as Durkheim would have it, create collective solidarities. These representations circulate in public and assume a stability of person. The self, by contrast, is a malleable yet deep structure, and highly individualized.[3] This is all the more important as the power grows internationally of disciplines—psychology being the oldest, neuroscience the most recent—that focus on penetrating, controlling, and orienting the self, and that orient the growth of institutions (e.g., advertising, education, criminal justice systems) that employ and market this information.

To follow up Robbins and Rumsey's (2008) argument, one might ask about the relative value in any particular place assigned to the person versus the self. In the South Pacific, as they write in their edited volume, the person is valued over the self, public presentation over individual expression. To sustain this valuation, subjectivity—how one defines one's internal states and drives—is kept opaque from intersubjective claims—the way in which these internal states are defined relationally through others. In the West, by contrast, the self is increasingly valued over the person, individual expression over public presentation; to sustain this valuation, subjectivity is pressed to make itself transparent through personal introspection and in intersubjective communication. This contrast can be explained in part by considering the density of intersubjective claims in small groups versus the comparative ease with which one can escape claims by the other in Western societies, especially in the relatively anonymous urban areas.

This comparative frame, then, might shed new light on how shame and guilt are usually assessed in anthropology. To take two extremes, Pacific cultures such as Japan are often described as "shame cultures" while northern European cultures such as Germany are "guilt cultures." While there is obviously some basis for this stereotype, such essential contrasts, even when not overdrawn, tend to shield the two poles from a reckoning with internal differences. An argument for the recognition of cultural variability does not contradict the fact that all humans experience the phenomenon of shame, though not to the same degree, and all cultures contain some notion of guilt, however attenuated. A more significant point of comparison for comparative psychology is how and under what conditions shame is converted into guilt, into a form of being held accountable for what one does.

In the South Pacific, shame is dealt with as an interior emotion, as in the West, but it cannot be made transparent, and the social consequences of shame for the person are highly elaborated, whereas guilt remains ambiguously defined and the conversion of shame into guilt is neither highly valued nor ritually elaborated. By contrast, in the West, the assumption is that feelings such as shame can be made transparent to the subject (in terms of internal drives) and understood intersubjectively, as the product of and in relations with others. By making feelings of shame transparent, guilt can be assessed and ritually elaborated to hold offenders responsible. On this basis rigorous public accountability mechanisms are developed to redress harms. The use of therapy in the ritual rehab of child sex molesters is one example of where shame is converted into guilt and ritually elaborated in a demand for self-transformation. Guilt in the South Pacific setting, by comparison, is not attached to the self, which is granted significant autonomy (while the public person is socially constrained); accountability mechanisms that hold the self responsible for his or her actions are therefore weak.

The point of psychological comparison, ultimately, is not to come up with discrete categories that allow typification, moral judgment, or radical separation of cultural areas or of individual subjects, but to understand how such categories work in culture regions or individuals processually and historically, through different and changing evaluative and developmental schemas.

Ritual Rehab and the Self

Rehabilitation rituals ask of therapy that it serve legal ends. For legal scholars it is important to understand the possibilities and limits of therapy. The German term *Behandlung* (treatment) encompasses all forms of treatment, including therapy. It is important to differentiate, however, between treatment that might better be called simply "normative adjustment without thinking," where neither introspection nor reflection is asked for, and treatment that requires thinking or symbolization. Popular treatments such as pharmacological interventions or cognitive behavioral modification are forms of administration of populations classified as dangerous. Influenced by such disciplines as behavioral psychology, criminal forensics, and psychopharmacology, they employ a simple model of the motivated and culpable person or agent who needs only to understand the norms and make a behavioral adjustment.[4] They involve thought modification but not thinking. Offenders remain basically unchanged except for agreement to obey the social norms. It is not important whether they are deceiving themselves (or the therapists) or unable to symbolize what they did wrong. There is no obligation to think or bring what happened into speech. If there is a threat of repetition of the crime, only the dosage must be adjusted or terms of punishment (more or less severe) or probation (longer or shorter, indefinite detention) changed.[5]

This narrower concept of treatment occludes the powerful potential of contemporary secular rituals, which rely on the more refined idea of the self and its transformative potential that I elaborate in these pages. That potential, while acknowledging the importance of adjusting to norms, takes up the self as an object of knowledge, value, control, and power to effect a rehabilitation of the individual. In decisions concerning early release or release without supervision, or in decisions to end supervision, judges are often dissatisfied with evidence of mere adjustment to norms. They seek evidence of a deeper transformation, without being able to name what this exactly is. Transformation of the self, I am arguing, is what they are looking for in rehab rituals. Self-transformation is a more powerful and rigorous way to think about change than related concepts referring to change of the agent, person, personality, or subject. Because the self refers neither to a stable entity nor to an integrated subject fully conscious of its desire, it allows one to go beyond a superficial concern with personality traits or fixed characteristics or the external determinants of power. Diagnosis or prognosis of the self cannot rely on traits or fixed characteristics. In short, the human "self" presents a much more refined object for legal intervention and use than the shell or vessel that is presented as the person or legal subject in a court of law.

In all fairness, formal legal procedures delimit the kind of evidence permitted to prove guilt in court, which often forecloses consideration of unconscious motivations and limits evidence to the order of a person with a conscious will. Not only in the trial or sentencing procedures but throughout the ritual process, the legal concept of guilt is linked to notions of culpability, motivation and the intentionality of acts, consent and coercion. In contemporary Western legal systems, such notions are necessary to turn the accusation of abuse into a crime. But many of the kinds of treatment that law turns to for rehabilitation do not essentially rely on these concepts. Chemical castration or other kinds of pharmacological intervention can sufficiently dampen the libido so as to make sex offenses very unlikely, but in substituting a chemical intervention for a change in will, they unwittingly remove the offender's possible culpability without actually admitting to doing so. Neurological intervention promises to bypass volition altogether and make adjustments in the brain itself. If such treatments do not work, the contemporary response is to adjust the pharmacological intervention rather than work to encourage the offender to think through and assume responsibility for the offense. Even incarceration and punishment often harden the resentment of the offender at his fate, driving whatever event has occasioned his crime deeper into the unconscious. If the goal is to contribute to changing the deeper motivations of the offender so as to make a repetition of the crime highly unlikely, rehabilitation must aim toward a psychic change of the self.

Different disciplines often cooperate with one another and the law, as their approaches seem compatible. Just as often, however, legal authorities pressure medical-psychological authorities for certain results, either assessments that allow for the release of offenders or, equally likely, ones that emphasize uncertainty and high risk factors and hence allow for more extensive surveillance accompanying probation. The turn to therapy within the German mode of rehabilitation of child sex molesters presents a more effective alternative to the punitive model such as is practiced in the United States. But it does not escape the tensions inherent in interactions among different kinds of experts with the legal field.

Preventive Detention and the Courts

On May 4, 2011, the German Federal Constitutional Court (BVerG; Bundesverfassungsgericht) declared unconstitutional the practice of *Sicherungsverwahrung* ("preventive detention," also called "supplementary preventive custody") when imposed subsequent to an original verdict. It was reacting to a 2010 decision of the European Court of Human Rights (ECHR), which had ruled that the practice of "subsequent incapacitation"—an indeterminate sentence following a regular imprisonment—violated Article 7 of the European Convention on Human Rights. The BVerG argued that extending the prison terms of offenders deemed a threat to public safety after the sentence had expired violated a basic right to freedom by not differentiating the preventive detention from normal imprisonment. Although the legislation in question offered therapeutic rationales for further detention, the court in effect saw only security interests behind the desire to incapacitate the offenders.

Kirstin Drenkhahn (2013), Basdekis-Jozsa et al. (2013), and Alexander, Graf, and Janus (2011) have written succinct analyses of the history of preventive detention and current legal controversies, which I will now draw freely from before explicating the significance of these for rehabilitation. Aspects of preventive detention can be found in nineteenth-century Prussian law, but only after the Nazi Party came to power in 1933 was it formally introduced into the Penal Code as the *Gesetz gegen gefährliche Gewohnheitsverbrecher und uber Maßregeln der Sicherung und Besserung* (Habitual Offenders and Measures of Security and Correction Act). Although ostensibly about confining the mentally ill, it was also used against political enemies or "asocial individuals." Some 3,723 court orders were imposed in 1934 alone; minimally 14,351 from 1933 until 1942. No statistics were kept after 1943, but the level of Nazi regime criminality, including the regular execution of repeat offenders as well as political opponents, suggests detentions of another numerical scale (Baumann 2006).

After the war, the Federal Republic did not change the code (§66). Preventive detention was ordered for between 100 and 270 cases a year, until legal reform in 1969 tightening specifications led to a drop to between 25 and 50 cases annually. Following unification, in 1990, the doctrine was extended to the territory of the former East Germany, which, ironically, had not carried the measure over during the Cold War. In 1998, a new Law for Combating Sexual Offences and other Dangerous Crimes abolished the previous ten-year limit on preventive detention and included the option to impose such detention after the fact. These revisions reversed the decline in cases: in 2010, 101 new court orders were issued; by April 2011, a total of 504 individuals sat in preventive detention in Germany.

In decisions in 2009 and 2010, the ECHR ruled against both of the 1998 revisions, rejecting the claim of German courts that preventive detention was about treatment and protection and not a punitive measure; preventive detention, it argued, was not different from incarceration or normal imprisonment. The BVerG then seemed to try in fact to implement these ECHR rulings, but German politicians held on to the legal provisions that contravened them. The German parliament, the Bundestag, appeared to want to check individual progress toward rehabilitation and to reassess "danger to society" during the period of imprisonment; if there was no certifiable progress, then the Bundestag wanted the right to continued custody of the offender. To justify placing the sentenced offender in what was transparently a situation of "double jeopardy," the parliament included the option of specifying "supplementary preventive custody" in the initial verdict and redefined punishment as detention for therapeutic reasons (Basdekis-Jozsa et al. 2013, 355).

These conflicting directives culminated in the *Therapieunterbringungsgesetz* (Therapy Placement Act) that came into force on January 1, 2011. It introduced for the first time in German law the term *psychische Störung* (psychic disorder) to justify continued holding of persons who otherwise would have had to be released. In replacing mental illness (*psychische Krankheit*) with "psychic disorder" and in claiming a danger to public safety, the courts sought to relegate to psychiatrists the diagnosis and prognosis regarding the nature of the offender and likelihood of repetition of a serious sexual or violent crime. The act even specified that extended institutionalization was to be decided by civil and not criminal courts, following civil and not criminal procedures, as if further incapacitation had nothing punitive about it. The BVerG saw through this framing and, five months later, ordered new legislation that is "freedom orientated and therapy focused." It set forth seven requirements that will in effect restrict the scope of preventive detention, though it did not rule on constitutionality of the Therapy Placement Act.

The distinction between punishment and corrective measures grew out of early twentieth-century attempts to refocus prisons on "resocialization" rather than mere incarceration. Eghigian (2011) dated this distinction back to the promulgation of a set of principles for governing German prisons in 1923, though the idea of alternatives to mere incarceration was probably present with the introduction of the idea of imprisonment as an alternative to capital punishment or exile. Whatever the case, the relationship between the two has never been straightforward. It seems to oscillate between opposing incarceration to resocialization, putting incarceration in the service of resocialization, or using the appearance of resocialization to legitimate imprisonment. All of these alternatives, their contradictions and rationalizations, come to a head in the use of preventive detention. This is true in other national contexts also, such as the United States, where the antiterror policies following September 11, 2001, have resulted in the rationalization of a permanent preventive detention—in Guantanamo Bay—even before the accused is charged with a crime.

That said, the occupying forces pushed German postwar penal policy, in both East and West, explicitly in the direction of *Erziehung* (education) instead of penalization. The criminological abuses of the Third Reich were and remain always in the background. The Nazis generally placed those defined as "security risks" in psychiatric institutions rather than prisons except in those cases where such "asocial" individuals were simply killed. The practice of psychiatric institutionalization as a form of detention for risk management is found to varying degrees in all European countries. The strong emphasis given to "rehabilitation" in the 1976 amendment to the West German Penal Code puts an added burden on those who argue for punitive measures alone.

One cannot underestimate the role of psychiatry and psychiatrists in the contemporary emphasis on rehabilitation (Luhrmann 2001; Rose 1998). It is their theories, combined with the promise of confirmation by the emerging neurosciences, that are quickly replacing other kinds of therapeutic orientations and that most inform public policy on the treatment of and risks posed by sex offenders. The standardized diagnoses of psychiatry and its wide reliance on psychotropic drugs (which are measurably effective in relieving or changing symptoms, at least in the short term) reaffirm a popular understanding of normal science useful for the legitimation of public policy.

Yet, as Eghigian (2011, 210–11) emphasized, the practice of psychiatry cannot be inferred from the techniques available to the psychiatrists. They do not make decisions about practice in social isolation but employ techniques in the context of huge incentives from the powerful pharmaceutical industry and under pressures from law enforcement agencies, in addition to demands from a public that tends to clamor for more security from and longer confinement for offenders. Nonetheless, the practices of contemporary psychiatry are not that far afield from the cranial measurements of nineteenth-century criminal anthropologists; both share an appeal to biological causes and inherited conditions. According to this classificatory scheme, a psychic disorder cannot then be expiated. It is located within the offender, who is incapable of a believable transformation and needs continual monitoring. To the extent child sex molesters are characterized as having a *Pädosexualität*, preventive detention appears to be a relatively humanistic punishment, certainly better than exile or death; these offenders can at most be resocialized through cognitive behavioral therapy (CBT) that teaches them to renounce sexual desire altogether. To work with the malleability of the self through psychodynamic therapeutic processes becomes a costly and time-intensive luxury the public cannot afford. Hence, in therapeutic institutions connected to prisons, as I have mentioned elsewhere, CBT specialists are replacing psychoanalysts and those therapists who employ more psychodynamic treatments.

A Suspended Sentence

A case from the prison files: A thirty-eight–year-old man was sentenced to three years imprisonment for child sex abuse and abuse of a minor, but the judge suspended the sentence. Two brothers accused the man of abusing them, but the judge concluded that there was proof of a sexual relationship with only one of them, who had begun having sex with the defendant at the age of eleven. Witnesses testified that this boy, now eighteen, had kept returning to the adult man on his own over the years, never complaining of the relationship. The other brother, the judge said, had no corroborating evidence of a sexual relationship with the defendant; he appeared to borrow from his brother details of his relationship with the defendant. The judge concluded that the brother who had a sexual relationship with the defendant, which was not disputed, had also many sexual relationships with other men, and he did not appear in any way to be traumatized by these, nor with the relationship with this particular man. In fact, the charge of sex abuse was made only after the two brothers had been accused of the murder of a fourth man, which involved a separate trial and another judge. The judge suspected that by means of a charge of sex abuse the two brothers were perhaps trying to place the blame for this murder on the adult defendant. Nonetheless, the defendant was guilty of sex abuse and abuse of a minor.

Suspended sentences for child sex abuse are rare today; this case is the only one I read that involved suspension. Sentencing procedures in Germany are not standardized but vary considerably between the different provinces (*Länder*). The vast majority of cases result in standard sentences of between two and three and one-half years, the number of months specified by the type of violation. Actual cases I encountered ranged from one and one-half to ten years. As a rule, the more severe the abuse, the longer the sentence. Judges justify the length of their sentences with standard criteria such as, for example, having no prior record, admitting to the crime, avoiding making the victim testify, and the relative severity of the act (the most severe being penetration, measured in centimeters). Offenders can apply for release after having served two-thirds of their sentence.

The terms of the release usually involve probation, and many also involve supervised release. These terms are usually framed by the question of whether the convicted offender has changed, which in turn is contingent on assessing the success of therapy and imprisonment. Dünkel (2009, 33–34) estimated that 60 percent of those with sentences longer than one year are given a conditional release after serving up to two-thirds of their time. By comparison, in Spain 20 to 30 percent are given early conditional releases, in Austria 40 to 50 percent, in Slovenia 32 percent, in Belgium 94 percent, in Finland 99 percent. Dünkel concludes from this comparison that those countries with early release actually have lower recidivism rates. That is, early release rather than serving the full sentence *reduces* the recidivism rate by 8 to 13 percent.

Directives of the European Union (EU) and National Law

On March 10, 2010, the European Commission issued a new Directive on Combating Child Pornography and Sexual Exploitation of Children. Approved by the European Parliament on October 27, 2011, by a vote of 541 to 2, with 31 abstentions, the directive proposed not only to block access to Internet websites containing child pornography (and the ever more "graphic and more violent" images being circulated), but also to oblige all twenty-seven member-states to criminalize erotic depictions of adults. Under the new directive, EU member-states would be legally obligated to ensure the prompt removal of such erotica on webpages hosted in their territories. To be banned were "any kind of sexually connoted pictures," with no exception for the arts (e.g., including coming-of-age movies like Harry Potter) or science (including humanistic or social science studies). Mere private possession of banned erotic films was to be banned, and outside parties would be legally obligated to report it.

In the spirit of a policy of "zero tolerance" of all crimes against children, the directive proposed tougher penalties across the EU, including minimum penalties for about twenty criminal offences, such as ten years in prison for "coercing a child into sexual actions or forcing a child into prostitution," at least three years for producers of child pornography, and at least one year for viewers. Convicted offenders were to be listed in "sex offender registers" and to be "temporarily or permanently" prevented "from exercising at least professional activities involving direct and regular contacts with children." These EU-wide requirements were to be transposed into national laws within two years.

Cecilia Malmström, European Commissioner responsible for Home Affairs, praised the directive as making "a real difference in protecting children from these horrible crimes." Many scholars (including this one), on the other hand, signed a petition circulated on the Internet to protest such overreach, warning that it would make criminal the display of much modern art.

The Committee of Ministers considered the recommendation in a meeting on June 13, 2012 (published two days later), claiming it had "carefully examined" the directive, welcoming the promotion of "greater co-ordination of measures to strengthen regulation of 'child pornography' while focusing particular attention on child abuse images." It then drew attention to the reasons it ultimately rejected the directive.

The Lanzarote Convention (CETS No. 201), the Committee wrote, stressed the importance of "precise" and not "overbroad" terminology in the definition of "child abuse images" to "satisfy the requirements of Article 10 of the European Convention on Human Rights or the corresponding case law of the European Court of Human Rights." The Committee asked for the "implementation of the existing conventions" rather than new "protocols," pointing specifically to its "Declaration on protecting the dignity, security and privacy of children on the Internet," adopted on February 20, 2008, which signaled that "other than in the context of law enforcement, there should be no lasting or permanently accessible record of the content created by children on the Internet which challenges their dignity, security and privacy or otherwise renders them vulnerable now or at a later stage in their lives" (Ministers' Deputies 2012).

In the last several decades, citizens within the various European states have come to complain bitterly that the EU in its various bodies has become primarily a massive regulatory regime with few controls over its reach. Taking the initiative to formulate and standardize rules for society and economy, it has consistently provoked resistance at the national, regional, and local levels. As this example indicates, such efforts are prone to overreach. Despite the formal embrace within the EU of the "principle of subsidiarity"— that decisions should be made by the smallest, lowest, or least centralized authority capable of making them—in the domain of family law, gender equality, or children's rights, various representatives and administrators frequently consider national laws insufficiently vigilant. This example suggests that there are also at times internal checks on the hegemonic thrust of the EU, and that many proposed rules that appear on their way to the status of "law" never indeed make it.

Protecting Children

Some readers may want to believe that current attempts to protect children, to create environments free of coercion in which children can grow up to realize themselves, is evidence of the march of social progress. From this progressive viewpoint, male genital sexuality, embodied in the father figure and father substitutes, is the major current threat to the child. Such "sexuality" (which, as I've documented in these pages, is frequently not about sexuality) can result in cruel attachments, for which rehabilitation, including therapy, of the adult offender is the most humanistic of alternatives. But to support what is assumed to be progress in providing security for the child, more punitive alternatives—long-term or permanent imprisonment, chemical castration, preventive detention, widespread surveillance—are often thought to be necessary.

It would be difficult to prove that the legal protections for children put in place since the 1970s in the contemporary West have created a better childhood there than in those places outside the West or in prior times in the West where and when these protections are missing. We know at least since the publication of Philippe Aries's *L'Enfant et la vie familiale sous l'ancien regime* (translated into English as *Centuries of Childhood*) that there is no universal concept of childhood. Adult relations with children are variable and culturally coded. Aries overstated his case, however, by arguing that childhood is an invention of modernity and that, for example, only in modernity do adults (in the West) grieve for their children's suffering (Pollock 1983). Had he engaged with either the psychoanalytic or ethnographic literature, he would have had to incorporate in his theory of modernity the singular phenomenological experience of the child that coexists with diverse social significations attached to childhood as a unique life-course experience. The treatment, survival, and experience of children is everywhere dependent on a complex dynamic of loss and love, as well as on seduction and empathy, attachment and separation. These dynamics remain phenomenological aporia, as fraught with problems for adults as for children and not resolvable in a universal regulatory code.

This study does not ask, then, whether child sex abuse is real or whether children need some degree of legal protection from adult aggression. Of course it is and they do. Child protections are, at base, what taboos used to address. These taboos appear to be no longer adequate to regulate a new indeterminacy in adult relations with children. But surely, given the fundamental challenges to and reorganization of the Oedipal complex and the incest taboo, codifying protections in law and creating new illegalities cannot be the primary means to respond to contemporary problems regulating acceptable forms of adult intimacy with children. Curtailing excessive parental or adult power over children alleviated some problems while creating new ones.

The more fundamental issues not openly addressed are how to love the child and how to agree on what kind of love children need from adults. Sequestering children from the adult male population to prevent harm may yield a kind of security, but it hardly responds to the child's needs for touch, care, attachment, and an adult "no." Security is not love. And the demand to distance oneself from the father or father figures would appear to make it even more difficult to provide children, especially those with a migration background, with the optimal conditions for a positive psychic development: to encourage curiosity, to discover and learn, to develop a confident and trusting self, and, as in the classical psychoanalytic goal, to develop the capacity and willingness to love others as well as to receive their love.

CHAPTER ONE

1. In the therapy groups that I observed, offenders tended to agree at various points with the ascription of "monster" or that what they had done was "evil," though only a very few actually thought of their transgression as placing them outside the category "human." Waldram (2009) draws a similar conclusion in an ethnographic study of Canadian offenders: The offenders admit that they are "bad" but deny being "evil."

2. For an overview of pharmacological treatments of paraphilias in Germany, and recommendations for a protocol on their use, see Hill et al. (2003).

3. Treatments vary within Germany, and surgical castration is permitted in only some *Länder* (states). In Berlin since 2001, five of the nine applications for castration were rejected by the expert commission that must approve them (CPT/Inf 2012, 59).

4. For arguments about the promises of neuroscience for criminal law, see Bonhoeffer and Gruss (2011); Eagleman (2012, 151–92); Markowitsch and Merkel (2011). Although neuroscience tends to call into question many of the classificatory systems of law and psychiatry, the classification of "pedophiles" is one of the most commonly cited examples turned to when trying to convince the public of the promise and good this science can realize.

5. With regard to my research in both institutions, Kind im Zentrum (KiZ) and the minimum-security prison, I am obliged to strict protection of human subjects (*Datenschutz*) and hence have altered all personal names, dates, and places except for the public figures in the first chapter and the public institution of KiZ, which, given the difficulty of maintaining its anonymity, specifically requested to be named. In the case of the use of government archives, I am not permitted to quote long passages and hence paraphrase mostly and cite selectively from the files. All discussions and documents were in German; all translations are mine.

6. Each therapy center in Germany, of which there are many, offers a slightly different treatment protocol. Most therapy for sex offenders takes place not in such centers but in prisons, and most is a form of behavioral treatment focused on the act. Perhaps most unusual in the Berlin landscape is the program at the Berlin Charité, the Prevention Project Dunkelfeld, which offers voluntary counseling for men who self-identify with "pedophilia" or "hebephilia" before committing any criminal offense. At KiZ, the number of men accused or convicted of the crime of using of child por-

nography has increased considerably in the period of my research, but the numbers were never sufficient to isolate these men in a separate group; instead they were always included in the group for pedophiles. At many therapy centers there is currently much discussion about whether men who use child pornography but usually have no sexual contact with actual children should receive the same diagnosis and treatment as men who have transgressed this boundary in person.

7. Jurisprudence (*Rechtsprechung*) varies considerably across Germany in interpreting this 2002 law. A 2013 judicature in Berlin mandated therapists in prisons to treat all sex offenders, and all sex offenders to obtain treatment. If prisons follow this legal interpretation, it may effectively eliminate for the offender the presumption that therapy is voluntary, and for the therapist the assumption that only some offenders are capable of therapy. Both assumptions are arguably necessary for the ritual efficacy or success of therapy. By assuming all men are treatable, and all therapists can treat all men, this judicature risks turning all treatment into an instrumental performance to produce the veneer of success. Undoubtedly this legal interpretation is motivated in response to a recent Constitutional Court decision limiting *Sicherungsverwahrung* (preventive detention for nonpunitive purposes). If psychiatrists now can pass judgment on the extent to which offenders have resisted treatment (*Behandlung*), an objective criteria (about which they are ritual experts) is introduced into sentencing procedures that enables judges to continue incarceration beyond the time of the original sentence (see chapter 3, footnote 4, and chapter 7).

8. Literature on the self is too extensive to review here. I draw primarily from psychoanalytic and anthropological discourses (see Kohut (1977) for a review of more ego-psychology informed US approaches, and Mitchell (1991) for a summary and comparison of ego-psychology, object relations theory, and Lacanian perspectives—the three major approaches within psychoanalysis).

9. Around the same time as Moore and Myerhoff took up secular ritual, the historian Jacques Donzelot (1979) pursued a Foucauldian argument on state intervention in the regulation of family affairs in France from the eighteenth century to the present. Focused on policy and practices rather than ritual, he nonetheless demonstrates one aspect of state-engineered change: that the state enlisted a wide range of experts to intervene in the family, previously considered a private sphere, which in turn changed quite radically working-class and bourgeois family structures.

10. Thomas Luckmann (1967, 112) anticipates this line of thought (and Foucault's claims about the history of sexuality), arguing that in the "modern world" (aka the secularized societies of the West) the domain of transcendence has shrunk while at the same time religiosity (articulations of the "sacred cosmos") have migrated from institutional religion to the everyday (or secular). Of these articulations, "sexuality, in connection with the 'sacred' theme of self-expression and self-realization, now comes to play a unique role as a source of 'ultimate' significance for the individual who is retrenched in the 'private 'sphere.'" I thank Parvis Ghassem-Fachandi for drawing my attention to this argument, which he elaborates as a failure in the articulation of prayer in a study of an American Holiness Church community (Ghassem-Fachandi 2007).

11. Modeled after programs established in the 1990s in Egypt, the Saudi rehab is limited to a maximum three-month effort and focuses primarily on religious instruction (proper reading of the Qu'ran) followed by counseling, evaluation, and, after release (determined by the Ministry of Interior), extensive monitoring. One of its precepts is to convince jihadis that only the government can authorize a jihad (Wagner 2010).

Indonesia and Singapore have also subsequently established similar rehab centers, modeled on the Saudi effort.

12. Among older Germans the term "rehabilitation" no doubt brings one into unconscious association with the changes demanded by the Allied forces following World War II. The term at that time was *die Umerziehung* (reeducation) for the East Germans, *die Entnazifizierung* for the West Germans, both of which demanded only distancing from fascism and agreement to an anti-National Socialist ideology, something much less than the self-transformation of rehabilitation rituals. In West Germany this was euphemistically referred to as having received a *Persilschein* (Tide certification, or certificate of having been cleansed; see Borneman 1992, 12–18, 231–35).

13. In the spirit of emancipatory movements in the 1960s and 1970s, many influential scholars began emphasizing the peculiar negative consequences of the Oedipus complex and its renunciations as they come to serve either state ends or capitalist production. Along with the work of Michel Foucault, among the most influential philosophically were Giles Deleuze and Felix Guattari and their polemic in *"Anti-Oedipus."* They argued that a change in focus from the hierarchical, arboreal to the multiple and fluid rhizome would encourage a freer flow of desire without the renunciations and limits set by authority figures. Instead of psychoanalysis they propose a "schizoanalysis," where the libido is not desexualized and sublimation is no alternative to repression. They write, "In reality [Oedipus] is universal because it is the displacement of the limit that haunts all societies, the displaced represented (*la représénte déplacé*) that disfigures what all societies dread absolutely as their most profound negative: namely, the decoded flows of desire" (Deleuze and Guaratti 1983, 193). Extending Wilhelm Reich's insightful argument that fascism is the desire to repress desire (later picked up by the anthropologist Michael Taussig [1993, 129–44]), they ultimately seem to be arguing that eliminating family prohibitions (as the perverse repression of desire) would result in emancipation from capitalist production also.

14. The child sex offender's relation to abjection can also be viewed through the frame of Julia Kristeva's theory of the incest taboo, which she places at the center of a theory of abjection (1982, 56–75). The incest prohibition, she concludes, "throws a veil over primary narcissism and the always ambivalent threats with which it menaces subjective identity." The prohibition is necessary for collective existence, but it is weak, not always of "sufficient strength to dam up the abject or demoniacal potential of the feminine." That is, the child (and presumably adults) is pulled toward a primary narcissism, defined as the "unnameable otherness" of the feminine, toward regression to the presymbolic relationship with the mother. Although societies of course vary in their specific economies of desire, hence in what the incest taboo exactly regulates, Kristeva argues that it is nonetheless menstrual and excremental pollution that are archetypal—menstrual because one shares the mother's blood ("the danger to identity that comes from within"), excremental because "maternal authority is experienced, after the first essentially oral frustrations, as sphincteral training." The incest taboo is, therefore, among other things, "the *confrontation with the feminine*, . . . an 'other' without a name." The "demarcating imperative" or the "symbolic 'exclusory prohibition'" resulting from this confrontation and taboo, she writes, is "subjectively experienced as abjection." Following this logic, the pollution of the incest offender, his abject status, is due to how he opens the veil over primary narcissism: He falls into a presymbolic stage (with the child) in refusing "the triangulating function of the paternal prohibition," that is, his function as a symbolically (linguistically) con-

stituting subject in relation to the child. In sum, Kristeva does us the service of expli-cating the subject's experience of pollution within the social rather than reducing the experience to or deducing it from the regulatory effects of social organization.

15. For comparative purposes, one might begin with Roger Lancaster's analysis of sex panics in the United States and the model of the punitive state. As to differences, the sex panic in Germany does not serve as "an important model—part metaphor and part blueprint—for the pervasive politics of fear" (Lancaster 2011, 12). The fear mobilized against the Bolshevik threat and internal enemies in Germany of the Nazi period, and then later the fear mobilized in the hunt for Red Army Faction terror-ists in the 1970s, predated the kind of sex panics that did in fact spread in Germany in the late 1980s. When it comes to terror today, those prior experiences may be formative, but they have a delimiting effect on present public hysteria. Another dif-ference: The genealogy of sex panics in Germany results from gender and genera-tional conflict and follows that of witch burning (the male sex offender takes the place of the female witch), rather than, as Lancaster writes about the United States, the gay molester and racial other taking the place of the homosexual (Lancaster 2011, 40–45).

   Even at the height of the sex panics of the 1980s, the public focus in Germany and throughout Western Europe was not on gay men, homosexuals, or race but on child-adult relations generally. That said, the phantasmatic investment in child sex, and child sex abuse, is as great in Germany as in the United States; it just has not re-sulted in hysterical, posse-like persecution. One of the early attempts to describe how pedophiles themselves come to desire children, by the sociologist and sex researcher Rüdiger Lautmann, did in fact result in identifying and naming him as the cause for what he was trying to describe (Lautmann 1994).

16. The statistics for all aspects of sex abuse vary across country, of course, but within a fairly narrow range. One frequently cited report that summarizes different studies in the United States, for example, found that of adults who are convicted child sex of-fenders, 90 percent are male, and 95 percent heterosexual. In studies of twelve states between 1991 and 1996, 96 percent of the perpetrators of sexual assaults reported to law enforcement were male (Holmes and Slap 1998). A 2002 Germany study found that men were convicted of 98 percent of the sex crimes in Germany (Osterheide et al. 2012).

17. For a careful analysis of this scandal as a sex panic, see Witte (2014). That this scandal became, by 2013, a political party scandal in sexual garb about the past (against the Greens and Free Democrats) rather than a witch-hunt for present-day child molest-ers speaks to the specific way in which the party is still dominant in structuring the political in the German context.

18. Lancaster (2011, 181–227) argues, interestingly, that the call for victim rights in the United States has its origins in the welfare state of the 1960s, specifically in the war on crime and the feminist movement, which then increasingly takes a punitive, right-wing political turn. In Germany, extensive welfare state provisions predate by a half century or more the proliferation of victim discourses and what now is often referred to as a punitive turn. Following WWII through national division and unification in the 1990s, discourse revolved around the German role as "perpetrators" of war crimes, even though of course many Germans experienced the war as victims. Still to-day, the use of punishment and imprisonment in Germany pales in scale compared to the United States, largely because rehabilitation remains the explicit goal of the German penal system.

19. Behavioral research utilizes questionnaires or formal interviews to elicit responses, which is called self-reporting. The problem with such research on either child sex offenders or victims of child sex abuse is not that the design lacks sufficient internal controls on consistency (produces the same results when applied to the same population over time) or validity (measures what it claims to measure). Rather, the "bias" is inherent to the topic itself—child sex abuse, stigmatized sexual behavior considered criminal—and the shame associated with it, which militates against accuracy in self-reporting. In the case of child sex offenders, the picture that arises from their participation in therapy is that they initially do not see themselves as others do. They do not even see themselves as part of a "population." Given that the act of sex abuse is inconsistently defined across time, offenders are also likely to be inconsistent in interpreting the questions they are asked about abuse and particularly sensitive to impression management. Ethnographic study of therapy groups relying on participant observation is unconcerned with consistency across population, and it relies on the verification of perceptions to validate its findings (see chapter 2).

20. I take my inspiration here from the recent debate sparked by Gopal Guru (2012) and Sundar Sarrukai (2012) about the current status of untouchability in India.

21. Theoretically, then, the rehabilitation of sex offenders should result in social reincorporation. In practice, of course, skepticism about this process makes incorporation difficult if not impossible. But given the presumption of the Western legal system that absolute or essential social exclusions are not permitted, it is a politically useful ruse. In all social contexts the ideal of incorporation is in tension with political reality. In India today, for example, the strategy of the Indian political movement Hindutva is to incorporate (rehabilitate) Dalits, those formerly classified outside the caste system, into the caste order (now a political identification) as Hindus. This incorporation creates the semblance of social integration for electoral-political utility; Hindus unite with (incorporate) Dalits to turn them against Muslims (see Ghassem-Fachandi 2012).

22. For an important comparison to this study, see James Waldram's (2012) ethnographic monograph of sex offender "habilitation" in Canada. Although there are many similarities in context and treatment in both Canada and Germany, important differences in our objects of study and theoretical framings preclude some more detailed comparisons. Above all, Waldram's study is of prison-based treatment, and the treatment he observes is solely cognitive behavioral therapy (CBT). One of his major foci is on the narrative shaping of the inmate experience into a peculiar type of autobiography, which results largely from methods employed in CBT and from the prison setting. He characterizes these narratives as distortions to comply with expectations, a "confession . . . [aiming] to admit guilt to the crimes by accepting the 'facts' without qualification" (133). The goal is not, as in my observation in Germany, a (more radical) ritual transformation of self. Rather, the goal of the CBT he studies is to make it possible for the prison therapists to claim that an individual is unlikely to relapse into the same behavior (of low risk). Waldram calls this "moral habilitation, an adjustment to the norms of "appropriate sexual and ethical conduct" so that offenders may ultimately "fit in" (101). While less concerned with the question of efficacy of treatment (ritual rehab) than I am, Waldram's study nonetheless provides invaluable insight into the experience of treatment and therefore the conditions under which it can render the sex offender capable of reintegration into the social after imprisonment.

23. Despite this research, the vast majority of professionals who study or work with sex offenders still assume that treatment for violent offenders is ineffective. A 2007 pilot

study of members of the Association of Treatment of Sex Offenders, most of whom are US Americans, found that 63 percent found "little hope for a cure," and 88 percent feared recidivism after treatment (Engle, McFalls, and Gallager 2007, 23).

CHAPTER TWO

1. By "imaginary" I do not mean that it is fabricated but that the origin of this complex is found in its relation to the body and unconscious phantasy rather than to language and the symbolic (see Berkel 2006). For the most part, I am concerned here with phantasy, what the subject makes inaccessible to him- or herself and, therefore, largely unconscious, rather than fantasy, what is accessible to the conscious subject (Issacs 1948, 73–97), though the distinction between the two is for heuristic purposes and not rigorously empirical.

2. On whether the harmful effects of sex abuse result from neglect or other kinds of violence that accompany the such abuse, see, e.g., Finkelhor (1979, 1984); Gschwind and Becker (1995); Herman (1982); Herman, Russell, and Trocki (1986); Hirsch (1999); Kempe and Kempe (1978); for a review of the anthropology of sex and abuse, see Bolin and Whelehan (1999, 185–96).

3. I use empirical case studies to generalize at several levels about the social significance of psychological processes that are universal but take culturally specific forms and of changing forms of intimacy and its regulation by sociolegal processes that are at times specific to Germany or to Northern Europe and North America and still at other times specific to the West. The cases are contextualized and interpreted by using relevant statistical and historical data in order to theorize, in this chapter, the contemporary experience of incest, child sex abuse, and rehabilitation.

4. See chapter 1, where I elaborate this point in terms of the ethnographic and psychoanalytic literatures. I have neglected other approaches that assume the universality of the taboo is due to instinct, which argues on too general a scale to be able to account for the sociohistorical specificity of practices examined in this study. Following Fox's ([1980] 1983) seminal attempt to situate the taboo between the cultural and biological, recent work in the sociobiological tradition revives a Westermarkian perspective (avoidance due to proximity) to explore the relation of the taboo to inbreeding and incest practices (Wolf and Durham 2004). For social anthropologists, the lack of a clear distinction in this approach between instinct (the pacification of a need) and drive (the fulfillment of a desire), along with the failure to incorporate the specifically intersubjective and linguistically mediated meanings of the act, effaces the evolutionary specificity of humans. Because of the contingency of drives and phantasmic relation to objects, humans acquire a unique (nonfunctional, often counteradaptational) subjectivity in sexuality that is absent in other animals. For a human, then, the meaning of "avoidance" of sex with another is an ambivalent, culturally coded response to complex stimuli, explained not by instinct but by the relation of historically determined drives to specific objects or categories of objects (cf. Aberle et al. 1963; Paul 2010).

5. This argument recalls the debate within anthropology about the difference between customary and modern state law (cf. Moore 1978). The incest taboo resembles a "customary law" in that it achieves its coherence in the context of increased state legal regulation. Modern state law does not replace this taboo, however, but specifies a fixed content and the conditions of enforcement and punishment. A "law," as I am using the term, operates in a system with special procedures for determining how it is made, interpreted, legitimated, and enforced.

6. For studies of the discourse on incest from the Middle Ages through the nineteenth century in Germany, see Eming, Jarzebowski, and Ulbrich (2003); Sabean (2002).

7. Here the psychoanalytic distinction between suppression (*Unterdrückung*) and repression (*Verdrängung*) is relevant. The problem is not one of misperception. An affect is not disguised through suppression and then misperceived by the potential offender. If that were the case, the offender could correctly identify this affect and change or prevent his behavior. Rather, the affect is made inaccessible to consciousness, and there is a psychic investment in this inaccessibility.

8. Three categories of criminal statistics are relevant: (1) the sex abuse of children, (2) the abuse of children as the exploitation of a dependency relationship, and (3) incest. For Germany the numbers of convictions in 2006 and 2007 were, respectively, (1) 12,772 and 12,765, (2) 828 and 897, and (3) est. 90 (extrapolated proportionally from the Berlin numbers) (BKA 2007; also see http://www.bka.de /nn_205960/DE/Home/homepage__node.html?__nnn=true). In the same three categories, the numbers of individuals sentenced for violations in 2006 in Berlin were (1) 2,686, (2) 126, and (3) 18 (Statistische Bundesamt 2007).

9. Classification of sex crimes varies as legal and social norms change. In Germany criminological discourse today tends to classify the sex abuse of children as a crime against sexual self-determination, rape as a crime of violence, and pornography as an economic delict. In the 1970s and 1980s, prostitution and homosexuality were fully decriminalized, making them no longer important for criminological classification. In this same period the number of sex crimes has remained constant while public awareness of them has increased because of nearly daily reporting, with the focus on the most spectacular cases. In 2002, for example, of the more than six million criminal acts, only 0.8 percent were of sex crimes (PKS 2002, table 1, cited in Stolte 2005, 174). In 2003, those sentenced for child sexual abuse, rape and sexual assault comprised 1 pecent (7,333 of 736,297) of all sexual delicts and 0.4 percent of all crimes. Between 1960 and 1985, "pedophile crimes" declined, and they have since remained relatively constant, with a very slight increase after 1987. Police-reported rapes increased in the 1950s and then remained constant until they increased again in the 1980s, before again declining. It is uncertain to what extent these trends are due to increased public sensitivity, which surely leads to more willingness to prosecute but has an uncertain relation to the commission of such criminal acts (Urbaniok 2005).

10. See the guidelines issued by the Bundesministerium der Justiz for the protection of child victims when they are called as witnesses in criminal procedures, http://www .bmj.bund.de/media/archive/541.pdf (accessed May 20, 2009), which make general, practical suggestions: e.g., empathy for the victim (3), protection of the victim's dignity (11), sensitivity in questioning (12), consideration of related family crises (15), care in determining whether to request an evaluation of the victim (27), care in determining whether to call the child as witness (32).

11. By 1955 Weinberg had already noted that the mother was integral to the conditions under which incest remained secret or became public knowledge (Weinberg 1955).

12. Devereux (1939, 510) is, as usual, the exception here. In his bold essay on Navaho incest, he writes, "Anthropological literature is strangely lacking in concrete data concerning the occurrence of incest. With the exception of a few brilliant anthropologists like Malinowski, field workers have provided us with nothing but elaborate listings of taboos."

13. There are several theoretically relevant frames for Juliet's experience, to specify at

what point and through what kind of mirroring with her mother and the psychologist the interaction with her uncle became an experience. Fonagy (2008) might frame this as the "introjection" of an "alien self" through the highly distorted and self-centered mirroring of her mother, which the child will later, for his or her own psychic stability, need to externalize through projection onto another; Laplanche (1999) might claim that the "intromission" or "implantation" by the child of the adult's excitation becomes a "message" that in translation creates the unconscious; Butler (1993) might ask how the child is "appellated" into a gendered sexual subjectivity.

14. The point here is to ask what replaces anatomy and gender complementarity as organizing principles when they become less salient and relevant for ordering the social. See the very prescient critique by Jessica Benjamin (1995).

15. For an outstanding interpretation of a male initiation ritual in New Guinea, see Juillerat (1992). For a more extensive analysis of the fate of male ritual initiations in Europe, see Borneman (2010); for the relation of masculinity to sex abuse, see Bruder (2001). Despite changes in the nature of masculinity in the West, extensive reporting of acts such as Uncle Bodo's transgression tends to equate male sexuality itself with violence. As for female initiation rites, before the twentieth century, defloration (*zu entjungfern*, literally "to take away youth") on the evening of marriage often served as a comparable rite of passage (see Gay 1993, 95–115, 288–352).

16. This argument follows Dammasch (2008a), who analyzes a growing male deficit, in comparison to female peers, in upbringing, education, and social relationships in Germany. Drawing from a number of statistical studies, along with cases from his own clinical practice, he identifies the central factor in the crisis of young men as the instability and weakness of someone whose inner father-representation is bound to the mother-representation and the resulting uncomfortable closeness of the son to the mother.

17. In the historiography of Germany, most important for initiating masculinity as research theme were Theweleit (1987) for World War I and Mosse (1985) for World War II. On Cold War restructuring of the German family and nation, see Borneman (1992); Herzog (2005).

18. The new legal status of women and children correlates only roughly with the changing empirical patterns of child care and family forms. The number of officially acknowledged single mothers in both German states more than doubled during the Cold War, and this growth has continued since 1990s. Concerning other household forms, between 1996 and 2007, the number of heterosexual couples living together outside of marriage increased by 36 percent. In 2006, only 1 percent of households included three generations, 37 percent of all households were single persons, with 49 percent in large cities (all numbers taken from Statistisches Bundesamt Deutschland (http://www.destatis.de/jetspeed/portal/cms/Sites/destatis/Internet/EN/Navigation /Statistics/Bevoelkerung/Bevoelkerung.psml, accessed August 13, 2009).

19. The current status of gender conflict in the West is the product of an uneven evolution, though there has been a definite trajectory toward the rectification of historical injustice, that is, toward what is recognized as "women's rights." Although male behavior generally has perhaps always been criminalized more than female behavior, the criminalization of male sexual behavior (outside same-sex behavior) is relatively recent. One way to understand this current criminalization is as the inverse of the past criminalization of female sexual behavior, though the latter most often made women scapegoats and exculpated men for socially defined abuses that were intrin-

sic to heterosexual relations (e.g., prostitution, wanton behavior, having children out of wedlock). The trials of witches throughout much of Europe over three hundred years, in which women became objects of ritual sacrifice, often involved the accusations of eating, killing, and having sex with children. I thank Thomas Hauschild for this suggestion.

20. For the current status of European law on self-determination, see Graupner (2004, 2005); for a history of the "right to sexual self-determination" in German law, specifically 13. Abschnitt StGB-Straftaten gegen die sexuelle Selbstbestimmung (§§174-184g), see Renzikowski (2003).

21. Despite opposition by legal scholars, the Deutsche Bundestag passed a law on April 1, 2004, that increased the length of sentences for crimes against sexual self-determination. This follows a pattern within the German legal community that began in the 1970s; in response to charges of being culturally *Täter identifiziert* (biased toward the perpetrator), more attention was given to the status of the victim and issues of victim protection, redress, and compensation. The most relevant laws include the 1976 Opferentschädigungsgesetz for victims of violence (compensation through a higher pension); the 1986 Opferschutzgesetz expanding the possible charges, especially of sexual delicts, and increased the protections of victims; the 1992 law to fight organized criminality (known by its German abbreviation, OrgKG); the 1998 Zeugenschutzgesetz to allow video taping and other means to protect witnesses; the 1998 Opferanspruchsicherungsgesetz (to grant victims a lien on the marketing of stories by offenders); the 1999 Täter-Opfer Ausgleich facilitating the process of arriving at a settlement between victim and offender; the 2000 Gewaltschutzgesetz expanding protections for victims of violence; the 2001 Prostitutionsgesetz providing sex workers with a legal right to a fee. Following the public Round Table on child sex abuse in Berlin in 2012–13, a series of laws that address victims were proposed and enacted.

22. In therapy men work through the many different kinds of relationships and sexual acts that might have led to their crimes. The kinds of sex abuse men in the incest therapy groups revealed varied widely, including, for example, taking pornographic pictures, inappropriate touching, kissing, oral-genital contact, repeated genital penetration; the victims included biological sons and daughters, stepdaughters, stepsons, nieces, neighbors' children, daughters' girlfriends.

23. The Court ruled that § 173 Abs. 2 Satz 2 StGB, which forbids *Beischlaf* (intercourse) between siblings, is compatible with the Basic Law (constitution). The brother, who had already served two sentences for previous incest with his sister, was sentenced for a third time, in the most recent case, to two years and six months, and the sister was sentenced to supervision. The majority decision of the Court appealed to "cultural-historical [grounds] and the internationally widely shared *Verbotsnorm* (norm to ban it)." Such acts, it argued, constituted a "deep violation of marriage and the family," especially the "genetic harm" and "psychosocial" injury to the child who is a product of incest. Moreover, it asserted that the right of "sexual self-determination" was oriented to protect children from sexual abuse and society from human trafficking.

The Court's vice president criticized this decision, however, arguing that a "eugenics perspective"—prevention of genetic defects—is not a task of the modern state; that criminal law is not the appropriate means to "build a social consensus about value-orientation," more specifically about the incest taboo; and that this decision violates the "right of self-determination" in order to defend "merely existing and assumed moral conceptions" (BVerfG, 2 BvR 392/07; for commentary, see Greco 2008).

The German Society for Human Genetics also criticized the decision, on scientific grounds, arguing that the issue of inheritance of genetic disorders has a different relevance in countries, such as Germany, where exogamy is widely practiced and therefore the likelihood of couples sharing a genetic disorder is miniscule. Research in other parts of the world on the effects of long-term endogamous marriages on health, however, confirms some dangers while attributing others to nongenetic factors. For example, while early infant and postnatal mortality is significantly higher in consanguineous progeny (a union of second cousins or closer) than among more distantly related or nonrelated couples, fertility is not affected, and estimates of the incidence of mortality generally in such unions have consistently been revised downward over time. More recent work on genetic disorders has confirmed that many single-gene disorders, including mental retardation, are prevalent among such progeny (Bittles 2003).

24. Ferenczi ([1909] 1952), who coined the term "introjection" in 1909, explained children's identification with abusers as identification with the aggressor. Freud ([1914] 1957, 90) identified several types of narcissistic love and contrasted the paths leading to the object-choice of the narcissistic type with the object-choice of the anaclitic, or attachment, type. In the case of narcissistic object-choice, identification is with "(a) what he himself is (i.e., himself), (b) what he himself was, (c) what he himself would like to be, (d) someone who was once part of himself."

25. In bringing incest into speech in therapy, Alex had to work to symbolize that which he had relegated to his unconscious, first, by recognizing, however timidly, his own temporal regression to an infantile sexuality, and second, by making himself more conscious of his own agency in his relation to people and objects.

26. Lacan (1970, 194; 1977) distinguishes between desire and *jouissance:* Desire is created by the lack that founds the subject as a member of the symbolic order, and it defines the subject in relation to an Other as well as to the renunciations that define the social order. *Jouissance,* by contrast, is not oriented to an Other but to fullness and excess.

27. Laplanche (1989, 126) writes, "I am, then, using the term primal seduction to describe a fundamental situation in which an adult proffers to a child verbal, nonverbal and even behavioural signifiers which are pregnant with unconscious sexual significations."

28. The field of transgender studies is at the forefront of these two shifts in agency, with the avatars prepubescent children who assert a right to operations that bring their anatomy in line with gender subjectivity. I thank Billie Jean Isbell for drawing my attention to this.

CHAPTER THREE

1. The sexual offense provisions pertain to those sentenced under §§174–183 StGB of the German Penal Code.

2. The strong interest in criminal typologies for the purposes of diagnosis and policy leads many scholars to assume that pedophilia results in a fixing in early life of a sexual preference for prepubescent children. The fact that most pedophiles do not actually act on this preference leads to arguments for treatment as opposed to incarceration. The Canadian psychologist Michael Seto (2008), for example, argues that interventions of various sorts work for three kinds of explanations—conditioning, child sexual abuse, and neurodevelopmental disorders.

3. In a Wisconsin study, Zevitz and Farkas (2000) conclude that community notifica-

tion programs have had no effect in managing sex offenders and antitherapeutic effects on their rehabilitation. They argue that a more effective strategy to reintegrate ex-offenders would be to provide stable housing and employment.

4. *Sicherungsverwahrung* (preventive detention for reasons of security, i.e., for nonpunitive purposes), a controversial legal doctrine that entered the Penal Code in the Weimar period, provoked vigorous dissent in the 1970s as it was used to detain members of the Red Army Faction suspected of terrorism. Today the doctrine has been less important for the suspicion of terrorism than for pedophilia. In 2004 in Germany, 310 adult prisoners out of 54,000 remained in prison for preventive detention after having served their sentences, and two-thirds of these were sex offenders (Dünkel and Maelicke 2004, 132). On May 4, 2011, the German Constitutional Court, citing the Convention on Human Rights as interpreted by the European Court on Human Rights, ruled unconstitutional incapacitation subsequent to the original sentencing (see chapter 7).

5. Where Goffman's insights do resound with the German situation is in his description of some aspects of inmate culture (on US maximum-security facilities, see Rhodes 2004; Wacquant 2002). For example, Goffman claims that most inmate conversations with each other revolve around "accounting for [their] present low estate," which leads to "much self-pity" (1961, 67). Self-pity interferes with a reckoning with how one has become a victimizer. Inmates only reluctantly and not immediately converse about the reasons they are in prison.

6. In the attempt to be more scientific, many experts divide "cognitive distortions" from "affective traits," specifically when it come to understanding the significance of empathy. Such effort is bound to fail, as there is no cognitive process in the absence of affect (for a critique of this use of cognitive therapy in prisons, see Waldram 2010). My argument here is that there is no disembodied cognition, and that affect intensification can lead in fact to more perspicacious judgments as well as to cognitive distortions (Stein 1998).

CHAPTER FOUR

1. The research of Gilbert Herdt (1994) and others on groups in the Highlands of Papua New Guinea posed a set of relevant cultural comparisons in any discussion of universal aspects of child-adult relations. Specifically, it challenged a universal idea of adolescent initiation and of "child sex abuse." In the Highlands at the time Herdt worked there, in the late 1970s, male initiation into adulthood was marked by ritualized homosexual insemination (oral ingestion of semen) of boys by older men. His research has been highly productive for questions in a number of domains: of ethics, of the nature of sexual desire, and of sexuality itself. As these questions will take me too far afield from my topic, I will focus solely on the regulation of adult-child relations. What Herdt depicted would undoubtedly be considered child abuse and illegal in contemporary Europe and the West generally. A boy initiate begins between the ages of six and ten, and the ritual separation continues for some ten to fifteen years. During this process of initiation, boys in engage in ritual practices—from rituals of separation from the mother to nose bleeding to ingestion of semen to hunting—that are meant to transform them into strong men (at least stronger than women and children), and to create bonds with one another and with adult men generally.

The ritual does not transform a taboo into an illegality, as in the rehab ritual of the West, but a secret practice (kept secret from women) into a mechanism for the organization of the entire society. Maurice Godelier, who worked in the same region, argued that this organization is fundamentally based on male dominance of both women and children. Sexuality, he wrote (Godelier 1986, xi), supports a "cosmic foundation"; the sexed and sexualized uses of the body become a language to speak about the social (hierarchy and identity). Along these lines, Godelier (1995) argued that the sexual act is socially defined, even in the case of sexual intercourse, and that there are two kinds of sexual intercourse among the Baruya, one homosexual practiced before marriage, one heterosexual practiced after. The meaning of these acts derives from how the imaginary representation of sperm and menstrual blood, which in no way privileges the symbolic over the imaginary register, is enacted in ritual and everyday life. His point is not that compulsory homosexual initiation of young boys in New Guinea is traumatic while compulsory heterosexual initiation of boys and girls in the West is not, but that both are traumatic rituals of initiation that reproduce the social person. Herdt frames the New Guinea ritual initiation as an erotic rite and a socially mandated trauma. The traumatic experience appears to be marked more by separation from the mother and radical differentiation from women than from the coerced cross-generation (homo)sexuality.

In the same way, in the West the "abused child" also initially has no repertoire of meanings to define what happened as an experience of abuse. That framing is introduced by the entire apparatus of ritual experts (e.g., psychologists, lawyers, judges), which then redefines what happened, the deed, as a key transformative act of adult transgression of the bodily and psychic integrity of children.

2. Butler's basic argument that the body does not preexist ideation is well taken, but the use of norm in determining "cultural intelligibility" cannot be equated with the individual performative "citation of law." Likewise, regulatory norms are merely one element and not determinative of the process of "assujetissement" (subjectivation) (1993, 15). "The force and necessity of these norms . . . is thus functionally dependent on the approximation and citation of the law" (14). While the logic between law and norm may be formally analogous, the specific modes and contexts of citation, approximation, or assumption have such radically different functions in different cultures and in different cultural occasions as to defeat the utility of the analogy.

Certainly KiZ therapists are aware of all sorts of regulatory norms, but the variety of deeds that are subsumed into the category of sexual abuse—for example, rape, kissing, fondling, viewing Internet pornography—constantly challenge the applicability of these norms. Moreover, the therapists do not have the enforcement authority that such Foucauldian theory would attribute to them. As they treat Uwe, they are also trying in all good faith, above all, to come up with a narrative that can help him account for his actions.

CHAPTER FIVE

1. In Freud's interpretation of the Oedipal dynamic, the son kills the father to have unimpeded sexual access to his mother, after which the dead father is reinstated as law, or superego (Freud 1913). That reading is, as I discussed in chapter 3, a nineteenth-century fantasy that grew out of a simplistic, narrowly heterosexual understanding of power and sexual desire.

CHAPTER SIX

1. Lacan writes, "It is in the name of the father that we must recognize the basis of the symbolic function" (2006, 230). He develops his insight partly out of a theory of

psychosis, defined as a state in which the patient cannot locate him or herself in the symbolic order (1966, 197–269, 464–65, 723). A single, succinct exposition by Lacan of what he means is not to my knowledge readily available. For such an exposition by means of an anthropological analysis of a social group that is unable to claim an inheritance through "name of the father," see Vincent Crapanzano's (2011) depiction of the Harkis in France.

CHAPTER SEVEN

1. The praxis of ethnographic research is in tension with this ideology of transparency, one effect of which is to restrict the pursuit and advancement of knowledge that requires a spirit of risk taking and open inquiry. Access to the other's world is the key to most ethnographic work, and this means not only that ethnographers play the child who is always in the position of discovering what the other knows but also not reveal different things about themselves to different audiences (Pels 1999). In the United States, anthropologists working in universities are required to produce rationalizations for human subjects monitoring boards, which have proliferated and whose mandates keep expanding, often driven by legal departments whose major concern is to protect institutions from being sued. Such boards tend to rationalize this control of research as necessary for the protection of "subjects," based on past abuse in experiments, primarily medical and psychological. An ethics that is situational would go some way toward enabling this tension rather than stopping research. For example, the decision in research to withhold names or specific identities or actions is considered the norm, required by ethical review boards, and rationalized as necessary to protect the "anonymity" or "confidentiality" of informants. But in some situations names are revealed to protect people, enabling persecuted individuals or groups access to external publicity. Likewise, the decision in research to disclose the conditions of research is usually demanded by ethical review boards at the beginning of research and legitimized as an issue of "informed consent." In my research on child molesters, signing informed consent forms might have in fact put convicted offenders at risk, exposing them to legal and political authorities that might want to know who informed my research and use this information against them. I did obtain written consent from institutional heads (i.e., government ministry, leader of therapy institute, group therapy leaders), but this hardly resolves the issue.

2. By "intersubjective third" I mean "a joint though decidedly unequal construction generated in the context of the encounter, which privileges the experience of the interlocutor but is powerfully defined by the relationship of the roles of anthropologist and interlocutor." Awareness and cultivation of such a third "opens a space in which both unconscious and conscious aspects of experience can be recontextualized, leading to a better understanding of interlocutors' wishes and anxieties" (Borneman 2011, 235). This ethics is similar to what Peter Pels (1999) appealed to in his argument that experience must replace the tendency to institutional codification, although I prefer to remain within a Weberian relation of "empathic understanding" than to turn, as he does, to a language of "negotiation" or "public relations," which implies that one can work with conscious motivations and intentions alone.

3. From a philosophical standpoint, the "Western self," wrote Charles Taylor (1989, 36) in his influential book on this subject, "exists within webs of interlocution," meaning self-definition occurs through communication with others. This characteristic of the "Western self" does not make it singular to the West, however, as the assumption of an embedded self in webs of interlocution can be found in many other

cultural systems. Surely the more significant singularity of the Western self is the assumption of an interiority that is malleable—an assumption that has been globally if unevenly disseminated through the Western "psy" industries. And due to the waning of the paternal function (despite the resilience of patriarchal sociopolitical structures) and the spread of capitalism, to create the self as object and to control the objects of the self have become important political projects.

4. For a critique of cognitive behavioral therapy as pursuit of the US normative ideology of happiness, see Greenberg (2010). Psychotropic drugs are often prescribed to accompany such therapy. For an explication of how the pharmaceutical industry marshaled public support by manufacturing diagnoses and bribing the medical profession, see Angell (2004).

5. Among proponents of cognitive behavioral treatment in the health care field, psychoanalytic or psychodynamic approaches remain largely eschewed because they are assumed costly, too time intensive, and often do not lend themselves to quantifiably measurable success. Yet increasing criticism can be found of the sole focus on techniques aimed at "thought suppression." For example, Jerry Jennings and Adam Deming (2013, 12) repeat a complaint that I heard repeatedly among prison therapists in Berlin, that "the quantity of sex offender group treatment that is explicitly 'behavioral' has become minimal in relation to that which is overwhelmingly 'cognitive.'"

REFERENCES

Aberle, David, Urie Bronfenbrenner, Eckhard Hess, Daniel Miller, David Schneider, and James Spuhle. 1963. "The Incest Taboo and the Mating Patterns of Animals." *American Anthropologist* 65 (2):253–65.

Alexander, M. A. 1999. "Sexual Offender Treatment Efficacy Revisited." *Sexual Abuse: A Journal of Research and Treatment* 19:101–16.

Alexander, Shawn, Leah Graf, and Eric Janus. 2011. "M. v. Germany: The European Court of Human Rights Takes a Critical Look at Preventive Detention." *Arizona Journal of International & Comparative Law* 29 (3): 605–22.

Andrews, D. A., J. Bonta, and J. S. Wormith. 2006. "The Recent Past and Near Future of Risk and/or Need Assessment." *Crime & Delinquency* 52:7–27.

Angell, Marcia. 2004. *The Truth about the Drug Companies: How They Deceive Us and What to Do About It*. New York: Random House.

Aries, Philippe. 1965. *Centuries of Childhood: A Social History of Family Life*. New York: Vintage.

Bachofen, Johann Jakob. 1861. *Das Mutterrecht: eine Untersuchung über die Gynaikokratie der alten Welt nach ihrer religiösen und rechtlichen Natur*. Stuttgart: Krais & Hoffmann.

Basdekis-Jozsa, Raphaela, Andreas Mokros, Knut Vohs, Peer Briken, and Elmar Habermeyer. 2013. "Detention in Germany: An Overview and Empirical Data from Two Federal States." *Behavioral Sciences and the Law* 31:344–58.

Bataille, Georges. 1957. *L'érotisme*. Paris: Editions de Minuit.

Baumann, Imanuel. 2006. *Dem Verbrechen auf der Spur: Eine Geschichte der Kriminologie und Kriminalpolitik in Deutschland, 1880–1980*. Göttigen: Wallstein Verlag.

Baurmann, Michael C. 2004. "Sexuality, Adolescence and the Criminal Law: The Perspective of Criminology." In *Adolescence, Sexuality, and the Criminal Law: Multidisciplinary Perspectives*, edited by Helmut Graupner and Vern Bullough, 71–87. Binghamton, New York: Haworth Press.

Becker, Sophinette, und Herbert Gschwind. 2003. "Sexuelle Störungen." In *Psychosomatische Medizin*, edited by Thure von Uexküll et al., 727–40. Stuttgart: Urban & Schwarzenberg.

Beech, Anthony. 1998. "A Psychometric Typology of Child Abusers." *International Journal of Offender Therapy and Comparative Criminology* 42:319–39.

Beech, Anthony, and D. D. Fisher. 2002. "The Rehabilitation of Child Sex Offenders." *Australian Psychologist* 37:206–14.

Beech, Anthony, and R. E. Mann. 2002. "Recent Developments in the Treatment of Sexual Offenders." In *Offender Rehabilitation: Effective Programs and Policies to Reduce Reoffending*, edited by J. McGuire, 259–88. Chichester, UK: Wiley.

Bell, Vikki. 1993. *Interrogating Incest: Feminism, Foucault, and the Law.* London: Routledge.

Benjamin, Jessica. 1995. "Sameness and Difference: An 'Overinclusive' View of Gender Constitution." *Psychoanalytic Inquiry* 15:125–42.

Berkel, Irene. 2006. *Missbrauch als Phantasma: zur Krise der Genealogie.* Paderborn, Germany: Wilhelm Fink.

———. 2009. "Die Erosion des Inzesttabus." In *Postsexualität: zur Transformation des Begehrens*, edited by Irene Berkel, 87–105. Gießen, Germany: Psychosozial Verlag.

Berlant, Lauren. 1997. *The Queen of America Goes to Washington City: Essays on Sex and Citizenship.* Chapel Hill, NC: Duke University Press.

Bernstein, Elizabeth. 2010. "Militarized Humanism Meets Carceral Feminism." *Signs: Journal of Women in Culture and Society* 36 (1):45–71.

Bettelheim, Bruno. (1976) 2010. "Hansel and Gretel." In *The Uses of Enchantment*, 159–66. New York: Vintage Books

Bion, Wilfried. 1962. "A Theory of Thinking." *International Journal of Psycho-Analysis* 43:306–10.

———. (1961) 1984. *Learning from Experience.* London: Karnac.

Bittles, A. H. 2003. "Consanguineous Marriage and Childhood Health." *Developmental Medicine and Child Neurology* 45:571–76.

Bolin, Anne, and Patricia Whelehan. 1999. *Perspectives on Human Sexuality.* Albany: SUNY Press.

Bollas, Christopher. 1987. *The Shadow of the Object: Psychoanalysis of the Unthought Known.* New York: Columbia University Press.

Böllinger, Lorenz. 2007. "Gefährlichkeit als iatrogene Krankheit: Sicherungsverwahrung ohne Grenzen." *Vorgänge: Zeitschrift für Bürgerrechte und Gesellschaftspolitik* 178 (2):73–81.

Bonhoeffer, Tobias, and Peter Gruss, eds. 2011. *Zukunft Gehrn: Neue Erkentnisse, Neue Herausforderungen.* Munich: C. H. Beck Verlag.

Borneman, John. 1992. *Belonging in the Two Berlins: Kin, State, Nation.* Cambridge: Cambridge University Press.

———. 1996. "Until Death Do Us Part: Marriage/Death in Anthropological Discourse." *American Ethnologist* 23 (2): 215–38.

———. 2004. "Gottvater, Landesvater, Familienvater: Identification and Authority in Germany." In *Death of the Father: An Anthropology of the End in Political Authority*, edited by John Borneman, 63–103. New York: Berghahn.

———. 2007. *Syrian Episodes: Sons, Fathers, and an Anthropologist in Aleppo.* Princeton, NJ: Princeton University Press.

———. 2009. "Fieldwork Experience, Collaboration, and Interlocution: The Metaphysics of Presence in Encounters with the Syrian Mukhabarat." In *Being There: The Fieldwork Encounter and the Making of Truth*, edited by John Borneman and Abdellah Hammoudi, 237–58. Berkeley: University of California Press.

———. 2010. "European Rituals of Initiation and the Production of Men." *Social Anthropology* 18 (3): 289–301.

———. 2011. "Daydreaming, Intimacy, and the Intersubjective Third in Fieldwork Encounters in Syria," *American Ethnologist* 38 (2): 234–48.

Borneman, John, and Abdellah Hammoudi, eds. 2009. *Being There: The Fieldwork Encounter and the Making of Truth.* Berkeley: University of California Press.

Bota, Alice, Khuê Pham, and Özlem Topçu. 2013. *We New Germans*. Berlin: Rowohlt.

Bowlby, John. 1973. "The Place of Attachment and Loss in Psychopathology." In *Attachment and Loss*, 2:25–56. New York: Basic.

Brown, Sarah, Leigh Harkins, and Anthony R. Beech. 2011. "General and Victim-Specific Empathy: Associations with Actuarial Risk, Treatment Outcome, and Sexual Recidivism," *Sexual Abuse: A Journal of Research and Treatment* 20 (10):1–20.

Bruder, Klaus-Jürgen. 2001. "Masculinity and Sexual Abuse in Postwar German Society." In *Conceptions of Postwar German Masculinity*, edited by Roy Jerome, 105–30. New York: SUNY Press.

Brüggen, Wilhelm. 2009. "Über 'traurige Flaneure,' 'glückliche Wilde' und 'die geheimen verführungen der Moderne.'" In *Die Modernisierung des psychischen Apparats*, edited by Wilhelm Brüggen, Klaus-J. Lindstedt, and Georg Schneider, 137–98. Frankfurt: Brandes & Apsel.

Buck-Morss, Susan. 2002. *Dreamworld and Catastrophe: The Passing of Mass Utopia in East and West*. Cambridge, MA: MIT Press.

Bundeskriminalamt (BKA). 2007. *Polizeiliche Kriminalstatistik*, 138ff. Berlin: Bundeskriminalamt.

Bundesministerium des Inneren. 2009. *Polizeiliche Kriminalstatistik*. http://www.bka.de/pks/pks2009/download/pks2009_imk_kurzbericht.pdf (accessed March 6, 2010).

Bundesregierung. 2010. *Runder Tisch Sexueller Kindesmissbrauch in Abhängigkeits- und Machtverhältnissen in privaten und öffentlichen Einrichtungen und im familiären Bereich*. Berlin: Bundesregierung Deutschlands.

Butler, Judith. 1993. *Bodies that Matter: On the Discursive Limits of "Sex."* New York: Routledge.

Carsten, Janet, ed. 2000. *Cultures of Relatedness: New Approaches to the Study of Kinship*. Cambridge: Cambridge University Press.

Chodorow, Nancy. 1978. *The Reproduction of Mothering*. Berkeley: University of California Press.

CPT/Inf (European Committee for the Prevention of Torture and Inhuman or Degrading Treatment or Punishment Information). 2012. *Report to the German Government on the Visit to Germany Carried Out by the CPT from 25.11.10 to 7.12.10*. Strassbourg: Council of Europe.

Crapanzano, Vincent. 2011. *The Harkis: The Wound that Never Heals*. Chicago: University of Chicago Press.

Dammasch, Frank. 2008a. Die Krise der Jungen. In *Jungen in der Krise: das schwache Geschlecht: psychoanalytische Überlegungen*, edited by Frank Dammasch, 9–28. Frankfurt: Brandes & Apsel.

———. 2008b. Der ruhelose Junge, die frühe Differenzerfahrung und der entwertete Dritte. In *Psychoanalyse des Vaters: klinische Erfahrungen mit realen, symbolischen und phantasierten Vätern*, edited by Hans-Geert Metzger, 237–54. Frankfurt: Brandes & Apsel.

Dannecker, Martin. 2001. "Sexueller Missbrach und Pädosexualität." In *Sexuelle Störungen und ihre Behandlung*, edited by Volkmar Sigusch, 465–74. Stuttgart: Klett-Cota.

Darwin, Charles. 1871. *The Descent of Man and Selection in Relation to Sex*. New York: Appleton.

Deleuze, Gilles, and Felix Guattari. 1983. *Anti-Oedipus: Capitalism and Schizophrenia*. Minneapolis: University of Minnesota Press.

Devereux, George. 1939. "The Social and Cultural Implications of Incest among the Mohave Indians." *Psychoanalytic Quarterly* 8:510–33.

Diamond, Michael J. 2006. "Masculinity Unraveled: The Roots of Male Gender Identity and the Shifting of Male Ego Ideals throughout Life." *Journal of the American Psychoanalytic Association* 54:1099–1130.

Diedrich, Ulrike. 2005. "Öffentliches Sprechen über sexuellen Missbrauch in der frühen DDR." *Streit* 23 (1):3–11.

Donzelot, Jacques. 1979. *The Policing of Families.* New York: Pantheon.

Douglas, Mary. 1966. *Purity and Danger: An Analysis of the Concepts of Pollution and Taboo.* London: Routledge and K. Paul.

Drenkhahn, Kirstin. 2013. "Secure Preventive Detention in Germany: Incapacitation or Treatment Intervention?" *Behavioral Sciences and the Law* 31:312–27.

Dumont, Louis. (1966) 1970. *The Caste System and Its Implications.* Chicago: University of Chicago Press.

———. (1983) 1986. *Essays on Individualism: Modern Ideology in Anthropological Perspective.* Chicago: University of Chicago Press.

Dundes, Alan, ed. 1992. *Fire in the Dragon and Other Psychoanalytic Essays on Folklore.* Princeton, NJ: Princeton University Press.

Dünkel, Frieder. 2005. "Reformen des Sexualstrafrechts und Entwicklungen der Sexualdelinquenz in Deutschland." In *Sexualstraftaten: forensische Begutachtung, Diagnostik und Therapie*, edited by Detlev Schläfke, Frank Häßler, and Jörg Michael Fegert, 1–32. Stuttgart: Schattauer.

———. 2009. "Risiko und Sicherheit im Strafvollzug—Prognose, bedingte Entlassung und Übergangsmanagement." Workshop, University of Greifswald, Germany, unpub. ms.

Dünkel, Frieder, and Bernd Maelicke. 2004. "Irren ist (un-)menschlich! 10 Irrtümer einer neo-konservativen Strafvollzugspolitik und ihre Widerlegung—Thesen des Ziethener Kreises." *Neue Kriminalpolitik* 4:131–34.

Durkheim, Emile. 1969. "Individualism and the Intellectuals." Political Studies 17:14–30.

Eagleman, David. 2012. *Incognito: The Secret Lives of the Brain.* New York: Vintage.

Eghigian, Greg. 2011. "Deinstitutionalizing the History of Contemporary Psychiatry." *History of Psychiatry* 22 (2):201–14.

El-Ariss, Tarek. 2007. "The Making of an Expert: The Case of Irshad Manji." *Muslim World* 97:93–110.

Eliade, Mircea. 1957. *The Sacred and the Profane.* New York: Harcourt, Brace, Jovanovich.

Ember, Melvin. 1974. "On the Origin and Extension of the Incest Taboo." *Behavior Science Research* 9:249–81.

Eming, Jutta, Claudia Jarzebowski, and Claudia Ulbrich, eds. 2003. *Historische Inzestdiskurse.* Königstein in Taunus: Ulrike Helmer.

Engle, Michael, Joseph McFalls Jr., and Bernard Gallagher III. 2007. "The Attitudes of Members of the Association for the Treatment of Sexual Abusers Towards Treatment, Release, and Recidivism of Violent Sex Offenders: An Exploratory Study." *Journal of Offender Rehabilitation* 44 (4): 17–24.

Erdheim, Mario. 1995. "Gibt es ein Ende der Adoleszenz? Betrachtung aus ethnopsychoanalytischer Sicht." *Praxis der Kinderpsychologie und Kinderpsychiatrie* 44: 81–85.

Ferenczi, Sandor. (1909) 1952. "Introjection and Transference." In *First Contributions to Psychoanalysis*, translated by Ernst Jones. London: Hogarth Press.

———. (1933) 1955. "Confusion of Tongues between Adults and the Child." In *Final Contributions to the Problems and Methods of Psycho-analysis*, translated by Michael Balint, 156–67. New York: Basic.

Fergusson, David M., and Paul Mullen. 1999. *Child Sexual Abuse: An Evidence-Based Perspective.* Thousand Oaks, CA: Sage.

Finkelhor, David. 1979. *Sexually Victimized Children.* New York: Free Press.

———. 1984. *Child Sexual Abuse: New Theory and Research*. New York: Free Press.

Finkelhor, David, and Linda Jones. 2004. *Bulletin of the Office of Juvenile Justice and Delinquency Prevention (January)*. Washington, DC: US Department of Justice.

Finkelhor, David, Linda Jones, and Anne Shattuck. 2011. *Updated Trends in Child Maltreatment, 2010*. Durham, NH: Crimes against Children Research Center.

Finkelhor, David, Heather Turner, Richard Omrod, and Sherry Hamby. "Trends in Childhood Violence and Abuse Exposure." 2010. *Archives of Pediatrics and Adolescent Medicine* 164 (3): 238–42.

Fisher, D., A. R. Beech, and K. D. Browne. 1999. "Comparison of Sex Offenders to Nonsex Offenders on Selected Psychological Measures." *International Journal of Offender Therapy and Comparative Criminology* 43:473–91.

Fonagy, Peter. 2006. "Psychosexuality and Psychoanalysis: An Overview." In *Identity, Gender and Sexuality 150 Years after Freud*, edited by Peter Fonagy, Rainer Krause, and Marianne Leuzinger-Bohleber, 1–19. Controversies in Psychoanalysis Series. London: International Psychoanalytical Association.

———. 2008. "A Genuinely Developmental Theory of Sexual Enjoyment and Its Implications for Psychoanalytic Technique." *Journal of the American Psychoanalytic Association* 56 (1): 11–36.

Fonagy, Peter, G. Gergely, E. L. Jurist, and M. Target. 2002. *Affect Regulation, Mentalization and the Development of the Self*. New York: Other Press.

Fonagy, Peter, and Margaret Target. 1996. "Playing with Reality: I. Theory of Mind and the Normal Development of Psychic Reality." *International Journal of Psycho-Analysis* 77:217–33.

Fortes, Meyer. (1959) 1984. *Oedipus and Job in West African Religions*. New York: Cambridge University Press.

Foucault, Michel. (1975) 1977. *Discipline and Punish: The Birth of the Prison*. Translated by Alan Sheridan. New York: Vintage.

———. (1976) 1978. *The History of Sexuality: An Introduction*. Translated by Robert Hurley. New York: Pantheon.

Fox, Robin. (1980) 1983. *The Red Lamp of Incest: An Enquiry into the Origins of Mind and Society*. Notre Dame, IN: University of Notre Dame Press.

Franklin, Sarah, and Susan McKinnon, eds. 2002. *Relative Values: Reconfiguring Kinship Studies*. Durham, NC: Duke University Press.

Frazer, James G. 1910. *Totemism and Exogamy*. New York: Macmillan.

Freedman, Estelle B. 1987. "'Uncontrolled Desires': The Response to the Sexual Psychopath, 1920–1960." *Journal of American History* 74 (1): 83–106.

Freud, Sigmund. 1913. *Totem und Tabu: einige Übereinstimmungen im Seelenleben der Wilden und der Neurotiker*. Leipzig: Hugo Heller.

———. (1914) 1957. "On Narcissism: An Introduction." In *The Standard Edition of the Complete Psychological Works of Sigmund Freud*, translated and edited James Strachey, in collaboration with Anna Freud, 14:73–102. London: Hogarth Press.

———. 1915. "The Unconscious." In *The Standard Edition of the Complete Psychological Works of Sigmund Freud*, translated and edited James Strachey, in collaboration with Anna Freud, 14:159–204. London: Hogarth Press.

———. 1931. "Female Sexuality." In *The Standard Edition of the Complete Psychological Works of Sigmund Freud*, translated and edited James Strachey, in collaboration with Anna Freud, 21:225–43. London: Hogarth Press.

———. 1985. *The Complete Letters of Sigmund Freud to Wilhelm Fliess, 1887–1904*. London: Belknap Press.

Friedrichsen, Gisela, and Gerhard Mauz. 1993. "Kot mit Ketchup: in Montessori-Kindergärten sollen Kinder in 55 Fällen von einem Erzieher sexuell mißbraucht worden sein." *Der Spiegel* 39:87–113.

Gay, Peter. 1993. *The Cultivation of Hatred: The Bourgeois Experience.* New York: W. W. Norton.

Gebhardt, Miriam. 2009. *Die Angst vor dem kindlichen Tyrannen: eine Geschichte der Erziehung im 20. Jahrhundert.* Munich: DeutscheVerlags-Anstalt.

Geertz, Clifford. 1973. "Deep Play: Notes on the Balinese Cockfight." In *The Interpretation of Cultures,* 412–53. New York: Basic.

Ghassem-Fachandi, Parvis. 2007. "About Prayer: Abjection and Urgency in an American Holiness Church." *Ethnography* 8 (3): 235–65.

———. 2012. *Pogrom in Gujarat: Hindu Nationalism and Anti-Muslim Violence in India.* Princeton, NJ: Princeton University Press.

Gil, Eliana. 1996. *Treating Abused Adolescents.* New York: Guilford Press.

Ginsburg, Faye, and Rayna Rapp, eds. 1995. *Conceiving the New World Order: The Global Politics of Reproduction.* Berkeley: University of California Press.

Godelier, Maurice. 1986. *The Making of Great Men: Male Domination and Power among the New Guinea Baruya.* Cambridge: Cambridge University Press.

——— 1995. "Qu'est-ce qu'un acte sexuel?" *Revue Internationale de Psychopathologie* 19:351–82.

———. 2004. *Métamorphoses de la parenté.* Paris: Fayard.

Goffman, Erving. 1959. *The Presentation of Self in Everyday Life.* New York: Doubleday.

———. 1961. *Asylums: Essays on the Social Situation of Mental Patients and Other Inmates.* New York: Anchor.

Gooren, Louis J. 2011. "Ethical and Medical Considerations of Androgen Deprivation Treatment of Sex Offenders." *Journal of Criminal Endocrinology and Metabolism* 96 (12): 3628–37.

Graupner, Helmut. 2004. "Sexual Consent: The Criminal Law in Europe and Outside Europe." In *Adolescence, Sexuality, and the Criminal Law: Multidisciplinary Perspectives,* edited by Helmut Graupner and Vern L. Bullough, 111–72. Binghamton, NY: Haworth Press.

———. 2005. "Sexuality and Human Rights in Europe." In *Sexuality and Human Rights: A Global Overview,* edited by Helmut Graupner and Phillip Tahmindjis, 107–41. Binghamton, NY: Haworth Press.

Greco, Luis. 2008. "Was läßt die Bundesverfassungsgericht von der Rechtsgutslehre übrig?" *Zeitschrift für Internationale Stafrechtsdogmatik* 5:234–39.

Green, André. 2005. *Key Ideas for a Contemporary Psychoanalysis.* London: Routledge.

———. 2008. "Freud's Concept of Temporality: Differences with Current Ideas." *International Journal of Psychoanalysis* 89 (5): 1029–39.

Greenberg, Gary. 2010. *Manufacturing Depression: The Secret History of a Modern Disease.* New York: Simon & Schuster.

Greenson, Ralph. 1968. "Disidentifying from the Mother: Its Special Importance for the Boy." *International Journal of Psychoanalysis* 49:370–74.

Gschwind, Herbert, and Sophinette Becker. 1995. "Verdacht auf sexuellen Kindesmissbrauch. Ein Gutachten." *Zeitschrift fur Sexualforschung* 8:168–78.

Guggenheim, Martin. 1995. *What's Wrong with Children's Rights.* Cambridge, MA: Harvard University Press.

Günter, Michael. 2005. "Jugendliche und erwachsene Sexualstraftäter im Vergleich: Psychiatrische Charakteristika und späteres Rückfallrisiko." In *Sexuelle Entwicklung—*

sexuelle Gewalt: Grundlagen forensischer Begutachtung von Kindern und Jugendlichen, edited by Marianne Clauß, Michael Karle, Michael Günter, Gottfried Barth, 62–79. Berlin: Pabst Science.

Guru, Gopal. 2012. "Archaeology of Untouchability." In *The Cracked Mirror: An Indian Debate on Experience and Theory,* edited by Gopal Guru and Sundar Sarukkai, 200–22. Delhi: Oxford University Press.

Habermas, Jürgen. (1962) 1991. *The Structural Transformation of the Public Sphere.* Cambridge, MA: MIT Press.

Hacking, Ian. 1991. "The Making and Molding of Child Abuse." *Critical Inquiry* 17 (2): 253–88.

Hallowell, Irving. [1955] 1967. "The Self and Its Behavioral Environment." In *Culture and Experience,* 75–111. New York: Schocken.

Haug, Wolfgang Fritz. 1987. *Commodity Aesthetics, Ideology and Culture.* New York: International General.

Herdt, Gilbert. 1994. *Guardians of the Flute.* Vol. 1, *Idioms of Masculinity.* Chicago: University of Chicago Press.

Héritier, Françoise. 1999. *Two Sisters and Their Mother: The Anthropology of Incest.* New York: Zone.

Héritier, Françoise, Boris Cyrulnik, and Aldo Naouri, eds. 2000. *De l'inceste.* Paris: Odile Jacob.

Herman, Judith. 1982. *Father-Daughter Incest.* Cambridge, MA: Harvard University Press.

Herman, Judith, Diana Russell, and Karen Trocki. 1986. "Long-Term Effects of Sexual Abuse in Childhood." *American Journal of Psychiatry* 143 (10): 1293–96.

Herskovits, Melville. 1955. *Cultural Anthropology: An Abridged Version of Man and His Works.* New York: Knopf.

Herzog, Dagmar. 2005. *Sex after Fascism: Memory and Morality in Twentieth Century Germany.* Princeton, NJ: Princeton University Press.

Hill, Andreas, Peer Briken, Christian Kraus, Kerstin Strohm, and Wolfgang Berner. 2003. "Differential Pharmacological Treatment of Paraphilias and Sex Offenders." *International Journal of Offender Therapy and Comparative Criminology* 47 (4): 407–21.

Hirsch, Mathias. 1999. *Realer Inzest: Psychodynamik des sexuellen Mißbrauchs in der Familie.* Gießen: Psychosozial Verlag.

———. 2010. "Ekel als Abwehr—Abwehr als Ekel." In *Ekel als Folge traumatischer Erfahrungen,* edited by Ralf Vogt, 95–110. Gießen: Psychosozial Verlag.

Hollan, Douglas 1992. "Cross-Cultural Differences in the Self." *Journal of Anthropological Research* 48:283–300.

Holmes, W. C., and G. B. Slap. 1998. "Sexual Abuse of Boys." *Journal of the American Medical Association* 280 (1): 1855–62.

Horkheimer, Max, and Theodor W. Adorno. (1944) 1972. *Dialectic of Enlightenment.* Translated by by John Cumming. New York: Continuum.

Isaacs, Susan. 1948. "The Nature and Function of Fantasy." *International Journal of Psycho-Analysis* 29:73–97.

Ivy, Marilyn. 1993. "Have You Seen Me? Recovering the Inner Child in Late Twentieth-Century America." *Social Text* 37:227–52.

Jenkins, Phillipe. 1992. *Intimate Enemies: Moral Panics in Contemporary Great Britain.* New York: Walter de Gruyter.

Jennings, Jerry, and Adam Deming. 2013. "Effectively Utilizing the 'Behavioral' in Cognitive-Behavioral Group Therapy of Sex Offenders." *International Journal of Behavioral Consultation and Therapy* 8 (2): 7–13.

Johnson, Allen, and Douglass Price-Williams. 1996. *Oedipus Ubiquitous: The Family Complex in World Folk Literature.* Stanford, CA: Stanford University Press.

Joseph, Betty. 1989. *Psychic Change and the Psychoanalytic Process.* New York: Routledge.

Juers, Evelyn. 2011. *House of Exile: War, Love and Literature, from Berlin to Los Angeles.* London: Allen Lane.

Juillerat, Bernard. 1992. "'The Mother's Brother Is the Breast': Incest and Its Prohibition in the Yafar Yangis." In *Shooting the Sun: Ritual and Meaning in West Sepik,* edited by Bernard Juillerat, 20–124. Washington, DC: Smithsonian Institution Press.

Jung, Heike. 1987. "Behandlung als Rechtsbegriff." *Zeitschrift für Strafvollzug und Straffälligenhilfe* 36:38–42.

Keane, Webb. 2008. "Others, Other Minds, and Others' Theories of Other Minds: An Afterword on the Psychology and Politics of Opacity Claims." *Anthropological Quarterly* 81 (2): 473–82.

Kempe, C. Henry, and Ruth Kempe. 1978. *Child Abuse.* Cambridge, MA: Harvard University Press.

Kepura, Jürgen. 2007. "Menschenhandel-Die Perspective bestimmt die Sicht." *Kriminalistik* 61 (4):256–62.

Klein, Melanie. (1937) 1975. Love, Guilt, and Reparation. In *Love, Guilt, and Reparation, and Other Works, 1921–1945,* 306–43. London: Hogarth Press.

Kleinman, Arthur. 1988. *The Illness Narratives: Suffering, Healing, and the Human Condition.* New York: Basic.

Kohut, Heinz. 1975. "The Psychoanalyst in the Community of Scholars." *Annual of Psychoanalysis* 3:341–70.

———. 1977. "Does Psychoanalysis Need a Psychology of the Self?" In *The Restoration of the Self,* 63–139. Chicago: University of Chicago Press.

Kracke, Waud. 1987. "Encounter with Other Cultures: Psychological and Epistemological Aspects." *Ethos* 15 (1):58–81.

Kristeva, Julia. 1982. *Powers of Horror: An Essay on Abjection.* New York: Columbia University Press.

Kroeber, Alfred. 1909. "Classificatory Systems of Relationship." *Journal of the Royal Anthropological Institute* 39:77–84.

Lacan, Jacques. 1966. *Écrits.* Paris: Éditions du Seuil.

———. 1970. "Of Structure as an Inmixing of an Otherness Prerequisite to Any Subject Whatever." In *The Languages of Criticism and the Sciences of Man,* edited by Richard Macksey and Eugenio Donato, 186–200. Baltimore: Johns Hopkins University Press.

———. 1977. *The Four Fundamental Concepts of Psychoanalysis.* London: Tavistock.

———. 1992. *Écrits: The First Complete Edition in English.* Translated by Bruce Fink. New York: W. W. Norton.

La Fontaine, Jean. 1998. *Speak of the Devil: Tales of Satanic Abuse in Contemporary England.* Cambridge: Cambridge University Press.

Lancaster, Roger. 2011. *Sex Panic and the Punitive State.* Berkeley: University of California Press.

Langan, P. A., E. L. Schmitt, and M. R. Durose. 2003. *Recidivism of Sex Offenders Released from Prison in 1994.* NCJ 198281.Washington, DC: US Department of Justice, Bureau of Justice Statistics.

Laplanche, Jean. 1989. *New Foundations for Psychoanalysis.* Translated by D. Macey. Oxford: Basil Blackwell.

———. 1999. *Essays on Otherness.* New York: Routledge.

———. 2009. "Inzest und Infantile Sexualität." *Psyche* 6:525–39.

Lautmann, Rüdiger. 1994. *Die Lust am Kind: Portrait des Pädophilen.* Hamburg: Klein.

Levine, Judith. 2002. *Harmful to Minors: The Perils of Protecting Children from Sex.* Minneapolis: University of Minnesota Press.

Lévi-Strauss, Claude. 1971. *The Elementary Structures of Kinship.* Boston: Beacon Press.

Luckmann, Thomas. 1967. *The Invisible Religion: The Problem of Religion in Modern Society.* New York: Macmillan.

Luhrmann, Tanya. 2000. *Of Two Minds: An Anthropologist Looks at American Psychiatry.* New York: Knopf.

Loewald, Hans W. 1980. "The Waning of the Oedipal Complex." In *Papers on Psychoanalysis,* 384–404. New Haven, CT: Yale University Press.

Malinowski, Bronislaw. 1926. *Sex and Repression in Savage Society.* New York: Harcourt, Brace.

———. 1927. *Crime and Custom in Savage Society.* New York: Harcourt, Brace.

Mallet, Carl-Heinz. 1984. *Fairy Tales and Children.* New York: Schocken.

Mandeville-Norden, Rebecca, and Anthony Beech. 2004. "Community-Based Treatment of Sex Offenders." *Sexual Aggression* 10 (2): 193–214.

Markowitsch, Hans J., and Reinhard Merkel. 2011. "The Brain Stands Trial." *Max Planck Research* 3:12–17.

Marquardt, Andreas, and Jürgen Lemke. 2006. *Härte: Mein Weg aus dem Teufelskreis der Gewalt.* Berlin: Ullstein.

Marshall, W. L., A. Eccles, and H. E. Barbaree. 1993. "A Three-Tiered Approach to the Rehabilitation of Incarcerated Sex Offenders." *Behavioral Sciences and the Law* 11:441–55.

Marshall, W. L., S. M. Hudson, and T. Ward. 1992. "Sexual Deviance." In *Principles and Practice of Relapse Prevention,* edited by P. H. Wilson, 235–54. New York: Guilford Press.

Marshall, W. L., R. Jones, T. Ward, Johnston, P., and H.E. Barbaree. 1991. "Treatment Outcome with Sex Offenders." *Clinical Psychology Review* 11:465–85.

Matson, Scott. 2002. "A Critical Management Tool." *Corrections Today,* 114–17.

Mead, George Herbert. (1934) 1964. *Mind, Self, and Society.* Chicago: University of Chicago Press.

Mead, Margaret. 1928. *Coming of Age in Samoa: A Psychological Study of Primitive Youth for Western Civilisation.* New York: Morrow.

Metzger, Hans-Geert. 2008. "Der imaginierte Vater und die Erfahrung der realen Begegnung." In *Psychoanalyse des Vaters: klinische Erfahrungen mit realen, symbolischen und phantasierten Vätern,* edited by Hans-Geert Metzger, 91–106. Frankfurt: Brandes & Apsel.

Meyer, Anneke. 2007. *The Child at Risk: Paedophiles, Media Responses and Public Opinion.* Manchester: Manchester University Press.

Ministers' Deputies. 2012. CM Documents, CM/AS(2012) Rec1980 final, June 15, 2012. http://hub.coe.int/en/.

Mitchell, Stephen A. 1991. "Contemporary Perspectives on Self: Toward an Integration." *Psychoanalytic Dialogues* 1:121–47.

Mitscherlich, Alexander, and Margarete Mitscherlich. 1965. *Auf dem Weg zur Vaterlosen Gesellschaft: Ideen zur Sozialpsychologie.* Munich: R. Piper.

Montagu, Ashley. 1971. *Touching: The Human Significance of the Skin.* New York: Harper & Row.

Moore, Sally Falk. 1978. *Law as Process: An Anthropological Approach.* Boston: Routledge.

———. 2009. "Encounters and Suspicion in Tanzania." In *Being There: The Fieldwork Encounter and the Making of Truth,* edited by John Borneman and Abdellah Hammoudi, 151–82. Berkeley: University of California Press.

Moore, Sally Falk, and Barbara Myerhoff, eds. 1977. *Secular Ritual*. Amsterdam: Van Gorcum.

Mosse, George. 1985. *Nationalism and Sexuality: Respectability and Abnormal Sexuality in Modern Europe*. New York: Howard Fertig.

Mullen, Paul E., and Jillian Fleming. 1998. "Long-Term Effects of Child Sexual Abuse." *Issues of Child Abuse Prevention* (National Child Protection Clearing House Paper, No. 9). Sydney: Australian Institute of Family Studies.

Mullen, Paul, Neville King, and Bruce Tonge. 2000. "Child Sexual Abuse: An Overview." *Behaviour Change* 17 (1): 2–14.

Nathan, Debbie, and Snedeker, Michael. 1995. *Satan's Silence: Ritual Abuse and the Making of a Modern American Witch Hunt*. New York: Basic.

Nedopil, Nobert. 2000. *Forensische Psychiatrie*. Stuttgart: Thieme.

Obeyesekere, Gananath. 1989. "The Conscience of the Parricide: A Study in Buddhist History." *Man*, n.s., 24 (2): 236–54.

Ogden, Thomas. 2004. "On Holding and Containing: Being and Dreaming." *International Journal of Psychoanalysis* 85:1349–64.

Osterheider, M., R. Banse, P. Briken, L. Goldbeck, J. Hoyer, P. Santtila, and H. Eisenbarth. 2012. "Frequency, Etiological Models and Consequences of Child and Adolescent Sexual Abuse: Aims and Goals of the German Multi-site MiKADO Project." *Sex Offender Treatment* 7 (1), http://www.sexual-offender-treatment.org/105.html.

Pardeck, James. 2006. *Children's Rights*. Binghamton, NY: Haworth Press.

Paul, Robert A. 2010. "Incest Avoidance: Oedipal and Pre-Oedipal, Natural and Cultural." *Journal of the American Psychoanalytic Association* 58:1087–1112.

Pels, Peter. 1999. "Professions of Duplexity: A Prehistory of Ethical Codes in Anthropology." *Current Anthropology* 40 (2):101–14.

Perner, Achim. 2006. "Trieb, Komplex, und Familie." In *Jahrbuch für klinische Psychoanalyse*. Vol. 7, *Familie*, edited by André Michels, Peter Müller, Achim Perner, and Claus-Dieter Rath, 120–55. Tübingen: Edition Diskord.

Perrot, Michelle, ed. 1990. *A History of Private Life*. Vol. 4, *From the Fires of Revolution to the Great War*. Cambridge, MA: Harvard University Press.

Pollock, Linda H. 1983. *Forgotten Children: Parent-Child Relations from 1500 to 1900*. Cambridge: Cambridge University Press.

Postman, Neil. 1982. *The Disappearance of Childhood*. New York: Delacorte Press.

Recht, Aktuell. 2007. "Suche im Internet nach kinderpornographischen Seiten." *Kriminalistik* 61 (3): 159.

Reinert, Thomas. 2010. "Der Ekel in der therapeutischen Realität und seine Auswirkungen auf die Gegenübertragung des Analytikers." In *Ekel als Folge traumatischer Erfahrungen*, edited by Ralf Vogt, 215–26. Gießen: Psychosozial Verlag.

Renzikowski, Joachim. 2003. Kommentierung der §§174–184g. In *Münchener Kommentar zum Strafgesetzbuch*. Vol. 2, edited by Wolfgang Joecks and Klaus Miebach. Munich: C. H. Beck.

Rhodes, Lorna. 2004. *Total Confinement: Madness and Reason in the Maximum Security Prison*. Berkley: University of California Press.

Richter-Unger, Sigrid. 1999. "Zur Entwicklung familienorienter Arbeit bei sexuellem Mißbrach." In *Wege aus dem Labyrinth: Erfahrungen mit familienorienteirter Arbeit zu sexuellem Mißbrauch*, edited by Kind im Zentrum, 8–15. Berlin: KiZ.

Robbins, Joel, and Alan Rumsey. 2008. "Introduction: Cultural and Linguistic Anthropology and the Opacity of Other Minds." *Anthropological Quarterly* 81 (2):407–20.

Róheim, Géza. 1950. *Psycho-analysis and Anthropology: Culture, Personality, and the Unconscious.* New York: International University Press.

———. 1992. *Fire in the Dragon and Other Psychoanalytic Essays on Folklore.* Princeton, NJ: Princeton University Press.

Rose, Nikolas. 1998. *Inventing Our Selves: Psychology, Power, and Personhood.* Cambridge: Cambridge University Press.

Rosenblum, Warren. 2008. *Beyond the Prison Gates: Punishment and Welfare in Germany, 1850–1933.* Chapel Hill: University of North Carolina Press.

Rüegger, Peter. 2007. "Das geltende Sexualstrafrecht." *Kriminalistik* 61 (6): 407–16.

Russell, Stacy. 1996/7. "Castration of Repeat Sexual Offenders: An International Comparative Analysis." *Houston Journal of International Law* 19:425–44.

Sabean, David. 2002. "Inzestdiskurse vom Barock bis zur Romantik." *L'Homme: Zeitschrift für feministische Geschichtswissenschaft* 13:7–29.

Scheper-Hughes, Nancy. 1993. *Death Without Weeping: The Violence of Everyday Life in Brazil.* Berkeley: University of California Press.

Schore, Allan. 1991. "Early Superego Development: The Emergence of Shame and Narcissistic Affect Regulation in the Practicing Period." *Psychoanalysis and Contemporary Thought* 14:187–250.

Schuman, Elliot P. 1972. "A Psychoanalytic Study of Hansel and Gretel." *Journal of Contemporary Psychotherapy* 4:121–25.Seifert, Dieter. 2007. *Gefährlichkeitsprognosen.* Darmstadt: Steinkopff.

Seto, Michael. 2008. *Pedophilia and Sexual Offending against Children: Theory, Assessment and Intervention.* Washington, DC: American Psychological Association.

Shengold, Leonard. 1991. *Soul Murder: The Effects of Child Abuse and Deprivation.* New York: Ballantine.

———. 1999. *Soul Murder Revisited: Thoughts about Therapy, Hate, Love, and Memory.* New Haven, CT: Yale University Press.

Shepher, Joseph. 1983. *Incest: A Biosocial View.* New York: Academic Press.

Shweder, Richard, and Eric Bourne. 1984. "Does the Concept of the Person Vary Cross-Culturally?" In *Culture Theory: Essays on Mind, Self, and Emotion,* edited by Richard Shweder and Robert LeVine, 158–99. New York: Cambridge University Press.

Siegel, James T. 2006. *Naming the Witch.* Stanford, CA: Stanford University Press.

Sigusch, Volkmar. 2001. "Was geußt sexuelle *Störung?*" In *Sexuelle Störungen und ihre Behandlung,* 3rd ed., 1–9. Stuttgart: Thieme.

Spiro, Melford. 1979. "Whatever Happened to the Id?" *American Anthropologist* 81 (1): 5–17.

———. 1993. "Is the Western Conception of the Self 'Peculiar' Within the Context of World Cultures?" *Ethos* 21 (2): 107–53.

Statista. 2013. *Anzahl der Fälle von sexuellem Missbrauch von Kindern pro 100.000 Einwohner in Deutschland von 1987 bis 2012.* Hamburg: Statista Gmbh.

Statistische Bundesamt. 2007. *Fachserie 10, Reihe 3: Rechtspflege: Strafverfolgung 2006.* Wiesbaden: Statistische Bundesamt.

Stein, Ruth. 1998. "Two Principles of Functioning of the Affects." *American Journal of Psychoanalysis* 58 (2): 211–30.

Stolte, Bernadette. 2005. "Legalverhalten nach Sexualdelinquenz: Erste Ergebnisse einer empirischen Untersuchung." In *Sexualstraftaten: Forensische Begutachtung, Diagnostik und Therapie,* edited by Schläfke, Detlev, Frank Häßler, Jörg Michael Fegert, 171–80. Stuttgart: Schattauer.

Taussig, Michael. 1993. "Alterity." In *Mimesis and Alterity: A Particular Organization of the Senses*, 129-43. New York: Routledge.

Taylor, Charles. 1989. *Sources of the Self: The Making of the Modern Identity.* Cambridge: Cambridge University Press.

Theweleit, Klaus. 1987. *Male Fantasies.* Minneapolis: University of Minnesota Press.

Thiee, Philip. 2006. "Keine Freiheit für Nabokov!—Zur routinemässigen Strafverschärfung von Kinderpornographie und der Strafpolitik der EU." *Neue Kriminalpolitik* 4:131-34.

Turner, Daniel, Raphaela Basdekis-Jozsa, and Peer Briken. 2013. "Prescription of Testosterone-Lowering Medications for Sex Offender Treatment in German Forensic-Psychiatric Institutions." *Journal of Sexual Medicine* 10:570-78.

Turner, Victor. 1967. *The Forest of Symbols: Aspects of Ndembu Ritual.* Ithaca, NY: Cornell University Press.

Urbaniok, Frank. 2005. "Validität von Risikokalkulationen bei Straftätern: Kritik an einer methodischen Grundannahme und zukünftige Perspektiven." In *Sexualstraftaten: forensische Begutachtung, Diagnostik und Therapie*, edited by Detlev Schläfke, Frank Häßler, and Jörg Michael Fegert, 143-57. Stuttgart: Schattauer.

Van Gennep, Arnold. (1908) 1960. *The Rites of Passage.* London: Routledge.

Wacquant, Loïc. 2000. "The New 'Peculiar Institution': On the Prison as Surrogate Ghetto." *Theoretical Criminology* 4:377-89.

———. 2001. "The Penalisation of Poverty and the Rise of Neo-Liberalism." *European Journal on Criminal Policy and Research* 9:401-12.

———. 2002. "The Curious Eclipse of Prison Ethnography in the Age of Mass Incarceration." *Ethnography* 3:371-97.

Wagner, Rob. 2010. "Rehabilitation and Deradicalization: Saudi Arabia's Counterterrorism's Successes and Failures." *Peace and Conflict Monitor*, August 1. http://www.monitor.upeace.org/innerpg.cfm?id_article=735.

Waldram, James B. 2009. "'It's Just You and Satan, Hanging Out at a Pre-School': Notions of Evil and the Rehabilitation of Sexual Offenders." *Anthropology and Humanism* 34 (2): 219-34._1039

———. 2010. "Moral Agency, Cognitive Distortion, and Narrative Strategy in the Rehabilitation of Sexual Offenders." *Ethos* 38 (3): 251-74.

———. 2012. *Hound Pound Narrative: Sexual Offender Habilitation and the Anthropology of Therapeutic Intervention.* Berkeley: University of California Press.

Wallace, Anthony F. C. 1970. *Culture and Personality.* 2nd ed. New York: Random House.

Ward, Tony, and Marie Connolly. 2008. "A Human Rights-Based Practice Framework for Sexual Offenders." *Journal of Sexual Aggression* 14 (2): 87-98.

Ward, Tony, and Theresa Gannon. 2006. "Rehabilitation, Etiology, and Self-Regulation: The Good Lives Model of Sexual Offender Treatment." *Aggression and Violent Behavior* 11:77-94.

Ward, Tony, Theresa Gannon, and Astrid Birgden. 2007. "Human Rights and the Treatment of Sex Offenders." *Sex Abuse* 19 (3): 195-216.

Ward, Tony, Theresa Gannon, and Pamela Yates. 2008. "The Treatment of Offenders: Current Practice and New Developments with an Emphasis on Sex Offenders." *International Review of Victimology* 15 (2):179-204.

Ward, Tony, and Thomas Keenan. 1999. "Child Molesters' Implicit Theories." *Journal of Interpersonal Violence* 14:821-38.

Ward, Tony, and Shadd Maruna. 2007. *Rehabilitation: Beyond the Risk Paradigm.* London: Routledge.

Weber-Kellermann, Ingeborg. 1977. *Die deutsche Familie: Versuch einer Sozialgeschichte.* Frankfurt: Suhrkamp.

Weinberg, S. Kirson. 1955. *Incest Behavior.* Secaucus, NJ: Citadel.

Western, Bruce. 2007. *Punishment and Inequality in America.* New York: Russell Sage Foundation.

White, Leslie A. 1948. "The Definition and Prohibition of Incest." *American Anthropologist* 50:416–35.

Winnicott, D. W. 1960. "The Theory of the Parent-Infant Relationship." In *The Maturational Process and the Facilitating Environment,* 37–55. London: Karnac.

———. (1960) 1965. "Ego Distortion in Terms of True and False Self." In *The Maturational Processes and the Facilitating Environment: Studies in the Theory of Emotional Development,* 140–52. Madison, CT: International Universities Press.

Witte, Sonja. 2014. "Panik vor Jedermann. Journalistische Beiträge zur Aufdeckung der Pädophilen." In *"Übergriffe" und "Objekte" in Kulturellen Konstellationen kindlich-jugendlicher Sexualität,* edited by Insa Härtel and Sonja Witte, 89–144. Bielefeld: Transcript Verlag.

Wößner, Gunda. 2010. "Classifying Sexual Offenders: An Empirical Model for Generating Type-Specific Approaches to Intervention." *International Journal of Offender Therapy and Comparative Criminology* 54:327–45.

Wolf, Arthur P., and William H. Durham, eds. 2004. *Inbreeding, Incest, and the Incest Taboo: The State of Knowledge at the Turn of the Century.* Stanford, CA: Stanford University Press.

Zevitz, Richard, and Mary Ann Farkas. 2000. "Sex Offender Community Notification: Managing High Risk Criminals or Exacting Further Vengeance?" *Behavioral Sciences and the Law* 18:375–91.

INDEX

abandonment, 4, 28, 37, 86, 133, 134, 138, 139, 156, 172, 173
abuse: as child sex abuse, 1, 2, 3, 4, 11, 27, 32–36, 40, 41, 45–50, 52, 53, 55, 56, 58, 59, 61, 66–68, 71–86, 91, 94, 97, 99, 100, 102, 106, 107, 108, 110, 112, 121, 122, 125–27, 135, 136, 138, 139, 141–46, 152, 156, 157, 174, 176, 178, 180, 186, 189, 199, 200, 206, 211, 219, 220, 223, 228–31, 233–36; as physical abuse, 3, 16–17, 23, 45, 66, 76, 84, 85, 157, 161, 173, 184, 185, 188, 189, 192
androgen deprivation treatment (ADT), 57
Aries, Philippe, 222
assault, 54, 68, 78, 79, 85, 94, 115, 150, 228n16, 231n9
authenticity, 42, 52, 53, 141

Beech, Anthony, 93, 121, 157
Behandlung, 62, 107, 120, 128, 214, 226n7
Berkel, Irene, vii, 55, 82, 106, 118, 122, 230n1
Bion, Wilfried, 100, 102, 143, 144
Butler, Judith, 153, 232n13, 236n2

castration, 56, 57, 141, 179, 189, 215, 222, 225n3
child care, 13, 19, 72, 86, 104–6, 110, 116, 118, 149, 159, 172–74, 179, 180, 188, 223, 232n18
child-object, 66
child protection, 46, 47, 102, 103, 105, 106, 107, 222, 223, 231n10, 233n21, 233n23
child sexuality, 72–73, 83, 87, 88, 91, 96,

103, 104, 117, 141, 153, 157, 161, 175, 234n25
cognitive behavioral therapy (CBT), 56, 93, 122, 125, 128, 141, 214, 219, 229n22, 238n4
compensation, 48, 82, 168, 233n21
containment, 100, 197, 199
countertransference, 31, 32, 196, 197
Crapanzano, Vincent, 237n1 (chap. 6)
culture shock, 209, 210

das Ding, 6, 24, 25, 46
death, 5, 9, 12, 13, 16–19, 21–23, 25, 28, 37, 62, 66, 67, 100, 133, 134, 138, 139, 219
Deleuze, Giles, and Felix Guattari, 227n13
Devereux, George, 231n12
Diagnostic and Statistical Manual of Mental Disorders (DSM-III), 56
Diamond, Michael J., 104
dreaming, 26, 64, 211
Dünkel, Frieder, 94, 220, 235n4

Eastern Europe, 64
empathy, 3, 5, 16, 32, 50, 55, 71, 72, 86, 93, 115, 121, 129, 130, 133, 135, 141, 152, 155, 157, 158, 160, 161, 198, 231n10
European Union, 220

fascism, 2, 227n12
father substitute, 118, 145, 172, 174, 175, 222
Ferenczi, Sandor, 117, 136, 234n24